GROWING
FOOD

ANNA PAVORD

GROWING FOOD

F

FRANCES LINCOLN LIMITED
PUBLISHERS

Frances Lincoln Limited
4 Torriano Mews
Torriano Avenue
London NW5 2RZ
www.franceslincoln.com

CONTENTS

INTRODUCTION

Ordered profusion is the hallmark of the best kitchen gardens. If you can add to this a sense of being cut off from the real world, then you are very close to Eden. For the ultimate sense of detachment, you have to have walls, sunny walls, where pears can ripen mellifluously against warm brick. But even without walls, even in the smallest of spaces, you can recreate a sense of richness and abundance in your own garden by growing trained fruit trees to make living screens between one part of the plot and another, or planting exotic-looking lettuce and frilly parsley among the flowers in your border or window box. A survey carried out in 2009 suggests there are 600 acres' worth of window boxes in Britain. That could represent a lot of salad crops.

A dilettante gardener may grow a passable show of flowers. Vegetables signify a deeper level of commitment. To cut yourself off from growing food is to cut yourself off from a long and resonant tradition of gardening to survive. Even if you no longer have to feed yourself from your plot, without fruit and vegetables to hand you deny yourself some of the great pleasures of gardening. Think of the warmth on your tongue of a strawberry freshly picked from under its canopy of leaves. Think of the sense of pride you get when sitting down to a supper that you have made entirely with produce from your own plot. You need to make the most of those moments. After the pride comes the inevitable fall, when somebody discovers a caterpillar mummified in the artistically arranged spears of calabrese on their plate.

It is only quite recently that vegetables and fruit have been herded into separate areas of the garden and that the kitchen garden has acquired its drear overtones of overblown cabbages and decaying runner beans. When, with increasing affluence and ease on the part of gardeners, the first flowers crept out of the physic gardens to decorate cottage plots, flowers, fruit and vegetables all grew together in happy profusion. For centuries, the kitchen garden continued to be as decorative as it was useful.

George Eliot set the scene in her novel *Scenes of Clerical Life* (1858).

No finical separation between flower and kitchen garden there; no monotony of enjoyment for one sense to the exclusion of another but a charming paradisiacal mingling of all that was pleasant to the eye and good for food. The rich flower border running along every walk, with its endless succession of spring flowers, anemones, auriculas, wall flowers, sweet williams, campanulas, snapdragons and tiger lilies had its taller beauties such as moss and Provence roses, varied with espalier apple trees; the crimson of a carnation was carried out in the lurking crimson of the neighbouring strawberry beds; you gathered a moss rose one moment and a bunch of carrots the next; you were in a delicious fluctuation between the scent of jasmine and the juice of gooseberries.

There is no reason why you too should not be in that same state of delicious fluctuation, if you abandon some preconceived notions about the 'proper' place of plants.

Perhaps you have a summer jasmine straddling an old fence at the back of a border. Perhaps the border itself has been a source of irritation. Something is wrong with it. You may decide that what it needs is a series of landmarks to punctuate its sleepiness. You could put in acanthus, but how much more fun it would be to use mop-headed standard gooseberries to bob up between the campanulas. Grown on straight metre-high stems, they have the sculptural quality of pieces of topiary, and are particularly enchanting if you leave the berries to hang and ripen until they are as richly coloured as amber. Alternatively, you could draft in some bold clumps of globe artichoke to liven up the scene. The leaves will bring to the border the drama that it needs and you will have the buttery bonus of the artichoke heads to look forward to. That is more than an acanthus will ever give you.

You may have two small plots at the end of the garden that you use for vegetables. These grow in straight parallel rows: cabbages next to lettuce, carrots next to parsley. Just by manipulating the rows of vegetables themselves, thinking about contrasts between the shape and texture of their foliage, you can make the plot start to sing. Try setting the frilly leaves of a red lettuce such as 'Lollo Rossa' against the drooping blue flags of leeks. Use the glossy crinkled leaves of a red-stemmed chard next to the puffs of feathery foliage that grow above the white bulbs of Florence fennel. Line out your Savoy cabbages with their swirling skirts of leaves next door to carrots, which have leaves as good as the finest ferns.

There are several other things you can do to improve the appearance of your plot. The first is to choose cultivars of vegetables and fruit that are in themselves more decorative than the norm. There is no need to take this to ridiculous lengths. The prime purpose of a leek is to give comfort on a cold, graceless day when the buses are late and your children more than usually intractable. Flavour is the prime criterion of any fruit or vegetable. But you can look for other attributes as well. Among leeks, for instance, there is an extremely handsome cultivar called 'Bleu de Solaise' (also known as 'St Victor'), which is hardy and wonderful to eat. You would expect this from an old French variety, but the bonus is its foliage, leaves of a rich deep purplish blue, which you can use to great effect among red frilly lettuces and the pale frizzed foliage of endives. You might think of experimenting with the old-fashioned runner bean 'Painted Lady'. Runner beans were originally brought from America to Europe as decorative climbers for the flower garden, and with 'Painted Lady' you can see why. The flowers are neatly bicoloured, red and white, charming when grown over an arch, perhaps mixed with the white flowers of a summer clematis. Even the prosaic Brussels sprout can dress itself up if you want it to. Try 'Rubine', which is suffused all over with a deep purplish red, the kind of saturated colour that looks sumptuous against tall pale cones of Chinese cabbage, the kind of solid form that stands out boldly against an insubstantial lacy clump of fennel or line of coriander.

The other thing you can do is to bring flowers back into the kitchen garden, recreating the 'paradisiacal mingling' that George Eliot wrote about. Line the paths between your plots with neat clumps of the alpine strawberry 'Baron Solemacher'. Set behind them a ribbon of pinks, choosing perhaps the deep blood-red flowers of 'Hidcote'. These contrast boldly with their own pale grey grassy foliage, but they will also strike up an alliance with the strawberries. As you bend to pick a strawberry, the heady, spicy scent of the pinks will be where it needs to be – right under your nose.

There are many different ways of combining fruit, flowers and vegetables in a single plot. You might like to plant purple-headed alliums among leeks (their cousins), set purple aquilegias with your red cabbage, grow marigolds with curly kale, lay down lengths of blue cornflowers in between your fennel and carrots, scatter seed of the California poppy, *Eschscholzia californica*, to sprout among the onions or use brilliant blue anchusa behind clumps of purple-leaved sage. Certain annual flowers, such as marigolds and nasturtiums, have a special affinity with vegetables, for they too can be eaten, the petals of marigolds sprinkled over a green salad, the leaves and seeds of nasturtiums used to add extra spice and bite to a sandwich.

George Eliot was writing about a time when the kitchen garden was at its full-blown, spectacular height. At Drumlanrig Castle, Dumfries, Scotland, during that period, the kitchen garden contained vineries, melon houses, carnation houses and hothouses for indoor plants. There was also a glass fruit house that was 150m (500ft) long and 5.5m (18ft) wide. A cast metal path ran down the middle with edges raised to make tracks for a railway wagon that carted muck into the glasshouse and produce out.

In the 1880s, the house was packed with nectarines and figs, peaches, pears and plums, all trained up wires strung from the roof. Pots of pelargoniums, begonias and other ornamentals were massed on stepped shelves against the wall. Fourteen gardeners worked for the Duke of Buccleuch at Drumlanrig under the eagle eye of David Thomson, one of the best gardeners of his day. They formed a Mutual Improvement Association and kept careful notes of the subjects they discussed at their meetings: Forcing of the Fig, Cultivation of the Raspberry, Man's Inhumanity to Man. It is a tradition from which we have much to learn.

If you are interested in good food, there is an overwhelming reason to grow your own fruit and vegetables. Without good ingredients you cannot expect to produce good food. Commercial growers of carrots, celery, peas and potatoes worry less about the taste of their vegetables than the size and uniformity of the crop. When you are growing your own, different standards prevail. To enjoy asparagus, sweetcorn and purple sprouting broccoli at their best, they need to go straight from plot to pot. If they don't, taste deteriorates along with texture. Some produce such as French beans, strawberries and raspberries can be expensive to buy. If you grow your own, you can indulge to your heart's content.

These are practical reasons to grow fruit and vegetables at home. The best reason, though, is the pleasure that they give and the beauty that they add to the garden. Few trees in spring can match the elegiac performance of a mature pear, pouring out its heart in white blossom against the blue sky. Few flowers can produce a smell to equal the scent of a ripe greengage drooping, intoxicatingly, from a tree fanned out against a warm wall. Few foliage plants can match the bravura performance of a kale such as 'Nero di Toscana', rising in a bold fountain of near black leaves ruched as intricately as smocking. All these pleasures can be yours. To re-create Eden, just plant, watch and wait.

1

GARDEN STYLES

In this first part of the book you will find ideas for many different ways of combining fruit, vegetables and flowers in your garden to create effects that may be whimsically nostalgic, or strictly formal, as in the design for a formal salad and herb plot on pages 34–5. The plans show how you can interpret each particular style in your own garden. They show a never-never land where everything fruits and flowers at once. Your own garden will behave more sensibly. The plans do not take into account the exact number of cabbages or lettuces that will fit into a row. For the spacings at which they should be grown, check the information given in Part Two.

AN EXUBERANT POTAGER

Potager, used in the English sense, means posh vegetables grown as part of a formal design and mixed with flowers, fruit or whatever else makes them look decorative as well as useful. Villandry, the great Renaissance château west of Tours in France, has the world's most famous potager. There are acres of it, divided into nine equal squares, each containing a different arrangement of formal beds edged with box. The idea has since been copied all over the world. At Kinoith in western Ireland, for instance, you will find a superb potager where nasturtiums jostle with peas, marigolds romp alongside curly kale and sweet peas smother an arbour, built in the shape of a cottage.

Re-creating the potager

In creating your own potager, the first task will be to draw up a suitable design for the beds. The main danger lies in over-complication. Some central vortex is useful in pulling the whole design together. It also gives you the chance to use a gazebo, a decorative screen or some very dramatic plant such as an artichoke to give height, a focal point, at the centre. Not all the paths need be of the same width or importance. You may want to make paths wide enough to take some kind of arbour or tunnel lashed together from hazel poles which you can cover with runner beans, or outdoor cucumbers wound round with clematis. Consider all the features you want to fit in before you fix on the design.

To furnish a potager you need three different sorts of plants: some to edge the beds, some to fill them and some to give height, whether on their own legs (perhaps standard bays) or borrowed ones, as with runner beans, which you might use trained over a decorative tripod.

Aim for a reasonable balance between vegetables and flowers. Avoid too many permanent plantings of perennials, which will cut down your options for change. *Verbena bonariensis*, which looks terrific interplanted with leeks, is a perennial, but not a thuggish one. You can pull it up easily if it gets out of hand. A potager is not the place for vegetables such as asparagus, which, although decorative, tie up a great deal of space for a relatively short season. Artichokes also need space, but you can make a meal from one artichoke – impossible from one spear of asparagus. Artichokes, perhaps underplanted as a centrepiece with hazy blue catmint, are the most sculptural of vegetables. Looks matter. Broad beans and Brussels sprouts are too butch for this kind of boudoir gardening.

Flexibility gives you a greater choice of crops. It suits the soil too: when you clear away a crop of beans or marigolds, you have a chance to fork over and feed the soil. But a potager focuses your attention with more than usual intensity on what is growing in the beds. Each vegetable is like a piece of china in a cabinet. There is no room for greenfly here.

PLANTING PLAN: EXUBERANT POTAGER

This plan shows how an area of roughly 11 x 8m (36 x 26ft) can be transformed into a kitchen garden full of formal yet exuberant charm. The shapes of the beds can be changed to suit the site, and the plantings adapted to meet individual needs.

VIOLAS, LEEKS & VERBENA
Violas border a bed of leeks interplanted with the tall, wiry stems of *Verbena bonariensis*.

MARIGOLDS, SWEETCORN & TOMATOES
Marigolds edge a mixture of tall sweetcorn and low-growing bush tomatoes that require no staking.

NASTURTIUMS, COURGETTES & BEANS
A wigwam of scarlet runner beans acts as the centrepiece for a bed of courgettes, surrounded by a ribbon of red and yellow nasturtiums.

LETTUCE & CABBAGES
Frilly red 'Lollo Rossa' lettuce surrounds a bed of cabbages, including varieties 'Ruby Ball' and 'Hispi'.

LETTUCE, ONIONS & ESCHSCHOLZIA
'Tom Thumb' lettuce fringes a mixture of
onions and eschscholzia. Plant the onions
as sets (small bulbs) and then scatter the
eschscholzia seeds in between.

**NASTURTIUMS, SQUASH
& BEANS**
This bed matches the one opposite,
but here squash have been used to
replace the courgettes. Catch crops
of rocket, corn salad and radishes
fill the plot early in the season.

**MARIGOLDS, CARROTS &
BEETROOT**
Marigolds edge the bed, as in the
opposite corner. Inside, carrots and
beetroot, both sown from seed, grow
in alternate rows.

VIOLAS, BEANS & CORNFLOWERS
Violas edge a mixture of cornflowers
and French beans. Sow the beans first,
then scatter the cornflower seeds in
between them.

ARTICHOKE & CATMINT
An architectural globe artichoke
forms the centrepiece of the
potager, underplanted with a ring
of hazy blue catmint.

There is a temptation in this kind of planting to cram in as many different flowers and vegetables as you can, but the pattern of the potager will be most effective if you restrict your choice. Stick to perhaps four edgers, or fewer, and use them to reinforce the symmetry of the layout. You might use exuberant flower edgings of marigold, nasturtium and viola for most of the beds, with sober, upright cos lettuces or slightly wilder red 'Lollo Rossa' fringing the rest of the plots.

Bright eschscholzia can brighten the onion bed and cornflowers flourish among French beans. Other beds should be furnished with vegetables that complement each other in looks or habit. Let bush tomatoes sprawl around among tall sheaves of sweetcorn, and purple-leaved beetroot make dark alternating stripes through rows of feather-foliaged carrots.

INGREDIENTS FOR AN EXUBERANT POTAGER
roughly 11 x 8m (36 x 26ft)

CENTREPIECE
- Standard bay or globe artichokes interplanted with catmint (plants)

Clockwise from top left:
BED 1
- **Edging** Marigolds (seed)
- **Filling** Sweetcorn underplanted with bush tomatoes (plants or seed)

BED 2
- **Edging** Violas (plants)
- **Filling** Leeks interplanted with *Verbena bonariensis* (seed or plants)

BED 3
- **Edging** Small butterhead lettuce such as 'Tom Thumb', grown from seed or plugs
- **Filling** Onions planted as sets with annual eschscholzia (from seed) scattered among them

BED 4
- **Edging** Nasturtiums (seed)
- **Filling** Squash with catch crops of rocket/corn salad/radishes sown early in the season (plants or seed) and a wigwam of runner beans as a centrepiece (plants or seed)

BED 5
- **Edging** Marigolds (seed)
- **Filling** Beetroot and carrots grown in alternating rows (seed)

BED 6
- **Edging** Violas (plants)
- **Filling** French beans interplanted with cornflowers (seed)

BED 7
- **Edging** Red oakleaf lettuce or 'Lollo Rossa' lettuce grown from seed or plugs

- **Filling** A mixture of cabbages (chosen for foliage contrast) planted in rows, to include pointed 'Hispi', a red drumhead and curly kale (plants or plugs)

BED 8
- **Edging** Nasturtiums (seed), with a wigwam of runner beans as a centrepiece (plants or seed)
- **Filling** Green and yellow courgettes followed by autumn-sown mizuna or oriental saladini (seed)

TRADITIONAL KITCHEN GARDEN

The traditional kitchen garden, walled around with stone or brick, is an oasis of order in a chaotic world. Here, ruler-straight paths divide the space into neat, beautifully tended plots. Onions and potatoes, parsnips and peas grow in rows running from north to south to catch the best of the weather. There will undoubtedly be perfectly trained fruit trees, spreading their arms over a sunny wall or perhaps used to make espaliered hedges along the edges of the vegetable patches. When you walk through a door into one of these private, peaceful places, you jettison any timetable constructed around dentists' appointments, car services and the possible arrival of trains and tune in to a much more deeply established pattern of sowing and growing, then harvesting and sowing again. Harmony and fruitfulness are the key notes, an observant eye and attention to detail the ways to success.

Recreating the kitchen garden

In this plan for making a quarter of a traditional kitchen garden, a lean-to glasshouse fills the south-facing wall and shelters crops of nectarines and peaches, tomatoes and peppers. Wherever room can be found, there are old clay pots filled with geraniums or clivias. This is emphatically not a space for living, in the manner of a modern conservatory. It is a forcing house, a larder, a growing space, though it will provide a welcome shelter in winter and early spring when you can loiter there, sowing seeds and dreaming of the harvest to come. The floor needs to be laid with something that you can hose down regularly in summer. Damping down a greenhouse is the best protection against red spider mite and whitefly, both of them persistent and damaging pests of glasshouse crops.

Although the traditional kitchen garden is primarily a place to produce food, flowers are not banished entirely. In the box-edged beds on the western edge of the garden there are picking borders of roses, larkspur and everlasting flowers such as statice and helichrysum. Thick plantings of tulips provide colour and flowers to cut for the house earlier in the year. Garlands of rambling roses decorate one of the main cross paths in the garden, trained up stout posts and tied in to swags of rope slung between them. A thick

PLANTING PLAN: TRADITIONAL KITCHEN GARDEN

This plan has been designed for a plot 7.5m (25ft) square, one quarter of the whole kitchen garden. Vary the vegetables according to taste (quantities represented are not exact). The decorative features will work equally well in a smaller space.

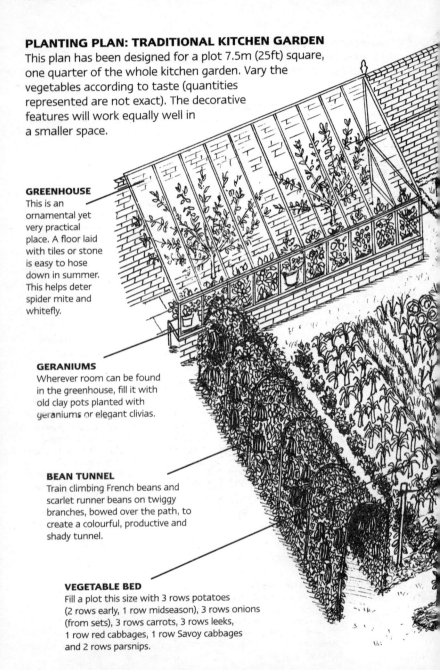

GREENHOUSE
This is an ornamental yet very practical place. A floor laid with tiles or stone is easy to hose down in summer. This helps deter spider mite and whitefly.

GERANIUMS
Wherever room can be found in the greenhouse, fill it with old clay pots planted with geraniums or elegant clivias.

BEAN TUNNEL
Train climbing French beans and scarlet runner beans on twiggy branches, bowed over the path, to create a colourful, productive and shady tunnel.

VEGETABLE BED
Fill a plot this size with 3 rows potatoes (2 rows early, 1 row midseason), 3 rows onions (from sets), 3 rows carrots, 3 rows leeks, 1 row red cabbages, 1 row Savoy cabbages and 2 rows parsnips.

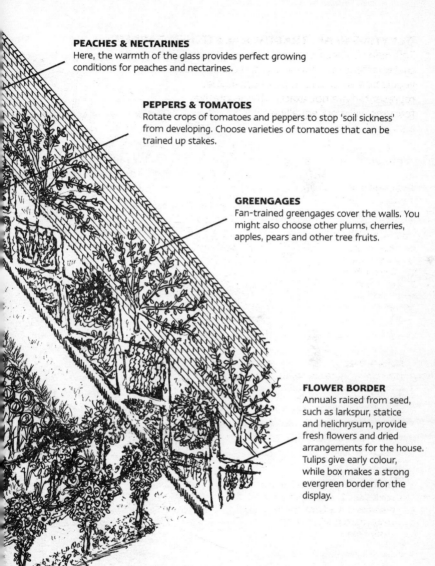

PEACHES & NECTARINES
Here, the warmth of the glass provides perfect growing conditions for peaches and nectarines.

PEPPERS & TOMATOES
Rotate crops of tomatoes and peppers to stop 'soil sickness' from developing. Choose varieties of tomatoes that can be trained up stakes.

GREENGAGES
Fan-trained greengages cover the walls. You might also choose other plums, cherries, apples, pears and other tree fruits.

FLOWER BORDER
Annuals raised from seed, such as larkspur, statice and helichrysum, provide fresh flowers and dried arrangements for the house. Tulips give early colour, while box makes a strong evergreen border for the display.

PATH OF ROSES
The rambling roses 'Rambling Rector', 'Albéric Barbier', 'Wedding Day' and 'Little White Pet' line the path, growing up sturdy poles and along swags of rope. A thick ribbon of sweet-smelling pinks runs along underneath.

ribbon of sweet-smelling old-fashioned pinks runs along underneath.

Gnarled espaliers are a feature of all old kitchen gardens, creating living screens around the vegetable plots with their outstretched, lichen-covered branches. Once the framework is securely established, they are easy to prune to shape each summer. Here, espaliered apples and pears are used round two sides of the plot, with fan-trained greengages spread out on the wall behind the picking border.

The way you organize the vegetable plots themselves is entirely a matter of personal taste. You might like to divide each big plot (these are 7.5m/25ft square) into a series of raised beds. You could fit five long 1.2m (4ft) beds with narrow beaten earth paths between in each of these big squares. You may wish to practise a traditional crop rotation, with members of the onion family in one big plot, brassicas in another, legumes in a third and potatoes together with root vegetables in the fourth. There are disadvantages, though, in grouping similar crops together as they tend to pass diseases from one to the other more quickly. In this plan, traditional vegetables such as potatoes, onions, parsnips and cabbages are grown in a mixed patch. Runner beans and climbing French beans are trained on hazel poles, bowed over to make a tunnel down the central path.

The main paths can be hoggin (rolled aggregate), gravel or grass. In old kitchen gardens, paths were often made from ash, spewed in vast quantities from the solid fuel boilers that heated the acres of glass. Grass looks wonderful, but needs regular mowing and edging. It may also transmute inexorably into mud in the winter, when you are busy (or should be) wheeling about barrows of muck and compost. Hoggin and gravel will need something to contain them on either side, perhaps wooden boards held in place with pegs bashed into the earth.

INGREDIENTS FOR A TRADITIONAL KITCHEN GARDEN
to fill a plot 7.5m (25ft) square, just one quarter of a full walled garden

GREENHOUSE
- 1 fan-trained nectarine 'Lord Napier'
- 1 fan-trained peach 'Peregrine'
- 12 tomato plants
- 6 peppers
- Pots of geraniums

PICKING BORDER
- 1 fan-trained gage 'Denniston's Superb'
- 1 fan-trained gage 'Cambridge Gage'
- 1 fan-trained gage 'Reine Claude de Bavay'
- 3 roses 'Iceberg'
- Larkspur raised from seed
- Statice raised from seed
- Helichrysum raised from seed
- Tulips in quantity

TO EDGE THE PLOT
- 1 espalier pear 'Fondante d'Automne'
- 1 espalier pear 'Beurre Hardy'

- 1 espalier apple 'George Cave'
- 1 espalier apple 'Sunset'

TO LINE THE PATH
- 2 roses 'Rambling Rector'
- 2 roses 'Albéric Barbier'
- 2 roses 'Wedding Day'
- 2 roses 'Little White Pet'

TO FILL THE PLOT
- 3 rows potatoes (2 rows first early, 1 row second early)
- 3 rows onions (from sets)
- 3 rows carrots
- 3 rows leeks
- 2 rows parsnip
- 1 row red cabbage
- 1 row Savoy cabbage
- 3.6m (12ft) run of runner beans either side of the central path
- 3.6m (12ft) run of climbing French beans either side of the path

IN THE BORDER

Occasional drama is what you want in a herbaceous border, to wake up the sleepy hordes of geraniums and well-bred campanulas. There is no reason why vegetables and fruit should not provide that drama as easily as flowers. The best borders, as gardeners are told a thousand times, are those that include plenty of good foliage. Only the slightest shift of focus is needed before you reach for a ruby chard instead of a bergenia, plant a globe artichoke rather than an acanthus or fill a gap with a frilly-leaved lettuce rather than a hosta. What could be more dramatic spearing through a mound of bright red verbena than the elegant drooping leaves of leeks, especially the burnished purple-leaved cultivar 'Bleu de Solaise'? If you leave the leeks in place, they will run up to flower, producing huge silvery white heads like an allium's. That is not surprising, for alliums are what they are. Be bold and cast aside inhibition. Liberate your leeks and let their flags fly among your flowers.

INGREDIENTS TO INCLUDE IN A BORDER

- **Runner beans** These (which might equally well be purple-splashed climbing French beans) can climb over tall wickerwork set between tall purple *Verbena bonariensis* and the fluffy heads of thalictrum.
- **Feathery bronze fennel** makes a good contrast with the spiky variegated leaves of iris.
- **Artichokes and cardoons** Both are dramatic plants in a border setting, but you must not put any other plant too close to them. Although they are ruthless smotherers, the plants have great style and presence. If you can bear not to eat the artichokes, they open out into huge blue thistleheads.

- **Sage and parsley** Both can enliven the front of a border with their contrasts of texture and tone: the sage's cool grey foliage makes a perfect foil for crisply curly-leaved parsley. Flat-leaved parsley, which is not such a bright green, would be less successful.
- **Chard** This may start off with bright green leaves but at the first touch of cold weather they turn a rich, shining purple which makes a dramatic setting for the bright red midribs, especially if you can arrange them so that the light shines through the leaves. Use them at the edge of a path, where other plants will not obscure the singing colour of the stems.
- **Kale** This is one of the best of all foliage plants. Choose 'Red Russian' with greyish-green leaves and purple midribs or tall 'Redbor' with curly beetroot-coloured leaves. 'Nero di Toscana' is even darker, and is as delicious to eat as it is to look at.

FORMAL FRUIT GARDEN

A beautifully trained espalier apple, perhaps with a row of Chinese chives at its foot, is on its own an elegant pleasure. In cold areas, a wall offers protection for the blossom against late frosts and its stored warmth hastens the ripening of the fruit in autumn. The charm of trained fruit trees lies in their formal precision and they can be used to great effect in a garden, either against a wall or tied to strong parallel wires stretched between posts. Grown like this, both apples and pears will make a protective screen around a fruit garden, filled with raspberries, strawberries and currants. The practical reason for growing soft fruit together in a patch is that you can net the whole lot together against birds, who can smell a new luncheon bar a mile off. Do not believe anyone who tells you that if you plant extra for the birds, both you and they will be happy. They will certainly be delirious at the prospect of more food – and will bring along even more friends to share in their joy. But you will still be left without a strawberry to your name. To enhance the decorative air of a fruit plot, you could introduce some sort of arbour at the centre. Find a rubber hawk to sit on top of the arbour and it may save you the trouble of a net.

Making a fruit garden

Grouping fruit together in the garden also gives you a chance to arrange it in a decorative yet practical and productive way. The whole plot can be screened from the rest of the garden by apples and pears trained as espaliers. Winter will reveal the geometry of their bare branches; then follows blossom and luscious fruit. Raspberry canes are generally planted in wide parallel rows. But if you make a squarish plot and plant two long lines of raspberries from corner to corner, you give yourself a much more interesting set of shapes, four generous triangles, which you can then fill with other soft fruit.

Choose two different types of raspberry: one that crops early in the season, the other much later. 'Autumn Bliss' is a particularly good variety, cropping from late summer into autumn. Support the raspberries in the usual way by stringing parallel wires between posts from corner to corner of the plot.

Gooseberries grown as standards on a long single trunk will reinforce the formal nature of this design. Put one in each quarter of the plot and stake it firmly, for the trees are top heavy, especially when laden with a crop. Prune them regularly to keep the mop-headed shape.

Use two of the quarters for strawberries, starting the plants off in one quarter and then transferring runners to the opposite quarter when the original plants begin to flag. Strawberry plants rarely crop well after three years and the old plants should be lifted and thrown away when the new bed is established. Refresh the ground with compost or muck before you reverse the process and use this bed again for new runners. Wherever there is a spare patch of ground, sow annual flowers such as rudbeckias and cornflowers.

Trim the outer edge of the other two triangles with a neat alpine strawberry such as 'Baron Solemacher', which does not make runners but clumps up liberally to form a thick band of fresh foliage, dotted in late summer with delicious small strawberries. Use the space inside the border for currants, planting three blackcurrants in one plot and a mixture of red and white currants in the other. If one side of your soft fruit patch happens to butt up against a wall, you can grow the redcurrants as cordons, training three stems vertically up wires. The currants, displayed thus, look particularly lush and translucent.

Planted up in this way, your soft fruit patch will crop intensively, but it needs to be well fed first. You must also mulch the ground liberally in autumn or spring with a thick layer of muck. It will be lapped up greedily. And in order to keep the arrangement looking neat, you must prune regularly. Each year cut out the fruited canes of the raspberries and tie in the new canes. Each year, too, cut out some of the old wood from the blackcurrant bushes, for the best fruit is produced on new wood. If you are short of space, choose a cultivar such as 'Ben Sarek', which is more compact than other types.

INGREDIENTS FOR A FRUIT GARDEN
in a plot 7.5m (25ft) square

- Pears 'Beurre Hardy' and 'Conference' grown as espaliers or fans
- Apples 'James Grieve' and 'Egremont Russet' grown as espaliers or fans
- Raspberries 'Glen Moy' and 'Autumn Bliss' (24 of each)
- Blackcurrants 'Ben Lomond', 'Ben Sarek' and 'Ben Hope' (1 of each)

PLANTING PLAN:
FORMAL FRUIT GARDEN

An arrangement like this should take up roughly 7.5m (25ft) square. Adapt it to suit your own tastes. If gooseberries are not a favourite, use bay trees, and plant parsley instead of alpine strawberries.

BLACKCURRANTS

Plant three bushes in one triangle. If you are short of space, choose a cultivar such as 'Ben Sarek', which is more compact than other types.

PEARS

Since few pears are self-fertile, plant two varieties to ensure pollination. Avoid planting where frosts may ruin the blossoms and subsequent fruit.

RASPBERRIES

Grow one line of summer-fruiting raspberries and one of an autumn-fruiting variety. This row of 'Glen Moy' will provide abundant fruit in summer, followed by a later crop from the row of 'Autumn Bliss'.

STRAWBERRIES

Use two of the triangles for strawberries, starting plants off in one and transferring rooted runners to the other when the original plants begin to flag. Renew plants after three years.

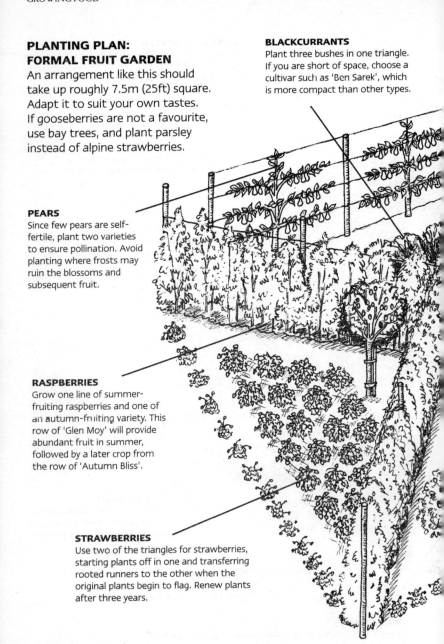

ESPALIERED APPLES
Growing apples in this way will not produce as big a crop as on a half-standard tree, but the fruit ripens well since it is better exposed to sunlight.

ANNUAL FLOWERS
Whenever there is a spare patch of ground, sow some flowers. Annuals such as rudbeckias and cornflowers put on a fine show through summer.

GOOSEBERRIES
Grown as standards on a single stem, these four bushes reinforce the formality of the design. Prune them regularly to keep the neat, mop-headed shape.

ALPINE STRAWBERRIES
Edge beds with plants of the variety 'Baron Solemacher'. It does not make runners, but instead clumps up to form a thick band of fresh foliage.

WHITE CURRANT
One bush has been planted here. Choose a variety such as 'White Grape' that has large, fine-flavoured fruit.

REDCURRANTS
There are two bushes here. Their clusters of translucent fruit have a jewel-like quality when the sun catches them.

- White currant 'White Grape' (1)
- Redcurrants 'Jonkheer van Tets' and 'Stanza' (1 of each)
- Gooseberries 'Leveller' and 'Whinham's Industry' (2 of each)
- Strawberries 'Elsanta' and 'Mara des Bois' (12 of each)
- Strawberries (alpine) 'Baron Solemacher' (30)

AN ALCOHOLIC HEDGE

For taking away the backs of your knees, there is nothing like a slug of sloe gin. In country areas sloes are a common component of mixed hedgerows, but there is no reason why they should not be planted in town. They could be part of an alcoholic hedge, mixed with elder for champagne and wine, cherry plums to make into liqueur and filberts or Kent cobnuts to nibble along with your drink. What has a hedge of Leyland cypress to offer compared with this decorative and productive mixture?

The key elements

Sloes are the fruit of the blackthorn (*Prunus spinosa*), whose spiny shoots make a hedge that neither animals nor vandals can push through. The wood is dark, a counterfoil to the wreaths of white blossom that cover it in spring before the leaves come out. The leaves are small and oval. The fruit, mostly stone, is darkest purple, no bigger than a grape and with a rich pewter bloom.

Since blackthorns are wild plants, often growing in tough, exposed situations, they do not need cosseting in the garden. They will need cutting back from time to time, more to restrict their girth than their height. The thickest and best hedges are those that are properly laid, but this is a farmer's skill, rarely a gardener's. You need to lurk around ploughing matches and other such agricultural meets where hedging competitions are held. Then it is a matter of bribing the winner to come and look at your patch.

It will be some time, though, before you need to worry about this. Blackthorns are best established when they are about 30–45cm (12–18in) high and though they quickly make a hedgey-looking mass, you can snip them whenever you want, to stop them straying over paths or other shrubs. Set the plants about 45cm (18in) apart. To get through the labour of planting (best done in late autumn), think of the gin. It is the most vital ingredient of a winter picnic.

Elder grows so easily that it is practically a weed, but if you coppice it regularly, pruning out some of the oldest growths each year, on a three-year rotation, it can be kept within bounds. It does not mesh in the same way as blackthorn, so on its own, unlaid, it won't keep animals in or people out. It grows very fast, though, and provides a good tall summer screen – and two sources of alcohol. From the flower heads – wide, flat creamy heads of blossom, which appear in early summer – you can make champagne. The berries, which come in late summer, provide a second excuse for a binge. There are always far more than you need, but the birds will be grateful for the leftovers and will then customize your car for you with surreal splodges of purplish-grey. But think of the brownie points you are gaining for your ecological correctness. As well as being decorative, a mixed hedge is good for birds.

As an ingredient of a hedge, the cheapest elder is the wild one, *Sambucus nigra*, with green leaves and creamy heads of blossom. It grows to about the same height as the blackthorn, but much faster. Sappy new shoots can make 1.5m (5ft) in a season. It is very easy to grow from cuttings, taken in November. You need lengths of hardwood about 30–40cm (12–15in) long. Stick them in a row in a nursery bed and transplant them to the hedge after a year.

For fitness of purpose there is nothing to beat common elder, but if you want something more decorative, more gardenesque, you can choose 'Aurea', a form with golden foliage, though it becomes green as the summer wears on. 'Aureomarginata' has leaves with yellow margins. The problem with these in a drunken hedge is that the best leaves come from cutting the elder hard back each winter. This will be at the expense of the flowers, so you won't get your champagne.

The form called *Sambucus laciniata* does not need such drastic treatment. It has leaves so finely cut they look like ferns, but it is not so vigorous as the wild kind. There are other forms too, with purple or white speckled leaves, and some that have pink flowers rather than cream. Berries are mostly reddish black, though there is an aesthete elder called 'Alba' that has white berries.

Elders are even less bother than blackthorns and will grow well in shade. The bark is pale, furrowed and corky, the new shoots pithy rather than woody. The bruised leaves have a sour smell. Elders like damp soil better than dry and, like the other ingredients of this hedge, will do better with an annual mulch of compost than without. Plant them about 4m (14ft) apart, hazels at a similar distance. Clusters of hazelnuts will decorate the hedge from late summer on, and in late winter and early spring it will be hung with delicate catkins. Both elders and hazel can be kept within bounds if branches are removed from the base at regular intervals.

The cherry plum has fruits twice the size of sloes and half as bitter. It is called *Prunus cerasifera*. It is more tree-like than the sloe, often growing taller, though of course you can trim it down to size. Both trees, left to their own devices, will become as wide as they are high. The cherry plum blossoms in early spring – white flowers, slightly larger than the sloe's. The fruit ripens in late summer. It makes an excellent hedge or screen and, mixed with sloe, gives a long season of blossom. Nursery plants are likely to be 45–60cm (18–24in) tall and you should set them about 60cm (2ft) apart. The hedge can be pruned back at any time of the year. The fruits are too fiddly for pies but make a good liqueur or wine, which becomes more like port the longer you keep it.

Once the hedge is reasonably established, say to about 1m (4ft), you could add to its alcoholic potential by planting cultivated blackberries at intervals along it and training the shoots along the hedge, tying them in roughly where necessary. Blackberries call for the same sort of treatment as raspberries. Each year, after you have gathered the fruit, you must cut out the old growths on which the fruit was borne and tie in the new ones that spring like a fountain from the base. Cultivated varieties provide fruit that is larger, earlier and less pippy than wild blackberries. Try 'Bedford Giant', or 'Loch Ness' for taste. For the most decorative effect, use the parsley-leaved blackberry.

At the foot of the hedge you could grow naturalized foxgloves, which flower in early summer.

INGREDIENTS FOR AN ALCOHOLIC HEDGE
roughly 4m (14ft) long

Choose plants to provide the raw materials for your favourite brews and adjust the quantities according to the length of hedge required. If possible make the planting strip about 1m (3ft) wide and set plants in a zigzag pattern, some at the front and some at the back, to make a hedge that is reasonably thick.
- 2 blackthorn (*Prunus spinosa*)
- 2 cherry plum (*Prunus cerasifera*)
- 1 elder (*Sambucus nigra*)
- 1 hazelnut (*Corylus avellana*)
- 1 blackberry 'Bedford Giant'
- 6 foxgloves (*Digitalis purpurea*)

A VEGETABLE PATCHWORK

Vegetables planted in bold blocks have more impact than those planted in single rows. If you divide up a plot into a series of rectangular beds of different sizes and proportions you can make a vegetable patchwork like a Mondrian painting. In this way you can build up contrasts of colour and texture just as you do in a flower border. You could add height to the patchwork by lashing together hazel poles to make the outdoor equivalent of a room divider and use it to support a crop of scrambling peas. It could equally well be used for climbing French beans or flowers. The annual climber *Cobaea scandens* would give the plot an exotic touch. Tall stems of sweetcorn will make a living hedge to screen your vegetable patchwork from the rest of the garden; Jerusalem artichokes can be used in much the same way. Make the main paths through the plot wide and paved and connect them with much narrower routes of beaten earth so that you can get in to pick or weed the vegetables. The beds should not be too wide to be tended from one path or another. Rotate the crops in the beds each year so that the nutrients in the soil are not exhausted.

Making a patchwork

This kind of layout will lend itself to any garden, whatever the size or however awkward the shape. Plan to use plants that look good in combination with each other and that will supply meals for most of the year. You can vary the quantities to suit your taste. Choose the most decorative vegetables such as bright ruby chard or courgettes with glowing golden flowers and fruit. Grow lettuce such as frilly, burnished 'Lollo Rossa', 'Red Salad Bowl' or 'Pablo' next to the ferny foliage of carrots or the steel-blue ribbons of leeks. In winter, cabbages in red, purple and silver and Savoys with crinkled lizard leaves will provide a feast for the eye as well as the table.

In this plan (based on Mondrian's 1921 painting *Composition in Red, Yellow and Blue*) the patchwork is made up entirely of vegetables and herbs. For greater contrast of colour, add flowers. Orange marigolds could replace one bed of parsley, or a stand of cheerful sunflowers could be planted instead of the red-stemmed chard. If you do use flowers, choose annuals rather than more permanent perennials that occupy the ground from year to year. The wide divisions between the beds are proper paths, which can be made from paving slabs or other hard material such as brick. The narrow paths can be left as beaten earth, although on heavy ground you might find a dressing of bark or woodchips helps to mop up the damp. All beds have one 'proper' hard path along one border, so that you can get a wheelbarrow in if necessary. None of the crops in this planting will need support, but you could introduce a screen alongside one of the paths and use it to prop up a crop of peas.

INGREDIENTS FOR A VEGETABLE PATCHWORK
for a plot roughly 7.5 x 5m (25 x 16ft)

- **Parsley** You need two sorts, flat and curly leaved, both sown from seed in situ. It is slow to germinate and runs to seed in its second year. Then you must sow again.
- **Chives** These can be sown from seed or set out as small plants. Cut down a portion of the plants in rotation, to encourage a constant supply of fresh green shoots.

- **Cabbage** It is easier to acquire these as plants than to grow them from seed. Use two different kinds, 'Red Drumhead' (9 plants) and silvery 'Spring Hero' (14).
- **Onions** There should be room for about 40 of these, planted as sets in spring. Choose between mild red onions such as 'Rossa Lunga di Firenze' or 'Red Baron' (though

PLANTING PLAN: VEGETABLE PATCHWORK

Designed for a plot roughly 7.5 x 4.9m (25 x 16ft), this plan shows the challenging variety of vegetables and herbs that can be combined in patchwork planting; quantities represented are not exact.

CABBAGES
Round red kinds, such as 'Ruby Ball', provide contrast in colour and shape, especially next to bright green parsley.

LETTUCE
Use this block to grow a crisphead type that adds texture to the salad bowl and garden alike.

ONIONS
The slender, strappy foliage of onions looks much more decorative set against the chunky shapes of oriental brassicas.

ORIENTAL BRASSICAS
Pak choi and Chinese cabbage have been chosen here, but other oriental vegetables would work equally well, providing an exotic contrast to their more traditional neighbours.

SWEETCORN
This gives the added dimension of height. Increase the productivity of sweetcorn by planting it in blocks, which will ensure good pollination.

CHARD
For the best effect, you need the red-stemmed ruby chard to achieve a bold central block of colour in the garden.

LETTUCE
It is worth sowing three blocks. Here, you could grow a small butterhead such as 'Tom Thumb', or the semi-cos 'Little Gem'.

PARSLEY
Include both flat- and curly-leaved. This block has been
set aside for the more decorative curly type.

ONIONS
Ring the changes and experiment in spacing onions. You
will get larger bulbs if you plant them farther apart.

COURGETTES
All types are decorative, with their golden flowers, but for
even greater impact choose a yellow-fruited variety.

CHIVES
Undemanding but striking, chives
make a neat edge to a plot.

CABBAGES
Use a standard type or
a more crinkly Savoy.
Both will withstand
harsh weather, so you
may enjoy their intricate
colours and shapes even
during the winter.

LEEKS
Leeks are in the ground
a long time, and their
strong green tops (flags)
are splendid enough to
justify a central position in
the patchwork.

PARSLEY
Plainer than its curly-leaved cousin,
flat-leaved parsley has the finest flavour.

LETTUCE
Use one of three blocks to grow frilly red types such as 'Lollo
Rossa'. They will last throughout the summer if their leaves
are harvested regularly.

CARROTS
Sow seed thinly, and grow several different varieties in
succession so that you can enjoy a continuous crop as well
as their decorative, feathery foliage.

it bolts) and standard varieties such as 'Sturon'.

- **Courgettes** These should be set out as young plants. Three should be plenty, as they take up an extraordinary amount of room. Use a yellow-fruited variety such as 'Soleil' as well as green ones.
- **Lettuce** There should be room for three blocks. Experiment with different varieties such as 'Lollo Rossa', 'Tom Thumb' and 'Merveille de Quatre Saisons', which can be grown from plugs or sown from seed and thinned in situ. Use one patch for a cut-and-come-again salad crop such as Italian 'Misticanza'.
- **Sweetcorn** This can be sown in situ, or raised in a greenhouse and transplanted out in late spring. There should be room for about 15 plants, planted in a block to aid pollination. Supersweet varieties such as 'Northern Extra Sweet' must not be mixed with ordinary kinds.
- **Chard** The showiest is multi-coloured 'Bright Lights' but it can look too hectic, all the traffic-light colours jumbled together. For the best effect, use 'Ruby Chard', which can be sown in situ and then thinned, in the same way as beetroot.
- **Leeks** These can be set out as young plants in early summer. There should be room for about 30 in two rows of 15 each. Try 'Bleu de Solaise' for its beautiful purplish leaves.
- **Garlic** The cloves should be planted in early winter. 'Arno' is a soft-neck type, 'Sprint' (early to mature) a stiff-neck type.
- **Oriental brassicas** Pak choi and Chinese cabbage are shown here, grown as individual plants (see pages 61–4), but oriental saladini would work equally well, grown as a cut-and-come-again crop to provide leaves for salads in autumn, winter and spring. Sprinkle the seeds in wide drills, sowing it at two-week intervals. Mixtures may contain pak choi, choy sum, mizuna and spicy mustard.
- **Carrots** Sow seed in situ, as thinly as possible, either broadcast or in rows. It is slow to germinate. 'Sytan' has some resistance to carrot fly, a useful attribute.

DECORATIVE COMBINATIONS

Shape, form, colour and texture are the attributes you have in mind when combining plants in a flower border. You put together those that will enhance each other's characteristics, perhaps using a broad-leaved hosta to set off the elegant fronds of a fern, or contrasting the grey foliage of artemisia with the saturated purple of cotinus. Vegetables, herbs and fruit are no less diverse in their qualities. Of course they are grown to eat. That is their prime purpose. But while they are growing we can heighten our pleasure in them by combining them in equally telling ways. For hosta, think cabbage. For fern, think carrot. Seek out lettuces – there are plenty – with rich red tones in their leaves and set them against the bright green foliage of curly endives. Use bright clumps of parsley among the marigolds, or edge the onion bed with bands of long-flowering violas. Liberate your leeks and let them fly their blue-green flags among the flowers of the herbaceous border.

INGREDIENTS FOR FIVE DECORATIVE COMBINATIONS

COMBINATION 1
Dwarf alpine strawberries make a fine broad edging for a bed of lavender. Choose a strawberry – such as 'Baron Solemacher' – that clumps up rather than one that sends out runners. The strawberry is not evergreen but the leaves stay fresh over a long period and provide an excellent foreground for the spiky lavender.

COMBINATION 2
At the end of their season, let some leeks run up to seed, with silvery-purple globes of flower balancing on strong hollow stems. Surround them with leaf crops of red-stemmed chard and lettuce and encourage marigolds to self-seed in between.

COMBINATION 3
For form, colour and texture, you can scarcely find a better plant than a cabbage. Swirling skirts of leaves surround the tightly folded hearts of red cabbages, which you can protect with tall screens of purple-flowered *Verbena bonariensis*. The verbena is a short-lived perennial, with a strong stem and very little leaf.

COMBINATION 4
Let the long elegant fingers of an oak-leaf lettuce brush against a line of the irrepressible miniature viola 'Jackanapes' along the margin of a path. The viola is ideal in a situation such as this for, though it is exuberant, it does not get too big or straggly. More aggressive plants will attack your ankles.

COMBINATION 5
The late-maturing Brussels sprout 'Rubine' has sprouts as richly dark as its leaves, which can be well set off by the bright blooms of the California poppy (*Eschscholzia californica*). This is an annual which will perpetuate itself by self-seeding wherever there is a small patch of bare earth.

SALAD AND HERB PLOT

A salad plot combined with a scattering of the most useful culinary herbs such as parsley, chives, mint and coriander will, with a little planning, provide a long succession of crops for a gourmet gardener. Lettuce in all forms – cos, looseleaf, butterhead and crisphead – provide the bulk of the planting, but for a smooth sequence of crops you need a small back-up plot or greenhouse to raise fresh seedlings for transplanting into the beds at the appropriate time.

Looseleaf lettuces, which do not form hearts, stand a long time in the ground, as you gather only a few leaves at a time from each plant. The red looseleaf lettuce 'Lollo Rossa' eventually grows up to make an extremely decorative tall pagoda, but by that time the leaves will be tough and bitter.

Combine crinkly looseleaf lettuces with smooth upright types such as the red cos 'Little Leprachaun'. Include other salad crops such as rocket, mizuna (good in winter) and corn salad. For extra decorative effect, let flowers such as nemophila (baby blue eyes), pink opium poppies and purple *Verbena* 'La France' grow among the salads. The poppies will keep themselves going by self-seeding. The other flowers will have to be replaced each year. In the main, this will be a late spring and summer garden, though some salads, especially if they are given the protection of cloches, will continue through into winter. Endive, rocket, corn salad and oriental mizuna will all help to extend the season.

In a formal design, you need to think carefully about a suitable centrepiece. You could use a big clay pot full of scented-leaved geraniums or a wigwam of sweet peas. If you used a pot, you could surround it with low mats of thyme and marjoram. You could also use a tall architectural plant such as angelica or fennel. Angelica is splendidly statuesque, with bright, light green foliage. It is a biennial and in the second year the plant throws up huge, rounded flower heads of pale yellow green. But remember that the whole thing stands taller than a man and that it takes up a lot of sideways space. There is a dramatic purple-stemmed form called *Angelica gigas*.

Fennel will grow equally tall but is less beefy. There is an excellent bronze-leaved variety called *Foeniculum vulgare* 'Purpureum', with filigree foliage topped by flat heads of golden flowers in July. Both these herbs will seed themselves about furiously if you let them. Be ruthless about pulling up and discarding excess seedlings.

Edging plants need to be compact. Floppers will block the paths and swish wetly round your ankles. If they flop the other way, they will smother crops. Box is a traditional edging plant, but it is hungry. As the crops inside the beds are predominantly leafy, you could experiment instead with flower edgings: the Spanish daisy *Erigeron karvinskianus* or a compact flowering viola such as 'Moonlight', which has pale cream flowers.

Two edgings are suggested for this design: violas and germander (*Teucrium chamaedrys*). The germander is a hardy little subshrub that makes neat, evergreen growth rarely more than 22cm (9in) high. The little oval leaves are deep shining green on top, grey underneath. The tiny flower spikes, bright pink, last from mid to late summer. When they are over, you need to clip the growth lightly to keep the edgings neat.

INGREDIENTS FOR A SALAD AND HERB PLOT
7m (24ft) square

CENTREPIECE
- Angelica, as in the plan, or fennel, or a big pot of scented-leaf geranium (surrounded by mats of thyme and marjoram), or a wigwam of sweet peas.

Clockwise from top left:
BED 1
- **Edging** Viola
- **Infilling** Three different lettuces such as 'Saladin', 'Merveille de Quatre Saisons' and 'Rouge d'Hiver'. 'Saladin' is a compact Iceberg type, a pale green crisphead, slow to bolt and best sown in spring and summer. 'Merveille de Quatre Saisons' can be grown all through the year but is best from spring and autumn sowings. It makes big, solid heads with large, curled reddish leaves. 'Rouge d'Hiver' is a cos lettuce that produces small, pointed, compact heads to cut through autumn, winter and spring. You can also crop it early for baby salad leaves.

BED 2
- **Edging** Germander
- **Infilling** Corn salad (spring and autumn) with radish substituted in summer, endive – a broad-leaved (Batavian) type such as 'Cornet de Bordeaux' – and pink (or red or black) opium poppies scattered throughout. 'Cornet de Bordeaux' is a very hardy French endive which can be cut all the way

through winter. It has broad leaves and an upright habit of growth. Land cress is a low-growing, powerfully flavoured winter salad to be sown in September and October for cropping between November and April. Radish 'Cherry Belle' or 'French Breakfast', sown between March and July, may mature in as little as six weeks.

BED 3
- **Edging** Viola
- **Infilling** Lettuces 'Merveille de Quatre Saisons', 'Lollo Rossa' and 'Little Gem' in alternate rows. 'Merveille de Quatre Saisons' is a butterhead type suitable for sowing from late winter (under cover) until late summer. It makes huge, generous plants, the green leaves overlaid with a distinct reddish brown. 'Lollo Rossa' is a loose-leaf lettuce with distinctive frilly leaves, tinged with red. 'Little Gem' is a well-known, compact semi-cos lettuce, all crispy heart. It is quick to mature, but the stem, once cut, won't sprout again.

BED 4
- **Edging** Germander
- **Infilling** Oakleaf lettuce 'Cocarde', nemophila (baby blue eyes) and parsley in alternate rows with pink, red or black opium poppies scattered throughout. 'Cocarde' is a large red oakleaf with arrow-shaped leaves. Heads splay out like a trumpet and

PLANTING PLAN: SALAD & HERB PLOT

This is a salad-lover's garden, designed to extend the season for picking fresh leaves for as long as possible. It measures just over 7m (24ft) square, but a simplified version could fit into a smaller space or the beds could be used for another range of crops.

LETTUCE

The three varieties here give a long season: crisp 'Saladin', the cos 'Rouge d'Hiver', and solid-headed 'Merveille de Quatre Saisons', all inside a viola edging.

ANGELICA

This makes a bold centrepiece in summer when the garden is at its peak. It grows to about 1.8m (6ft) tall with a 1m (3ft) spread. Be ruthless about pulling up the surplus seedlings it is certain to produce.

CORN SALAD, ENDIVE, PARSLEY, VERBENA & POPPIES

Here are rows of corn salad, the curly endive 'Sally', flat-leaved parsley and *Verbena* 'La France', with opium poppies and a germander edging.

LETTUCE, CHIVES & CORIANDER

Looseleaf lettuce 'Green Salad Bowl' and 'Red Salad Bowl' are combined with rows of chives and coriander, all contained within a viola border.

ENDIVE, RADISHES & POPPIES

The hardy French endive 'Cornet de Bordeaux' is mixed with radishes in summer (or corn salad in autumn) and a sprinkling of pink opium poppies. The edging is germander.

LETTUCE

The frilly looseleaf 'Lollo Rossa' alternates with the reddish-brown butterhead 'Continuity' and green cos 'Valmaine' inside a band of violas.

LETTUCE, PARSLEY, NEMOPHILA & POPPIES

The lettuce here is the oak-leaf 'Cocarde' with curled parsley and the annual *Nemophila menziesii* (baby blue eyes) for decoration. Pink opium poppies are scattered around. The edging is germander.

PATHS

Paving slabs have been used here. The paths need not be wide, but the angles they form may restrict the choice of materials. Gravel would make a good alternative.

LETTUCE, ROCKET & MIZUNA

Rows of the compact, red-leaved, semi-cos lettuce 'Little Leprechaun' alternate with rocket and the oriental brassica mizuna. The bed is edged with purple violas.

RADICCHIO, SALADINI & POPPIES

'Rossa di Verona', a type of radicchio or red chicory, is mixed with saladini, a cut-and-come-again mixture of different lettuces, chicory, endive and rocket. The bed is scattered with poppies and edged with germander.

35

the leaves are dark green with a red overlay. *Nemophila menziesii* grows up to 22cm (9in). The plants have a spreading habit, feathery, deeply cut, pale green leaves and sky-blue flowers with white centres. For decorative effect, the best parsley to use is the curly-leaved kind.

BED 5
- **Edging** Viola
- **Infilling** Rocket, lettuce 'Little Leprechaun' and mizuna, in alternate rows. Salad rocket has larger leaves and a milder taste than wild rocket. Late summer sowings will be less prone to attack by flea beetle. Mizuna, too, makes an excellent ingredient in early winter salads. 'Little Leprechaun' is a very compact semi-cos with red foliage that you can use as a leaf lettuce. It is slow to bolt.

BED 6
- **Edging** Germander
- **Infilling** Radicchio 'Rossa Trevigiana Tardiva', saladini mixture, pink opium poppies scattered throughout. Radicchio (chicory) 'Rossa Trevigiana Tardiva' has beautiful red and white marbled leaves, forms a tight head during winter and can be cropped through until spring if protected from severe frost. Saladini (French mesclun) is a mixture of several different salad crops which you sow by broadcasting and use as seedlings and then as a cut-and-come-again crop. It usually

includes lettuces (both cos and red and green looseleaf), chicory, endive, radicchio and rocket, but you can buy oriental mixtures too.

BED 7
- **Edging** Viola
- **Infilling** Lettuces 'Green Salad Bowl' and 'Red Salad Bowl' with rows of coriander and chives in between. Both lettuces are looseleaf types, differing only in colour. One is green, the other bronzy red. The showiest chives are the giant type, easy to establish as young plants. Coriander is best sown from seed, but you need a strain such as 'Cilantro' or 'Leisure', selected to produce plenty of leaf. 'Moroccan' is a quick-bolting type that produces lots of seed.

BED 8
- **Edging** Germander
- **Infilling** Corn salad, frisée endive, parsley and *Verbena* 'La France' in alternate rows. Corn salad (also known as lamb's lettuce) is one of the hardiest of salad plants, best sown between July and September. The endive could be 'Wallonne' or 'Fine Maraichere' (not hardy), both of which have tight heads of very curled crisp fringed leaves, naturally blanched in the centre. Use flat-leaved parsley for the best flavour. *Verbena* 'La France' is a low-growing, relatively compact purple-flowering verbena.

COTTAGE GARDEN

Profusion and a certain happy randomness should be the order of the day in a cottage garden. Here, vegetables are kings of the castle while flowers grow hugger-mugger in small, odd patches where space can be found for them. Paths are narrow, so that as much room as possible can be given over to the production of food, and can be covered in straw, which in the country at least is cheap and easy to find. It sops up the wet and stops the ground getting muddy. Each season it can be raked up, added to the compost heap and replaced with a fresh covering. Country hedgerows yield elderberries for wine and will also provide the hazel, willow and sweet chestnut needed to make screens tumbling with hops and wigwams to support runner beans or sweet peas. Seats can also be made from willow and hazel, cut from the hedge.

True cottage gardens were made by instinct and fuelled by necessity. Seed for the following season would be saved from the best of the year's crops. By this means, cottage gardeners gradually improved strains of vegetables and developed cultivars that best suited their particular growing conditions. Nowadays, they may introduce plants with a more foreign flavour: feathery Florence fennel to jostle against a more prosaic crop of parsnips and Chinese pak choi to accompany the cabbage.

Recreating the cottage garden

In this plan for a stylized cottage garden, a meandering path leads through a screen of woven willow and makes its way past beds of vegetables, bordered and interspersed with flowers, to a simple seat woven from hazel and willow that occupies a sheltered south-facing corner. A second path leads in through an arch in a willow screen covered with hops and blackberries. Next to it a stand of hollyhocks makes a welcoming entrance. Protecting the garden from cold winds is a mixed hedge of elder, hazel, honeysuckle, ash, willow and hawthorn. The honeysuckle is there for its swoony scent; the rest provide nuts and berries and useful sticks for the garden. In front of the hedge, a succession of biennials – foxgloves, honesty, mullein and evening primrose – will seed themselves from year to year. In the left-hand corner, a fine topiary peacock gazes blandly at the view. In the other corner, next to the seat, a pear tree is planted for its bountiful white blossom and tempting fruit, while an old moss rose provides sweetly scented flowers for a buttonhole.

The paths are beaten earth, laid with straw, and the crops either side are mostly traditional. There is a big bed of peas and potatoes, both of which can be stored for winter use. A wigwam of runner beans rises from a sprawling patch of bush tomatoes and marrow, while other beds include leeks, red cabbages, sprouts and kale.

PLANTING PLAN: COTTAGE GARDEN

With its easy informality, a cottage garden is the most adaptable of styles. This mix of vegetables, flowers, fruit, topiary, and quirky furniture fills an area 6 x 7.5m (20 x 25ft). Draw on the ideas to fill a space any size or shape.

BOUNDARY HEDGE
A mixture of useful species includes willow and hazel for sticks and honeysuckle for scent.

TOPIARY PEACOCK
Yew is best for large clipped shapes such as this sprightly bird.

VEGETABLES
In this bed, carrots, beans, kale, beetroot and Brussels sprouts have been joined by some marigolds and a patch of herbs.

TOMATOES, MARROWS & ONIONS
Use bush tomatoes that do not require staking. The marrow leaves will keep down weeds. Next to them, the onions need a space of their own.

BEAN WIGWAM
The wigwam is made of willow gathered from the hedge and is used to support a crop of scarlet runner beans.

PEAR TREE, ROSE & FLOWERS
A pear tree shades the seat and bears inviting fruit, while in front is an old-fashioned moss rose and space for growing annual flowers. A mixture of biennials lines the foot of the hedge.

BLACKBERRIES & HOPS
These cover a screen woven from willows cut from the hedge. Choose a blackberry variety such as 'Oregon Thornless' that has pretty, finely cut leaves.

VEGETABLES
Lettuce, leeks, parsnips and red cabbage fill this bed, together with Florence fennel, a recent arrival in the cottage garden patch.

PATH EDGINGS
Strawberries and double daisies line the paths. In the centre they are joined by patches of nasturtiums.

HOLLYHOCKS
The tall flower spikes, in the colours of an old tapestry, make a picturebook entrance at the side of the arch.

PEAS & POTATOES
These were both staples of a cottager's diet. The peas would have been dried before being stored for the winter. Now they will be stashed in the freezer.

PATHS
Made of beaten soil, these are covered with straw that can be raked up each season, put on the compost pile, and replaced with a fresh layer.

INGREDIENTS FOR A COTTAGE GARDEN

BACK BOUNDARY
This is a hedge of randomly mixed elder, honeysuckle, hazel, ash, willow and hawthorn, but should not be too tall. In the top left-hand corner, start a piece of yew topiary, as fanciful as you like. In front of the hedge, establish a mixture of biennials, randomly distributed and not in a straight line, which might include mullein (verbascum), honesty, foxglove and evening primrose, which will keep themselves going by self-seeding. They do not all come out at the same time, so will give a long season of interest. To the right of the seat, tuck a pear tree into the corner. Choose a variety such as 'Beth' with a tall, narrow, upright habit. In front of it plant a shrub rose, an old-fashioned moss rose with deep pink flowers.

PATHS
These should be narrow, gently curving and covered with straw, bark or anything else that will stop them becoming muddy. The entrances to the garden are through arches in the woven willow screen, which is partially covered with scrambling hops and a parsley-leaved blackberry, such as 'Oregon Thornless'. The short path on the right is bordered with strawberry plants – proper ones, not alpine strawberries – which benefit from the straw covering on the paths.

At the junction of the paths are two clumps of bright nasturtiums, the dark-leaved lustrous kind called 'Empress of India'.

LEFT-HAND BED
There are four separate elements: a small random herb bed to the left of the seat, some parallel rows of traditional vegetables, a wigwam of runner beans surrounded by tomatoes and marrows and a bed of onions at the bottom. The herb bed could have a fringe of parsley along the path, with sage, thyme and mint filling the rest of the space. Short parallel rows of vegetables, running north to south, could include:

- 2 rows of 'Chantenay' carrots
- 2 rows of kale ('Redbor' and 'Cavolo Nero')
- 1 row of 'Candyman Yellow' marigolds
- 1 row of 'Aquadulce Claudia' broad beans to be followed by a sowing of 'Purple Pod' French beans
- 1 row of 'Boltardy' beetroot
- 1 row of 'Red Rubine' Brussels sprouts

The wigwam is made from 18 sweet chestnut poles wound round with a spiral of willow withies. Cover it with runner beans – perhaps the purple- and red-flowered 'Painted Lady'. Around it plant a sprawl of bush tomatoes: a small-fruited kind such as 'Tornado' would be excellent. There will be room here for marrows or courgettes too.

The onion bed needs to be neatly set out with a block of onions filling the whole of the bottom left-hand corner.

RIGHT-HAND BED

At the top of the bed, by the seat, is a small patch of wallflowers, followed in summer by sunflowers – not giants perhaps, but one of the multi-headed types such as 'Moonwalker' or 'Harlequin' in different shades of orange and lemon. In the bottom corner is a stand of hollyhocks – not big, but filling in a spare patch. Between these two patches of flowers set short rows of vegetables running east to west. There should be room for:

- 1 row of 'Black-seeded Simpson' lettuce
- 2 rows of 'Hannibal' leeks
- 1 row of Florence fennel ('Romanesco' has some resistance to bolting)
- 2 rows of 'Gladiator' parsnip

- 1 row of a red cabbage such as 'Red Drumhead'

BOTTOM BED

This is lined on the one side with 'Hapil' strawberries and on the other by a thick double band of double daisies (*Bellis perennis* 'Tasso Mixed'), with fat splodgy flowers in various shades of white, pink and red. This patch is devoted to two staple crops: peas and potatoes. The potatoes should be a mixture of varieties including a first early such as 'Sprint' and a maincrop such as 'Pink Fir Apple', which can be stored for winter use. The peas would once have been dried and used for a kind of porridge, the 'pease pottage' of the nursery rhyme; now peas are more likely to be stored in the freezer. If you can provide a double row of well-twigged hazel branches, you can grow a tallish variety such as 'Hurst Green Shaft', which matures over a long period.

CITY LARDER

Even if you live with your head in the clouds, marooned seventeen floors up in a block of city flats, you may still be able to surround yourself with the fruits of your own labour by making a mini-kitchen garden in pots and grow bags or galvanized containers on a balcony. Hungry vegetables such as cauliflowers and celery will never be happy in these conditions, but lettuce, tomatoes, peppers and aubergines adapt remarkably well to life in a concrete jungle. Cucumbers, French beans and courgettes are other possibilities, together with a wide range of cut-and-come-again salad crops – rocket, mizuna and saladini mixtures – which can be sown at frequent intervals through the season. Even hanging baskets can be pressed into service: bush tomatoes such as 'Tumbling Tom' will crop happily in a basket, provided you

PLANTING PLAN: CITY LARDER

This plan shows how a mouth-watering ranges of vegetables, fruit and herbs can fit on a balcony only 2 x 1.5m (7 x 5ft). The growing methods used here can be adapted to the smallest of spaces, from roof gardens to minute backyards. Even the windowsill inside has been put to productive use, with pots of aromatic basil and jars of sprouting seeds.

TOMATOES
Choose a bush variety, such as 'Tumbler' or 'Phyra', whose cherry-sized tomatoes will cascade elegantly from the basket. If you remember to water and feed them regularly you will be rewarded with a delicious crop.

CUT-AND-COME-AGAIN SALADS
Sprinkle a mixture of rocket, mizuna and saladini seed into a grow bag and keep cutting the leaves as they sprout.

PARSLEY
The tightly curled kind is the easiest to grow in a pot. It will do best in a shady corner where the compost is less inclined to dry out.

PEPPERS
These will thrive in a pot, given shelter and sun. Raise seedlings indoors, or buy ready-grown plants to put into large containers.

CHILLIES
As with peppers, the best crops in cool climates often come from pot-grown plants. Choose a variety such as 'Yellow Cayenne' or the prolific 'Apache', which may bear up to 100 chillies.

BASIL, SPROUTING SEEDS, MUSTARD & CRESS
Fill the windowsill inside with trays of mustard and cress, pots of basil and jars of sprouting seed such as mung beans.

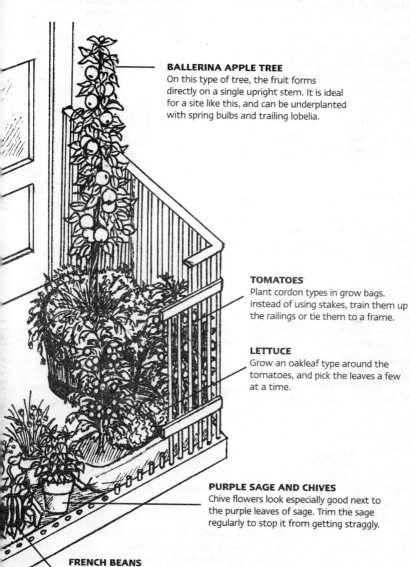

BALLERINA APPLE TREE
On this type of tree, the fruit forms directly on a single upright stem. It is ideal for a site like this, and can be underplanted with spring bulbs and trailing lobelia.

TOMATOES
Plant cordon types in grow bags. Instead of using stakes, train them up the railings or tie them to a frame.

LETTUCE
Grow an oakleaf type around the tomatoes, and pick the leaves a few at a time.

PURPLE SAGE AND CHIVES
Chive flowers look especially good next to the purple leaves of sage. Trim the sage regularly to stop it from getting straggly.

FRENCH BEANS
Use bush varieties. In mid-spring, sow individual seeds into 7cm (3 inch) pots, indoors. The plants should be ready to set out in a grow bag in late spring. Up to 12 plants will fit into one bag. Make sure that they are always watered well.

attend to the feeding and watering. In a hot, dry summer you may have to water containers twice a day. Herbs such as marjoram, savory, sage and thyme grow easily in terracotta pots. Parsley and chives need a little more attention, for they both hate to dry out. Basil can be grown in small pots on a kitchen windowsill, where it will thrive on regular liquid feeds. An indoor windowsill is ideal, too, for crops of mustard and cress, which can be sown on damp tissue paper laid in seed trays. This is also the place to set up a little production line of sprouting seeds. Use them fresh in salads or whirl them in a wok.

MAKING A CITY LARDER
assuming a balcony 2 x 1.5m/7ft x 5ft with railings around three sides

The balcony adjoins a room with a door opening on to it and a window alongside with a deep windowsill. Here basil, mustard and cress and sprouting seeds can grow. Fix a hanging basket to the wall alongside the window and plant it up with a bush tomato such as 'Red Alert' or 'Tumbling Tom'. Most of the crops will grow in growing bags or galvanized containers, laid out around the edge of the balcony. One contains tomatoes and lettuces, another French beans, a third a selection of cut-and-come-again salad crops. Mix your own selection: various mustards, mizuna, pak choi, tatsoi and rocket can all be cropped at the baby-leaf stage. If the balcony is very exposed, you may need to put up heavy mesh netting inside the railings to filter the wind.

In a large half barrel on the right-hand side of the balcony, a dwarf pillar apple of the Ballerina type is planted round with bulbs for a spring display and lobelia, which makes waterfalls of blue through the summer. The apple will need feeding with a slow-release fertilizer.

Because grow bags are relatively shallow, they dry out quickly and you need to be more particular about watering and feeding than you would be if the same crops were growing in open ground. Staking may be a problem if you choose tall cordon-type tomatoes. The compost in a growing bag is not deep enough to support a stake, and you will have to either tie tomatoes to a custom-made frame, which you can buy to fit a standard grow bag, or train your tomatoes up the balcony railings. Concrete makes a cold base. For sulky plants such as tomatoes, which only get going when the soil has warmed up, insulate the bags by slipping some polystyrene tiles under them.

Tomatoes are greedy, so they should have the first turn in a bag. You can use them a second time for a less demanding crop such as lettuce or radish. You can also use bags for perennial crops such as strawberries or mint. Before replanting an old bag, ease out the roots of the previous crop and fork over the compost in the bag. Do not feed the new plants until they are well established. Over-feeding causes a build-up of unhelpful salts, which will eventually retard growth rather than promote it.

French beans such as 'Slenderette' or 'Sonesta' are very successful in grow bags. You can get about 12 plants in each one. Raise the seeds inside, sowing them singly in 7cm (3in) pots. If you sow in mid-spring, the plants should be ready to go into the bags by late spring. If, however, you are not going to be able to water frequently, choose deeper containers such as galvanized troughs and grow your crops in those, rather than in grow bags.

Even the most hastily constructed salad or dish of pasta is transformed by a whiff of basil. You can easily raise plants on a windowsill, where they will last long after an outside crop has been wiped out by frost. Sow seeds in a 10cm (4in) pot in mid-spring. Water the compost and cover the pot with clingfilm until the seedlings emerge. Prick the seedlings out into 7cm (3in) pots and keep them lined up on the windowsill in as much light as possible. From time to time, soak the pots in the sink, adding a few drops of liquid fertilizer to the water. The plants may try to flower but you must not let them. Pinch out the flower heads to keep a good supply of leaves coming on. A warm windowsill is also the ideal place to sprout seeds of adzuki beans, nutritious alfalfa, chickpeas (high in vitamins A and C), curry-flavoured fenugreek, mung beans and snow peas. Think too about finding space for seedlings of amaranth, chervil and purple radish alongside your trays of mustard and cress.

Peppers will thrive in a pot, given shelter and sun. Raise seedlings indoors, or buy ready-grown plants to pot into large contains. Chillies often crop best from pot-grown plants. Choose a variety such as 'Yellow Cayenne' or the prolific 'Apache', which will bear up to 100 chillies.

The tightly curled parsley is the easiest kind to grow in a pot. Put it in a shady corner where the compost is less inclined to dry out. Chive flowers look especially good next to the purple leaves of sage. Trim the sage regularly to prevent it getting straggly.

MEDITERRANEAN COURTYARD

Lemons and large terracotta pots are the quintessential elements of a Mediterranean courtyard garden and if you can lay your hands on beautiful pots, you will be well on the way to making (or faking) the real thing. For you do not necessarily need to be by the Mediterranean to make this kind of garden. It could be in Chile, or South Africa or California or western Australia or any other place where the winters are kind and hard frosts as rare as sunshine in Siberia. A courtyard by its very nature will be a sheltered place, probably enclosed on two of its sides by the arms of the house to which it belongs. A retaining wall, perhaps pierced with railings, will break the force of winds coming from any other quarter. The comfortable stone paving which covers such a courtyard should be randomly laid, with enough cracks to encourage the growth of creeping thymes, marjoram or camomile. Flowers such as monkey-faced violas or the little Spanish daisy *Erigeron karvinskianus* can also seed themselves casually into the paving. Although the courtyard might be used primarily as an outdoor room, with deckchairs for lounging and a shady arbour for meals, there will still be plenty of space on the surrounding walls for fruit such as apricot, peach and nectarine. If you can add a small wall fountain, perhaps a benign lion's mask dripping into a stone trough beneath, you will be getting very close to Eden, Mediterranean style.

The key elements

The suggested courtyard contains two separate areas, linked by a long, low step. The area close to the house is paved with large, random slabs of stone with a stone kerb dropping slightly to a lower level, covered in gravel. Pots are an important feature: three handsome lemon trees in pots march along the edge of the paving, signalling the change in levels. Bay trees in pots stand either side of railings, let into the retaining wall to give a view of the landscape beyond. A pomegranate, which will be covered throughout the summer with showy red flowers, sits in a large pot by the house, while in the sunny gravel area massed lavender fills another swagged terracotta container. Smaller, shallower pots of aeoniums, echeverias or sempervivums can be grouped wherever there is space. One of the doors of the house opens directly into a shadowy arbour, made from rough poles lashed together. A grape vine is trained up the side wall and over the arbour to make a green, living roof. A passion flower, *Cobaea scandens* and summer jasmine, climbing up three support poles at the front, bring extra colour and scent to this relaxed and shady sitting-out area. Low creeping mats of thyme colonize the paving slabs, while the gravel is peppered by a whole series of flowers that will enjoy the sun-baked patch. Sunflowers fill the space between the bay trees, while iris and agapanthus sprawl in relaxed clumps elsewhere. In spring, dwarf bulbs carpet the gravel: species tulips, crocus and de Caen anemones.

MAKING A MEDITERRANEAN COURTYARD
assuming the main part by the house measures 4.5 x 2.4m (15 x 8ft), with an apron of gravel beyond

The courtyard is contained on two sides by the walls of the house, with doors opening into it from two directions. It is surrounded by a retaining stone wall, up to 2m (7ft) high, with railings let in along one stretch. The exit from the courtyard is to the right of the railings. The gravel apron is at a slightly lower level than the paved area, the change highlighted by a row of three lemon trees in decorative terracotta pots.

One of the doors of the house opens on to a vine-covered arbour, measuring about 2.4 × 1.8m (8 × 6ft). It is made from rough, gnarled poles (not regular like larch, nor square-cut timber) of bleached wood. The three uprights along the front edge of the arbour are connected by a long pole. A chequerboard arrangement of poles on top, like a chessboard, makes a framework for a vine such as 'Dornfelder'. Bunches of grapes will hang down inside the arbour, while over the makeshift roof, cobaea and the intricate blooms of the passion flower (*Passiflora caerulea*) blend with the vine's handsome leaves. You could also add a white summer jasmine (*Jasminum officinale*), which does not have such showy flowers but compensates with the swooniest scent this side of paradise. A long wooden plank table can be set under the arbour, ready for outdoor meals.

The pots will be the most important things in this courtyard, especially the pots of lemons. Lemons may take up to a year to ripen on the tree, the glossy yellow globes finishing their long growing period at the same time as the heavily scented flowers that will produce the following season's crop are opening their waxy petals. A citrus tree hung with fruit looks curiously unreal, as though it has all been modelled from wax. Limes and grapefruit are the most tender members of the family; lemons are easier to manage and in a frost-free courtyard can be left out all year. Elsewhere they will have to be trundled under cover for winter. They do not mind being slightly potbound and do not need regular pruning, though you can trim them to shape if necessary.

The deciduous pomegranate (*Punica granatum*) will grow slowly to make a compact small tree about 2.4 × 1.5m (8 × 5ft). It has shiny, pale green leaves and very showy scarlet flowers, tubular and borne in clusters right the way through the summer. The fruit is generally ready to pick in late autumn and makes a very good jelly. In a pot, the pomegranate will need regular watering and a liquid feed once every fortnight. It is not reliably hardy.

Either side of the railings in the gravelled part of the courtyard are mop-headed bay trees growing in plain terracotta pots, while on the gravel stands a large, more decorative pot, packed full with a lavender such as *Lavandula* x *intermedia* 'Hidcote Giant'. Cut it back hard each year, after it has finished flowering, so that it does not become leggy.

The walls of the courtyard should be fully utilized. Train a white wisteria against one of the house walls and a fig on the other. Splay out the fig to make a fan-shaped tree, tied in closely to the wall. Against the retaining wall of the lower part of the courtyard plant a 'Rochester' peach and a 'Lord Napier' nectarine (it could equally well be an apricot), ready-trained as fans. In colder areas, nectarines have to be grown like this if they are to fruit at all outside. In the warm, balmy climate of the Mediterranean, peaches, apricots and nectarines will fruit as freestanding trees, but there is not enough room

PLANTING PLAN:
MEDITERRANEAN COURTYARD

The shape and exposure of your courtyard will, to some
extent, determine the choice of plants. This plan shows just
one way of creating a relaxing garden filled with fruit and
the scent of herbs and flowers.

FLOWERS
Choose flowers such as iris and agapanthus
that positively like to bake and will not droop
if they spend a week without water.

NECTARINE
Trained fruit trees can be used in
a courtyard like wall-hangings in
a room. Through the seasons a
nectarine will provide a decorative
sequence of flowers, foliage and
then fruit.

LAVENDER
Plant one of the taller sorts,
such as *Lavandula angustifolia*,
for maximum effect and place
it so that you can catch its
scent whenever you pass. Cut
it back hard after flowering to
keep it in good shape.

SUNFLOWERS
With their golden heads always
turned toward the sun, a group
of sunflowers puts on a bold
show through the railings. When
the flowers have finished, dry the
heads. The seeds can be eaten
raw or roasted.

BAYS
Two bay trees, trimmed into neat balls at the top,
are placed on either side of the railings. Planted
in large, simple terracotta pots, their clear-cut
outlines stand out well among the more complex
shapes of other plants in the courtyard.

ARBOUR
Formed by a grapevine scrambling over a lattice of rough wooden poles, the arbour makes a relaxed eating area. A passion flower, *Cobaea scandens* and summer jasmine climb the three support poles at the front.

POMEGRANATE
This small tree will have clusters of showy scarlet flowers all summer long. Its fruit, ready in autumn, can be used to make a delicious jelly.

WISTERIA
The variety chosen here has white flowers, giving the courtyard a cool elegance in the heat of the sun.

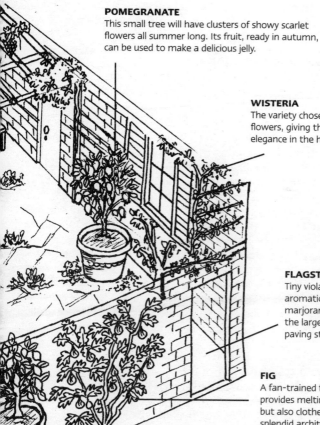

FLAGSTONES
Tiny violas, daises and aromatic thyme and marjoram creep among the large, randomly laid paving stones.

FIG
A fan-trained fig tree not only provides melting, sensuous fruit, but also clothes the wall with splendid architectural foliage.

LEMON TREES
The row of three lemon trees in pots signals the change in levels between the paved area and the semicircle of gravel.

PEACH
A fan-trained peach will produce a first-rate crop in a warm, sheltered spot. An apricot would be equally at home here.

for this in the courtyard. Here they become like wall hangings, providing through the spring and summer a decorative sequence of blossom, foliage and fruit.

You can allow the gravel area to contain as many flowers as is consistent with the way the space is used and the taste of the gardener. Choose between agapanthus, iris, daisy-flowered argyranthemums, arctotis and gazanias. Persuade wallflowers to colonize the walls. Scatter spring bulbs with abandon; they will sensibly disappear from view when their spring act is over.

FORMAL HERB GARDEN

How many of us when we plant hyssop, the aromatic herb that flowers in mid-summer in blue, white and pink, really believe we are going to brew hyssop tea, distil hyssop oil or marshal the local bees to produce hyssop honey? We just like the idea that one day we might. Having hyssop makes us feel comfortable. It reassures us that we have not entirely cut ourselves adrift from a tradition of folk knowledge and thrifty housekeeping. But it is a pretty plant, and if you have enough room there is absolutely no reason why you should not grow herbs such as hyssop or bergamot for their looks. Mix these with culinary herbs such as sage and rosemary. Massive buttresses of purple-leaved sage can prop up a showy centrepiece of cardoon and nasturtiums can cavort round the feet of a monumental stand of lovage.

Traditionally, low box hedges provide neat – and necessary – frames for tumbling plants inside the beds of a herb garden. Evergreens such as box provide year-round interest and form, but given the widespread problem of box blight, you may find it better to use parsley and chives, as in the plan here. Winter structure can come from different kinds of sage, an excellent foliage plant whether in or out of a herb garden, and gently clipped mounds of rosemary.

Making a herb garden
Designs for a formal herb garden can be expanded or shrunk to fill the space you have available. The one suggested here is planted with a collection of herbs for the kitchen, for the most indispensable herbs in a garden are the ones needed for cooking: thyme, basil, parsley, sage and their kind. Decorative standard roses mark the corners of the plot – try 'The Fairy' or 'Little White Pet' – to add a splash of summer colour and scent. Mounds of the tallish rosemary 'Miss Jessopp's Upright' surround the centrepiece, which here is a clipped bay tree in a pot, but it could be a small fountain with a simple jet of water, a statue or an urn tumbling with scented-leaved geraniums. The beds are edged alternately with parsley and chives.

The advantage of having chive edgings is that you can cut them down turn and turn about so that you always have a fresh supply coming on. One lot will be newly sheared to the base, the second will be resprouting, the third will be almost ready to pick and the fourth will be at its peak. Tarragon, sorrel, mint and chervil also respond to this treatment, though of course you would not apply it to shrubby herbs such as rosemary or sage. Herbs can be split roughly into two kinds: the Mediterranean aromatics such as thyme, rosemary and marjoram that like hot sun and grow in poor soil, and others such as mint and borage which like a cooler, richer soil to grow in. If one side of your projected herb patch is sunnier than the other, save it for the Mediterranean sunbathers.

Thymes particularly resent being in damp, clogged soil and will quickly show their displeasure by rotting away. In formal beds such as these, use the shrubby upright kinds of thyme, rather than creeping *T. serpyllum*. Lemon thyme (*T.* × *citriodorus*) is particularly good for stuffings and herb bread. Cut some of the shoots down in June to encourage plenty more leaf for the rest of the season.

Mints have a bad name for putting themselves where they are not wanted, but if you plant several varieties in a bed together, they can battle for space. Contrast dark-leaved peppermint with the variegated leaves of pineapple mint (*Mentha suaveolens* 'Variegata'). The common mint is *M. spicata* or spearmint and there is a beautiful yellow-variegated kind called gingermint (*M.* × *gracilis* 'Variegata'). It is lower growing than the common type but has the same spikes of purplish flower in late summer. Those with refined palates insist that the round-leaved applemint (*M. suaveolens*) makes the best mint sauce.

Coriander is very easy to grow each year from seed, but some strains are better for foliage, others for seed heads. You need both. If you don't use coriander, then substitute dill, which is equally easy to raise from seed. For a constant supply of fresh leaves, sow patches at monthly intervals between early spring and mid-summer. The plants grow up to about 90cm (36in) high and have feathery leaves like fennel.

Use different kinds of basil to make patterns in the herb beds, contrasting neat, self-contained bushes of Greek basil with the huge undulating leaves of the lettuce basil or the purple foliage of the decorative variety 'Dark Opal'. Basils are a collector's dream, as new types keep being introduced. You can get Peruvian, Mexican and Thai basil as well as lemon, lime, aniseed, liquorice and cinnamon types. Connoisseurs of pesto should grow the variety 'Sweet Genovese'.

Paths in a herb garden can be very narrow, just wide enough to shuffle along to pluck and weed. Brick, laid on edge, has a more interesting texture than plain concrete slabs. Gravel, as suggested in this plan, is simple to use but needs low wooden edgings to keep it off the beds. Leave the paths as plain beaten earth if the ground is not too sticky.

PLANTING PLAN: FORMAL HERB GARDEN

This mixture of annual herbs – which you can vary from season to season – and more permanent plants to give height and form has been chosen to fill a plot roughly 2.6m (8½ft) square. However, the design can be expanded or shrunk to fill the space available.

MARJORAM
Mix plain green marjoram with the golden form and set plants 30cm (12in) apart.

ROSEMARY
Choose a fairly vertical type such as 'Miss Jessopp's Upright'. Others tend to sprawl.

ROSE
'The Fairy', with tiny pink flowers, makes an ideal standard, as does 'Little White Pet'.

BASIL
Here, giant-leaved lettuce basil is mixed with lemon basil.

MINT
In this bed, spearmint grows with gingermint, variegated applemint, and purplish eau de cologne mint.

CHERVIL & CORIANDER
These annuals have a light and lacy air. Sow seed in small patches every month from spring to mid-summer.

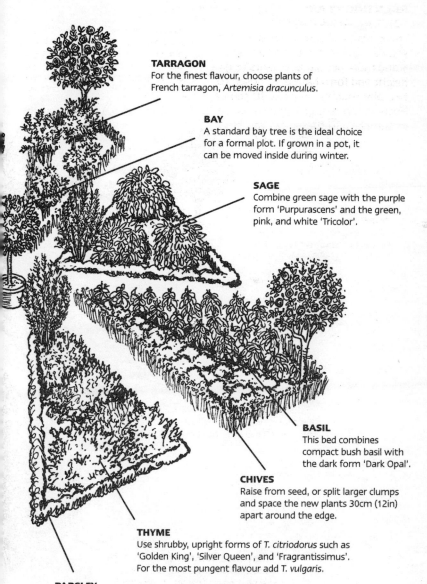

TARRAGON
For the finest flavour, choose plants of
French tarragon, *Artemisia dracunculus*.

BAY
A standard bay tree is the ideal choice
for a formal plot. If grown in a pot, it
can be moved inside during winter.

SAGE
Combine green sage with the purple
form 'Purpurascens' and the green,
pink, and white 'Tricolor'.

BASIL
This bed combines
compact bush basil with
the dark form 'Dark Opal'.

CHIVES
Raise from seed, or split larger clumps
and space the new plants 30cm (12in)
apart around the edge.

THYME
Use shrubby, upright forms of *T. citriodorus* such as
'Golden King', 'Silver Queen', and 'Fragrantissimus'.
For the most pungent flavour add *T. vulgaris*.

PARSLEY
Curled varieties are the neatest for edging. Set plants,
which can be raised from seed, 23cm (9in) apart.

INGREDIENTS FOR A FORMAL HERB GARDEN
roughly 2.6m (8ft 4in) square

- 1 clipped bay for centrepiece
- 4 rosemary, an upright type such as 'Miss Jessopp's Upright'
- 4 standard roses 'Little White Pet' or 'The Fairy'
- Chives planted 30cm (12in) apart (seed or plants) as edging
- Curly-leaf parsley planted 23cm (9in) apart (seed or plants) as edging

Clockwise from top left:
BED 1
- 2 types of basil, such as the giant-leaved lettuce basil and lemon basil. Alternatively you could grow blue-flowered hyssop (*Hyssopus officinalis*), a marvellous bee plant, mixed with bronze-leaved fennel (*Foeniculum vulgare* 'Purpureum').

BED 2
- Marjoram, either plain *Origanum vulgare* or a mixture of plain and gold-leaved *O. vulgare* 'Aureum', planted 30cm (12in) apart

BED 3
- 4 tarragon (French *Artemisia dracunculus*)

BED 4
- 3 sage (1 each of *Salvia officinalis*, *S. o.* 'Purpurascens' and *S. o.* 'Tricolor')

BED 5
- 4 different types of basil (seed), which might include 'Rubin' with purplish-bronze leaves, 'Sweet Genovese', 'Green Globe', which makes dense little bushes looking as if they have been clipped as topiary, and 'Green Ruffles' with heavily ruched leaves.

BED 6
- 5 thyme, including lemon-scented *Thymus × citriodorus*, *T. × citriodorus* 'Golden King', *T. × citriodorus* 'Silver Queen', *T. vulgaris* and orange-scented *T.* 'Fragrantissimus'

BED 7
- Half sown with coriander (seed), both 'Cilantro' which is best for leaf and 'Moroccan' which is best for seed, the other half with chervil (seed)

BED 8
- 4 mint (1 each of *Mentha × gracilis* 'Variegata', *M. × piperita*, *M. spicata*, *M. suaveolens*)

2

GROWING VEGETABLES, HERBS & FRUIT

The following pages give all the information you need to be able to grow a wide range of vegetables, herbs and fruit to combine with flowers in a decorative kitchen garden. Cultivation techniques include full instructions on choosing the right place for each crop, advice on sowing, transplanting, thinning and harvesting, as well as highlighting likely pests and diseases. There are details, too, for pruning and training fruit. You may already know which types of vegetables and fruit you want to grow. If you are not sure, you will find plenty here from which to choose.

VEGETABLES AND HERBS

If on a map of the world you drew lines showing how different foods had travelled from their countries of origin you would end up with a pattern more complex than a spider's web. Before the discovery of the Americas, the vegetable diet in Europe relied heavily on peas and beans. The New World proved a happy hunting ground, as maize and tomatoes as well as potatoes enriched gardens on this side of the Atlantic. Some vegetables travelled in the opposite direction. In the pages ahead you can learn how to grow more than fifty different vegetables and twenty different herbs.

Leaf and salad vegetables

These include some of the lushest vegetables in the kitchen garden: crinkly winter cabbages in red and plum, crisp oriental brassicas, elegantly curled kale, frilly lettuces and endives. Among this group you will find the ingredients for summer salads: cos lettuce, frizzy endive, peppery rocket, crisp chicory as well as a host of other leafy delights such as watercress, purslane and mizuna. Many leaf vegetables are high in vitamins.

Fruiting and flowering vegetables

Warm oranges, yellows and reds characterize the showiest members of this tribe, pumpkins and squash. Along with courgettes, marrows and cucumbers, they belong to the diverse family of cucurbits, originating in South and Central America. Tomatoes belong in this group, too, and can usefully be grown in the kitchen garden sprawling on the ground between tall sheaves of sweetcorn. Here too you will find the most dramatic vegetables – the artichoke and the cardoon, whose sculpted leaves rise from the ground in fountains of silver-grey.

Podded vegetables

The obliging pea and bean family produces two types of food, seeds and pods. You eat either or both, depending on when you gather the crop. This is not a large group, but in nutritional terms it is an important one and the plants, particularly the climbing members of the family, can be used to great effect in a decorative kitchen garden.

Bulb, stem and root vegetables

Although this group does not include the most eye-catching vegetables, it contains some of the most indispensable ingredients for a keen cook: onions, garlic, potatoes and carrots. There are some gourmet treats here too, such as asparagus, but only those with plenty of space will be able to indulge in this particular crop. Leeks can be used to great effect among annual flowers, as can the feathery tops of carrots.

Herbs and edible flowers

All the most useful herbs are to be found in this section, divided into annuals, which must be sown fresh each year, and perennials which, once planted, will provide years of pleasure.

Key to cultivation charts

✤ Sow inside
❂ Sow outside
➡ Transplant
✄ Harvest

LEAF AND SALAD VEGETABLES

Shock waves spread through the florists' world back in the 1950s when the renowned flower arranger Constance Spry first put cabbage leaves among the delphiniums in her arrangements. But she saw what vegetable gardeners had always known: for texture, form, substance and diversity, there is nothing like a cabbage leaf. Unless it is a lettuce leaf. These two vegetables provide endless opportunities for the gardener. For rich combinations, seek out the black Italian kale called 'Cavolo Nero' with narrow upright leaves that are as sumptuously textured as tapestry. Combine it with wobbling heads of allium, purple iris, rosettes of maroon-tinged oak leaf lettuce and deep blue aquilegias. Plant bronze fennel between rows of red cabbage. Try cornflowers among the endives. Use vegetables to provide a feast for the eye as well as the stomach.

INGREDIENTS FOR A GOOD-LOOKING VEGETABLE GARDEN

- Ruby chard has stems that glow with particular brilliance against its shiny green crinkled foliage. Remember to plant it at a sensible distance from the edge of a path so that when the outer leaves splay out from the centre of the plant, they do not get in the way. Well watered, this makes a striking plant for containers.
- Combine complementary pinks and purples in a planting scheme that may include young plants of the cabbage 'Red Drumhead', the frilly rosettes of the looseleaf lettuce 'Lollo Rossa' and the flowering heads of a clump of chives. Curly-leaved parley and the foliage of parsnips will provide green buffers between.
- Ornamental kales have leaves in a wide range of colours – pink, purple, sea green, grey, cream – which blend together in arrangements as subtle as any rose or peony. Although a kale such as this would not be your first choice

for cooking, it makes a decorative feature in an ornamental potager. Kales can also be grown in pots and window boxes.

- When dark looseleaf lettuces run up to seed, they make elegant tall pagodas among the chunky shapes of green looseleaf lettuces. The lettuce patch can be surrounded by a thick border of brightly coloured nasturtiums. Their spicy leaves are good in mixed salads.
- Pak choi is one of many oriental vegetables that are now being grown in western gardens. All parts of the plant are edible – its shiny rounded leaves, its crunchy stems and its flower heads, which may be produced in the first year of growth.
- The handsome kale 'Cavolo Nero' grows like a miniature palm tree, the narrow fronds a dark, almost black green. The texture, bubbly and finely crimped, is like that of a Savoy cabbage. In Tuscany, it is a favourite winter vegetable.

CABBAGES *Brassica oleracea* Capitata Group

Cabbages have an image problem. They make you think of clubroot and caterpillars, starvation soups and the sulphurous smell of rotting leaves. But once you have grown your own, you jettison all that negative baggage. Cabbages start to assume personalities. You begin to appreciate the difference between a sensuously crinkled Savoy and an introverted white Dutch, between an elegant black-leaved kale, 'Cavolo Nero', with leaves as upright as a feather crest, and the tight, bright, mossy curled foliage of green borecole.

Where growing space is limited, the winter types are the cabbages to go for. Too much else cries out for space in summer. For the pleasure of looking at them as well as eating, you need a Savoy type, perhaps 'Bolero' or 'Ice Queen'.

When Savoys, which have dark leaves that are puckered more intricately than smocking, arrived from the Haute Savoie via Holland, they were enthusiastically taken up by sixteenth-century garden writers. Not so rank as the native kales, wrote John Evelyn approvingly.

The beast as you see it at the greengrocer's, trimmed and tamed, is far more impressive standing unfettered in the vegetable garden, where the outer leaves form a vast protective circle around the core, a chiselled swirl of skirt. That was not considered waste when you had sheep and pigs and chickens to feed as well as yourself.

'January King' cabbages have leaves that are less tactile than a Savoy's, but the colouring is more complex. The foliage is steely blue-grey, the outsides of the leaves that curl over the central drumhead flushed deep red. The inside of the cabbage is as green as a spring lettuce.

White cabbage, the sort you use to make coleslaw, is not as hardy as the other two winter types, but the heads last well when cut. You can store them somewhere cool and frost free inside.

RECOMMENDED CULTIVARS
- **January King type** 'January King (3)': characteristic red-tinged hearts.
- **Dutch white** 'Holland Winter White': large heads that will stand outside in mild winters.
- **Red cabbage** 'Red Drumhead': early, uniform and solid, will stand from late summer until midwinter. 'Marner Lagerrot' dense hearts to store from November on.
- **Savoy** 'Best of All': tight, solid heads, hardy throughout the winter. 'Ormskirk': one of the darkest and crinkliest. 'Tundra': deep green fine Savoy with a looser head than others of its type.

Cultivation
Savoy cabbages are extremely hardy. Planted out in mid-summer, they can be harvested from autumn through until the following spring. Cultivars of the January King type need to be set out in early summer and are ready by mid-winter. The solid Dutch white types can be planted out in early summer and harvested in early winter. They store well under cover, as do the highly decorative red cabbages.

SITE AND SOIL
All brassicas are hearty eaters. They like ground that is rich and fertile, well manured in the autumn before planting. The ground need not be deeply dug before the plants are set out, as they prefer firmness round the roots. They will not thrive in shade, or in soils with a pH less than 7.

SOWING
Sow seed in shallow drills outside, scattering it as thinly as possible. You can also raise seedlings under cover in pots or modules. If they are in pots, you will have to prick them out and grow them on in individual pots before transplanting them to their final positions. You can let someone else shoulder the responsibility of raising plants from seed and buy in a few bundles of transplants in early summer, but you will have to accept someone else's choice of varieties and they will not necessarily be the most decorative ones.

THINNING/TRANSPLANTING
Thin the seedlings in the row until they stand about 7cm (3in) apart. In early summer lift the plants to set them in their final growing positions. Use a trowel so that you cause least disturbance to the root ball. Set the transplants in holes about 60cm (2ft) apart, slightly deeper than they were set before, and water them in well. When the water has drained away, firm the soil round the plants with your feet.

Hungarian cabbage soup

There is no need for another course after this soup, which provides a complete meal in a bowl. Do not use red cabbage, as it needs longer, slower cooking than the white and green kinds.

Serves 4
a little dripping, butter or oil, for frying
250g (8oz) smoked sausage, sliced
1 clove garlic, crushed
1.5 litres (2 1/2 pints) stock (the water from boiling a ham is ideal)
1 large potato, peeled and diced
1 bay leaf
500g (1lb) green cabbage, finely shredded (a little less if you use the beefier white kind)
salt and black pepper
chopped parsley
sour cream and caraway seeds, to garnish

1. Melt the dripping, butter or oil in a large pan and gently fry the sausage and the garlic. Add the stock, potato and bay leaf, and simmer slowly for 15 minutes.
2. Add the cabbage and simmer for a further 5 minutes.
3. Season to taste, add the parsley and serve, garnishing with sour cream and caraway seeds.

Culinary notes
* If you are cooking white or green cabbage to accompany meat, try braising it in butter rather than boiling it. This enhances the nutty texture and taste, and there is less danger that the cabbage will be overcooked and lose its crunch.
* Finely sliced or shredded cabbage is one of the classic ingredients of coleslaw salad. Dutch white cabbage is most commonly used, but Savoys are equally good.

ROUTINE CARE
Cabbages sit a long time in the ground, working up to their grand winter performance. Extra rations, particularly nitrogen, should be offered during the long growing period.

YIELD AND HARVESTING
Size varies enormously with growing conditions. Heads may weigh anything from 500g (1lb) to 1.5kg (3lb) each. Red and white cabbages should be cut by mid-winter and stored in a cool, frost-free place. Savoys and January King types are cut as needed.

PESTS AND DISEASES
Clubroot is the worst problem. Spores can lurk unseen in the soil for up to twenty years, even when there are no roots to club. There is no positive cure.

Infected roots throw out weird nodules like deformed fingers and toes. The roots collapse and so does the plant. The spores burst out of the infected tissue and wait in the soil for the next batch of victims.

As there is no cure, you must put your faith in prevention. Do not compost old cabbage plants. Grow them on a different patch each year. Liming helps: clubroot is less of a problem on alkaline soils.

Pigeons may attack the crop in cold winters unless it is protected by netting. Caterpillars are more easily dealt with, if you are not squeamish: jump on them. The cabbage root fly is more devious, because, as with clubroot, the damage goes on underground. Adult flies lay their eggs close to the stem of a brassica, where the maggots hatch and feast greedily on roots. Then the grubs turn themselves into cabbage soup and two weeks later emerge as flies for the whole hideous cycle to begin again.

Use circles of roofing felt or carpet underlay to deter them. The circles should be about 12cm (5in) across with a slit from the centre to the outside. Fit them flat on the ground round the stems of new brassica transplants.

	SPRING			SUMMER			AUTUMN			WINTER		
	EARLY	MID	LATE	EARLY	MID	LATE	EARLY	MID	LATE	EARLY	MID	LATE
EARLY CABBAGE	✳	➡	➡		✂	✂						
LATE CABBAGE	✳	➡	➡				✂	✂				

ORIENTAL BRASSICAS

Mizuna, mibuna, pak choi and Chinese mustard were once strangers in the average vegetable garden. Thanks to Joy Larkcom and her book *Oriental Vegetables* they are now widely grown. Mizuna is pretty enough to use as a foliage plant in its own right, perhaps mixed in a tub with trailing lobelia or set among the bright yellow daisy flowers of *Chrysanthemum segetum*. You could plant up a whole container of oriental specialities: flat-leaved Chinese chives with white bunched flowers at the end of the stems, mizuna, coriander and chrysanthemum greens, which look like ordinary garden chrysanthemums but it is the leaf that you eat. All are simple from seed.

RECOMMENDED CULTIVARS
- **Pak choi** 'Hanakan': has pale green stems with much darker leaves. 'Red Pak Choi': as a baby leaf, has dark green leaves veined in red; as the plant matures, the leaves turn dark maroon; excellent in winter salads.
- **Tatsoi** Has spoon-shaped leaves of glossy dark green; excellent in winter salads.

- **Mizuna** 'Kyoto': has thin white stalks with attractively jagged green leaves and can be sown all year round.
- **Mibuna** 'Green Spray': best in spring and autumn, with a slightly stronger taste than mizuna.
- **Mustard** 'Giant Red': has a spicy tang, good when young in salads, or when more mature in stir-fries. 'Green in Snow': exceptionally hardy, with dark jagged leaves veined in white.
- **Komatsuna** A fast-growing growing brassica with a cabbage-like leaf.

Cultivation

The easiest way to use oriental brassicas in a decorative kitchen garden is to sow pak choi and tatsoi, mizuna and mibuna, komatsuna and Chinese mustard to use at the baby-leaf stage as cut-and-come-again crops.

The advantage of these crops is that they can be sown over a long period. Late autumn sowings may have to be done under cover, but will provide a succession of baby leaves for winter salads. Most oriental brassicas are fast growing and in spring will provide a speedy follow-on from winter vegetables such as parsnips. Just six types are covered here, but adventurous gardeners will soon move on to other oriental vegetables such as choy sum. This has a longer growing season than pak choi and needs 60–80 days to mature. It is a brassica, but it is grown for the flowering shoots, in the way that broccolis are. Like other oriental greens, it needs to grow quickly to produce shoots that are tender rather than stringy.

SITE AND SOIL
Oriental brassicas need fertile, moisture-retentive soil and lots of water.

SOWING
Cut-and-come-again crops can be sown over a long season from spring to autumn. The earliest sowings will do best under woven polypropylene film – a floating mulch – which warms the soil and protects early crops from sudden frosts. Though they do little to enhance the appearance of the decorative kitchen garden, they extend the growing period considerably. Avoid sowing pak choi too early, as it has a tendency to bolt.

Broadcast the seed over a bed, or sow it in wide drills. For individual crops, sow seed in drills, little and often, about 1cm (1/2in) deep, scattering it thinly. Or you can sow groups of 3–4 seeds at 10cm (4in) intervals along the row and then thin to leave the strongest seedling.

THINNING
Cut-and-come-again crops need little thinning. Thin other seedlings as necessary. The easiest way to do this is by nipping them off at ground level so that you do not disturb the roots of those that are left. Leave plenty of space if you want whole plants to use in stir-fries. Pak choi, tatsoi, mizuna and mibuna can be set 23cm (9in) apart, mustard and komatsuna 30cm (12in) apart.

Winter Leaf Salad

A selection of cut-and-come-again oriental salad leaves, such as mizuna, mustard, komatsuna and tatsoi. You can add other ingredients such as rocket and watercress if you do not have enough of the oriental brassicas.

For the dressing (adjust the ingredients to taste):

1 dessertspoon of honey
1 heaped teaspoon of grainy mustard
1 clove garlic, crushed

juice of ½ lemon
a splash of balsamic vinegar
good olive oil

1 Mix the honey, mustard, crushed garlic, salt and pepper together in a bowl.
2. Add the lemon juice and balsamic vinegar.
3. Using a whisk, add olive oil, very slowly at first, and then in a constant dribble, until the mixture emulsifies into a suspended whole.
4. Dress the leaves with the vinaigrette. Any that is left will keep for months in a bottle.

Culinary notes

* The flavour of most oriental vegetables intensifies as the leaves age. This is particularly pronounced with mustards. In salads of oriental greens, use only young leaves, both for their texture and subtle taste.
* Older leaves can be cut into strips and cooked. Brief, rapid cooking in a wok gives the best results. Chinese cooks sometimes blanch vegetables before frying them, as this takes the edge off any bitterness.

ROUTINE CARE

Keep plants well watered at all times. This will also encourage fresh growth on cut-and-come-again crops.

YIELD AND HARVESTING

You can usually start cutting baby salad leaves after a month and take at least three more cuts before the plants either give up or leap, frustrated, into flower. Late summer and autumn sowings provide a long succession of baby leaves for winter salads. Cut above the first seedling leaves, or the crop will not sprout again. In winter, sow the mixture in boxes on a windowsill and treat it like mustard and cress.

Winter hardiness is the great bonus of many oriental leaf crops. Mizuna can be grown throughout the year, but is particularly valuable in winter, both as a salad vegetable – the leaves, deeply divided, are extremely decorative – or cooked in a stir-fry.

Mizuna is a brassica, like European cabbages and sprouts, and takes about ten weeks to reach maturity after sowing. It likes wet better than dry, but in the Napa valley of California, where it is extensively grown, it copes extremely well with temperatures over 90°F/32°C. It does not bolt, as some vegetables do when they are hard pressed. Sow it in a seed tray and pick it over regularly to make sure of a constant supply of new leaves.

Adverse weather conditions – heat, drought, cold, early frosts – have a more dire effect on crops of Chinese greens such as pak choi and choy sum. They tend to bolt and low temperatures when the seeds are germinating or lack of moisture as the plants are growing will be the most likely reasons. You must also harvest the vegetables promptly. They do not stand long in an ideal state.

PESTS AND DISEASES
Unfortunately, the cabbage root fly is just as partial to eastern brassicas as it is to western ones. Take precautions. Watch also for slugs, which adore pak choi.

	SOW	HARVEST
MIZUNA/MIBUNA	Dec–Feb (for spring salads) Jul–Sep (for summer salads) Sep–Oct (for winter salads) Spring sowings will be massacred by flea beetle	Aug–Nov (from Jul–Sep sowings) Nov–Apr (from autumn and winter sowings)
MUSTARD/KOMATSUNA	Jul–Sep (for late summer and autumn salads) Sep–Oct (for winter and spring salads)	Aug–Nov (from Jul–Sep sowings) Nov–May (from Sep–Oct sowings)
PAK CHOI/TATSOI	Jul–Sep (for late summer and autumn salads) Sep–Oct (for winter and early spring salads)	Aug–Nov (from Jul–Sep sowings) Nov–Apr (from Sep–Oct sowings)

BRUSSELS SPROUTS & KALE
Brassica oleracea Gemmifera and Acephala Groups

Sprouts and Brussels go together like tea and China. The Belgians discovered the first sprout plant (probably a Savoy cabbage determined to break the mould) around 1750 and have made sure the rest of the world does not forget it. Sprouts did not reach England or France until the 1800s, but gardeners were quick to see the point of them. You can pick them over a long period and any that you don't pick 'blow' in early spring to make delicious shoots a bit like spring cabbage.

Commercial growers want sprouts that are all the same size and all develop at the same time for stripping by mechanical pickers. Gardeners, though, should look for varieties such as 'Noisette' and 'Igor' that crop, as Brussels sprouts should, over a long period. Except for time of maturing, one sprout plant looks very much like another, but there is an unusual purplish-green type called 'Red Bull' that can be used to decorative effect in the winter garden.

Kales are the oldest kind of cabbage, and are sometimes dismissed (unfairly) as cattle fodder. They are bulky, hardy vegetables bearing the kind of names – 'Ragged Jack' and 'Hungry Gap' – that remind you of the less picturesque side of cottage gardening. Curly kales are the most useful, as you can eat the leaves as well as the young spring shoots. They are also more decorative than the plain, broad-leaved varieties, from which you take spring shoots only.

Kale does not make a head in the way that a cabbage does. The leaves splay out in the fashion of a palm tree and so the plants take up a great deal of space. The curly-leaved varieties can be used as tall foliage plants in a mixed border. Some are more markedly blue-tinged than others. The best-looking kales, though, are 'Red Russian', with jagged leaves of dark purple with red ribs and veins, and the black Tuscan kale 'Cavolo Nero' ('Nero di Toscana').

RECOMMENDED CULTIVARS
- **Brussels sprouts** 'Igor': early or mid-season variety with fine-flavoured sprouts. 'Noisette': produces gourmet sprouts of French breeding, small and nutty. 'Red Bull': gives deep reddish-purple sprouts, the colour more obvious in cold weather.
- **Kale** 'Cavolo Nero' ('Nero di Toscana'): Prince of Wales plumes in crinkled, darkest green. 'Dwarf Green Curled': shorter than the norm, but spreads wide with handsome curly leaves. 'Redbor': densely curled leaves of an intense red. 'Red Russian': grey-green, feathery foliage on dark purple stems.

Stir-fried Brussels sprouts

Overcooking has been the tragedy of the average sprout. If you are boiling them, give them little water, no lid and rapid cooking for no more than 8 minutes. Cooking by other means, as in the stir-fry below, reduces the chances you will take away the crunch that is an essential part of the sprout's appeal.

Serves 4

sunflower oil	200g (7oz) chestnuts, peeled
1 onion, chopped	1 clove garlic, crushed
2 rashers bacon, cut into narrow strips	soy sauce
500g (18oz) Brussels sprouts, finely sliced	

1. Heat the oil in a wok or large, shallow pan and fry the onion and bacon.
2. Add the sprouts and chestnuts and then the garlic.
3. Keep stirring all the time so that the sprouts soften slightly but do not burn.
4. Add soy sauce to taste.

Cultivation

Both these vegetables will keep an ornamental kitchen garden furnished through winter and early spring but, as with other brassicas, you need a back-up patch where you can bring on young plants before setting them out in mid-summer. You may be able to buy ready-grown plants, but the choice of variety will be more limited.

SITE AND SOIL

Brussels sprouts do best in medium to heavy soil that is well drained, firm and fertile, but not recently manured. Too much nitrogen makes the buttons 'blow' (become loose and elongated). The pH should be around 6.5. Kale tolerates poorer soil, but of course does better if it is given the same rich pickings as its brassica cousins.

SOWING

Sow seed of Brussels sprouts outside in shallow drills in a seedbed any time between mid-March and mid-April. Kale can be sown in the same way during May. Keep the seedlings well watered so that they grow steadily without check.

TRANSPLANTING

Lift young sprout plants with as much soil as possible around the root balls and plant them out in their final positions any time from mid-May to the end of June, setting them 75cm (30in) apart each way. If you prefer small sprouts, reduce the spacing. Kale plants will be ready to move in July, roughly eight weeks after you have sown seeds. Plant tall types 75cm (30in) apart each way. Water plants well until they are established.

ROUTINE CARE

Earth up sprouts through the summer as they grow. This helps to keep them stable.

YIELD AND HARVESTING

Expect about 1kg (2lb) of sprouts from each plant and the same weight of shoots or young leaves from kale. Sprouts start cropping in early autumn and continue through until the new year. Start picking from the bottom upwards and expect a final crop of greens from the leafy topknot. Kales such as 'Red Russian' are excellent picked very young and used raw in winter salads.

PESTS AND DISEASES

The most serious problem, as with other brassicas, is clubroot. Strict rotation of crops helps to prevent it building up in the soil. Mealy aphids may also hide themselves in tightly packed sprout buttons, where you cannot see them until they are cooked. Unpleasant. Fortunately, ladybirds love them.

	SPRING			SUMMER			AUTUMN			WINTER		
	EARLY	MID	LATE	EARLY	MID	LATE	EARLY	MID	LATE	EARLY	MID	LATE
BRUSSELS SPROUTS			❀	➡			✄	✄	✄	✄	✄	
KALE	✄		❀	❖	➡	➡			✄	✄	✄	✄

SPINACH *Spinacia oleracea* and *Tetragonia expansa*

Spinach has two useful attributes in the kitchen garden: it will grow in light shade, provided the ground is moist, and it grows fast. This means that you can sow a succession of spinach catch crops between rows of slower-maturing vegetables and use it to green up a potager speedily in spring.

True spinach is an annual. The one aim of an annual is to set seed and perpetuate itself. In hot dry conditions, this works against the spinach fancier. Instead of pausing to produce a feast of handsome, arrow-shaped leaves, the plant races on up to maturity, leaving only an unusable crop of creamish-green seed.

On hot, dry soils, the New Zealand spinach is more likely to succeed, although it germinates relatively slowly. These are the greens that the intrepid eighteenth-century voyager Captain Cook collected by the boatload in New Zealand to stop his sailors getting scurvy.

RECOMMENDED CULTIVARS
- 'Dominant': thick, rounded dark green leaves.
- 'Medania': more reluctant than most to bolt, with dark sweet leaves that overwinter well.
- 'Scenic': resistant to mildew.
- 'Tetona': fast growing and high yielding.
- 'New Zealand': spreading bushy plants with relatively small leaves.

Cultivation
Little and often is the best way to sow spinach. It is most likely to succeed in rich, damp soil and in cool weather conditions. Feast on spinach during spring and autumn and do not expect too much from the crops of high summer.

SITE AND SOIL
True spinach, like other leafy crops, is a great gobbler of nitrogen. Ground can scarcely be too rich for it. As a crop, it follows on well after peas and beans, which leave the soil better equipped with nitrogen than they found it. It tolerates light shade, but not dryness. New Zealand spinach is more tolerant of dry, poor conditions.

SOWING
For a summer crop sow seed at 2–3-week intervals from mid-March to May, setting the seeds no more than 1.5cm (3/4in) deep in rows 30cm (1ft) apart. For a winter crop, sow in August. It used to be thought that prickly-seeded cultivars were more suitable for winter cropping, but modern breeders have blurred the old distinction between prickly- and smooth-seeded types. Perpetual spinach can be sown from March to July.

Roast lamb with spinach forcemeat

Spinach can be used in many different ways: raw in a baby-leaf salad, cooked in a soufflé or puréed. Combined with spices it makes a tangy stuffing. This recipe is excellent inside a boned and rolled shoulder of lamb. You can also pile it into an earthenware dish and cook it in the oven alongside a roast chicken.

Serves 4–6
1/2 large, mild onion, finely chopped
30g (1oz) butter
250g (8oz) spinach, washed
250g (8oz) good sausagemeat
1 egg, beaten
1 tbsp finely chopped parsley
salt, black pepper, nutmeg and mace, to taste
1.75–2kg (3 1/2–4lb) shoulder of lamb, boned weight

1. Preheat the oven to 180°C/350°F/gas mark 4. Sauté the onion gently in the butter until it has become soft and transparent.
2. In a clean pan, cook the spinach until limp (it will cook in the moisture remaining on the leaves after washing) and then chop finely.
3. Combine the onion and spinach with the rest of the ingredients in a large bowl and mix well. Use this mixture to stuff the boned shoulder of lamb, spreading the stuffing over the flattened-out joint. Roll it up like a Swiss roll and secure firmly with skewers or string.
4. Weigh the stuffed joint and roast it in the oven, allowing 20–25 minutes for each 0.5kg (1lb), plus a final 20–25 minutes. Let the joint stand for 10 minutes before carving.

THINNING
Thin summer crops to 15cm (6in) between plants, and winter crops to 23cm (9in). Thin New Zealand spinach seedlings to 20cm (8in) apart.

ROUTINE CARE
Spinach must never be short of water, and on hungry soils extra feeding is also beneficial. In exposed areas, winter crops may need the protection of cloches.

YIELD AND HARVESTING
Expect about 2.5–5kg (5–10lb) of spinach from a 3m (10ft) row, depending on the season. Start picking as soon as the leaves have reached a useful size. They get smaller as plants run out of steam.

PESTS AND DISEASES
Downy mildew is the most prevalent disease, but you can deter it by thinning plants to allow plenty of air to circulate round the crop.

	SPRING			SUMMER			AUTUMN			WINTER		
	EARLY	MID	LATE	EARLY	MID	LATE	EARLY	MID	LATE	EARLY	MID	LATE
SPINACH	❀	❀	❀ ✂	✂	✂	❀	❀ ✂	✂				
NEW ZEALAND SPINACH			❀	❀		✂	✂					

CHARD AND LEAF BEET
Beta vulgaris Cicla Group

Red-stemmed chard has a dramatic beauty in the vegetable garden but it needs to be grown carefully. If you can nurse it through the early stages without upsetting it, it will develop into a superb plant: rich, glowing red stems topped by luxuriantly crinkled foliage, either green or, in the variety 'Burgundy Chard', deep purplish ruby.

The leaf stalks of the various chards are more highly developed than those of spinach and the stalks and the green leaf are best cooked separately. Enthusiasts say that the steamed stalks are as good as asparagus, but in fact the taste is more watery, less concentrated.

The chards belong to a different family to that of spinach and are biennial, running up to seed in their second season. At this stage they are still decorative, but too coarse to eat. They are used superbly in the vast potager at Villandry in France, where the rich ruby stems are set off against deep red roses and the purplish-blue spikes of *Salvia superba*. Leaf beet, or perpetual spinach as it is sometimes called, has a much smaller midrib. It is often used as a substitute for true spinach which, in some situations, is a trickier crop to grow, but the flavour of chard is not nearly so fine.

RECOMMENDED CULTIVARS
- **Chard** 'Rhubarb Chard': scarlet ribs contrasting with sumptuous crumpled foliage. 'Swiss Chard': a white-stemmed chard with dark green foliage. 'Yellow Chard': with distinctive, bright yellow stems.
- **Leaf Beet** 'Erbette': a traditional Italian variety producing fresh leaves for months on end.

Cultivation
Once through the ticklish early stages, chard will stand quite well in drought conditions, but if it is checked in the first two or three months of its life, it will forget all about being a biennial and run straight up to seed. Leaf beet, often called perpetual spinach or spinach beet, has a smaller midrib than chard. It is also biennial and has the advantage of being more tolerant of

drought, as well as easy to grow, though the flavour is not so fine as that of true spinach.

SITE AND SOIL CONDITIONS

Chard and leaf beet like fertile soil, rich in nitrogen. Add plenty of farmyard manure or compost. If it can be arranged, they make good follow-on crops after peas or beans.

SOWING

Sow chard and leaf beet from April to August, setting the seed no deeper than 1.5cm (3/4in) in rows 38–45cm (15–18in) apart. Alternatively, sow 'at stations', setting three or four seeds at 60cm (2ft) intervals along the row. The plants should crop through the winter until late spring of the following year, when they will start to run up to seed. Chard will run to seed in the same year if it is sown too early.

THINNING

These are much bigger, bossier plants than true spinach. Thin seedlings to at least 30cm (12in) apart in the rows. If you have sown 'at stations', thin weaker seedlings to leave one plant at each point.

Chard soup with coconut milk

Serves 6
250g (9oz) chard, green part only
125g (4oz) other winter greens (kale, sprout tops, pak choi, mustard)
2 onions, finely chopped
1 clove garlic, finely chopped
2 tbsp olive oil
1.5 litres (3 pints) good stock
400ml tin coconut milk
Salt and black pepper, to taste

1. Shred the chard and winter greens.
2. Fry the onion and garlic gently in the oil until the onion is transparent.
3. Add the greens, stock and coconut milk.
4. Bring gently to the boil and simmer for 10 minutes before liquidizing.
5. Taste and season the soup.

Culinary notes
* If you are cooking chard as a vegetable to serve alongside some other dish, treat the stems and leaf separately. Strip the greenery from the stems, slice up both and give the stems a three-minute head start in boiling water before you add the greens. Of course you can also serve the two separately.

ROUTINE CARE

The early stages are by far the most critical, especially for chard. Keep the young plants growing as smoothly as possible by providing sufficient water and plenty of liquid feeds. Mulch to conserve moisture.

YIELD AND HARVESTING

Expect about 3.5kg (7lb) from a 3m (10ft) row. Pull, rather than cut, the stems as required. Do not take too many leaves from any one plant at a time, especially in the middle of winter, or else the plant may not be able to recover. For the best results, cook the stems and the leaves separately.

PESTS AND DISEASES

These are generally easily grown, trouble-free crops.

	SPRING			SUMMER			AUTUMN			WINTER		
	EARLY	MID	LATE	EARLY	MID	LATE	EARLY	MID	LATE	EARLY	MID	LATE
CHARD AND LEAF BEET	✂	✂	❀ ✂	❀	❀	✂	✂	✂	✂	✂	✂	✂

LETTUCE *Lactuca sativa*

Of all decorative vegetables, lettuce is the most versatile, because it presents itself in so many different guises and adapts itself to so many uses in the garden. The ferny, frilly, looseleaf kinds can be used as foliage plants between bright groups of annual flowers or to add bulk to billowing daisy-flowered argyranthemums in a window box. You can use oakleaf lettuce to line paths, small 'Tom Thumb', all heart, to fill beds in a modest parterre, frilly 'Red Salad Bowl' to edge a raised bed or sculpted 'Frisée de Beauregard' to provide a frame for tomatoes in a grow bag.

There are five different types of lettuce to choose from: soft butterheads like 'Merveille de Quatre Saisons' ('Marvel of Four Seasons') or the dwarf 'Tom Thumb', dense crisp varieties like the old favourite 'Webb's Wonderful' or 'Black-seeded Simpson' and upright growing cos lettuces such as 'Freckles' or my own favourite 'Little Gem'. Then there are the looseleaf, cut-and-come-again lettuces such as 'Amorino' and the decorative, frilly 'Lollo Rossa'. Batavian lettuce such as 'Leny' (green) and 'Relay' (red) have particularly thick, crunchy leaves.

RECOMMENDED CULTIVARS

- **Butterhead** 'Buttercrunch': compact, dark green heads very slow to bolt. 'Cassandra': pale green variety to grow all the year round. 'Merveille de Quatre Saisons' ('Marvel of Four Seasons'): waxy, mottled leaves, bronze on green, a fine lettuce.
- **Cos** 'Corsair': flat dark green leaves, strongly flavoured. 'Freckles': light

green leaves freckled with reddish brown. 'Little Gem': the best of its kind, a semi-cos dwarf lettuce, all heart. 'Lobjoit's Green Cos': tall, crisp, deep green hearts, tightly folded.

- **Crisphead** 'Black-seeded Simpson': excellent taste and texture. 'Saladin': solid, pale green heads slow to bolt. 'Webb's Wonderful': solid hearts and slow to bolt.
- **Looseleaf** 'Amorina': deep red leaves can be cropped from spring to autumn. 'Catalogna': deeply lobed, elongated oakleaf type, pale green and quick to resprout after cutting. 'Cocarde': a French oakleaf type which makes trumpet-shaped heads, dark green overlaid with red. 'Lollo Rossa': crisp frilly leaves tinged with red. 'Salad Bowl Red': will last through the summer if picked over regularly.
- **Batavian** 'Relay': matures in about sixty days and can be harvested from spring to autumn.

Cultivation

Differences between lettuces have as much to do with texture as with taste. For this reason, it is useful to grow several different kinds, bearing in mind that the cos (except speedy 'Little Gem') take longer to mature than the butterheads and that the looseleaf can be cut from a much earlier age. Seed keeps well for about three seasons, so you can experiment with different varieties without feeling extravagant.

SITE AND SOIL

Lettuce grows best on soil that is light and fertile but retains moisture. It does not mind partial shade.

SOWING

In theory, if you sow seed every fortnight from spring until mid-summer, you should have a non-stop supply of lettuce until autumn. For autumn and winter crops, you need protection: a cold frame, unheated greenhouse or polytunnel. In practice, however complicated the cropping charts, lettuce either bolts or sulks, one lot colliding into the next so that you end up with the usual chaos of feast or famine. Despite this, little and often is the best way with lettuce seed.

Unpredictable weather conditions are the most frequent cause of unpredictable crops. In hot weather, germination is erratic. In drought, growth is sluggish. Smooth, steady, unchecked growth is what a lettuce likes best.

Direct sowing outside is the simplest method. Sow short rows, little and often, scattering the seed in the drill as thinly as possible. Rows can be 15cm (6in) apart for small cultivars like 'Little Gem', 30cm (12in) apart for large types like 'Lollo Rossa'.

For early sowings under cover, use modules such as Jiffy 7s, setting a few seeds in each and planting out the seedlings when conditions allow.

THINNING

Thin small cultivars to 15cm (6in) apart and large types to 30cm (12in) apart. Make the first thinning about a month after sowing when the seedlings are 5cm (2in) tall. Transplanting these thinnings works reasonably well at the beginning of the season, though the lettuces take longer to mature. Once the weather becomes hot and dry, it is difficult to persuade the transplants to settle. You can, though, use thinnings as leaf lettuce in salads.

ROUTINE CARE

Lettuce needs plenty of water while growing but not too much feeding: scientific tests have shown that excess nitrogen makes the leaves bitter. Water in the morning rather than the evening. In the evening, leaves dry off more slowly and so are more prone to attacks of downy mildew.

YIELD AND HARVESTING

A 3m (10ft) row gives 10–20 lettuces, depending on the variety. Harvest

---

Lettuce, bacon and blue cheese salad

John Parkinson, the seventeenth-century granddaddy of all garden writers, recommended lettuce for 'Monkes, Nunnes and the like of people . . . to keep them chaste'. Poor Nunnes: lettuce on its own is not much of a diet. Like pastry, it is a background, a carrier of other more lively ingredients – walnut oil, black olives, hard-boiled eggs, anchovies – as here.

Serves 4

250g (8oz) smoked streaky bacon
1 crisphead lettuce (such as Iceberg)
1 bunch watercress
500g (1lb) small tomatoes
2 avocados
4 tbsp lemon juice

250g (8oz) Gorgonzola cheese, finely sliced
4 tbsp olive oil
2 tbsp red wine vinegar
1 tsp grainy mustard
2 tsp clear honey

1. Grill the bacon until it is crisp and chop it finely.
2. Wash the lettuce and watercress and gently pat dry the leaves. Halve the tomatoes and mix with the bacon, lettuce and watercress.
3. Peel and slice the avocados and dress them with lemon juice to prevent them browning. Add them to the salad with the cheese.
4. Make a dressing by combining the remaining ingredients. Pour over the salad just before serving.

Culinary notes

* Use the small, inner leaves of cos lettuce as crunchy scoops for hummus.
* Braise lettuce leaves with fresh young peas, some chopped onion, a knob of butter and a little water for the French classic *petits pois à l'etuvée*.

looseleaf lettuces a few leaves at a time. Over the last ten years, there has been a massive shift towards looseleaf kinds, which can be cropped over a long period. This method is ideal for a small garden, particularly where there are raised beds. Broadcast seed over the bed, rather than sowing it in lines, and leave the plants to grow close together, without thinning. You can mix your own cocktail of varieties and start cropping about eight weeks after sowing, when the plants are 7–15cm (3–6in) high. Cut just above the lowest leaves, leaving the stem to resprout. 'Red Salad Bowl' and 'Lollo Rossa' are excellent varieties to use for cut-and-come-again beds, mixed with other baby salad leaves such as rocket and corn salad.

PESTS AND DISEASES

Slugs, aphids and cutworms are common pests. In cool, damp weather, lettuces are particularly prone to downy mildew and grey mould. Seek out cultivars with some resistance and do not plant too close.

	SPRING			SUMMER			AUTUMN			WINTER		
	EARLY	MID	LATE	EARLY	MID	LATE	EARLY	MID	LATE	EARLY	MID	LATE
OTHER LETTUCE	✸	✸	✿ ➡		✿	✿ ✂	✂	✂				
LOOSELEAF LETTUCE	✸	✸	✿ ➡	✂	✿ ✂	✿ ✂	✂	✂				

ROCKET AND OTHER SALAD LEAVES

Rocket, mustard and cress, purslane and corn salad are all useful extras to add tang to a sandwich or a salad bowl. In the garden, you can use them as catch crops, to make quick use of bare ground between other slower-growing crops. As the seeds germinate fast – you can cut mustard and cress within two weeks of sowing – you can use these seedling crops to make instant edgings or to 'paint' patterns in a vegetable bed. Mark out a diamond trellis in the earth and sow along the lines of the pattern. Children like seeing their initials rise magically from the ground.

Mustard (*Sinapis alba*) and cress (*Lepidium sativum*) can also be raised in small trays on a windowsill. The seed grows well on wads of damp newspaper, paper tissues or folded squares of towelling.

These leaves green up spare patches of ground in a productive way, though none of them rates very highly as a decorative vegetable. Winter purslane, or claytonia, is the prettiest, with succulent leaves each shaped like an ace of spades and coloured greenish bronze. This purslane grows very fast in early spring, which is a bare time for salad crops, and carries a profusion of small pink flowers over the foliage. Where it is happy (and that seems to be most places, including shade, damp or dry) it will seed copiously and may become a nuisance. Summer purslane (*Portulaca oleracea*) only grows well where it is warm. It is best used as a seedling, cut-and-come-again crop.

Corn salad or lamb's lettuce (*Valerianella locusta*) is extremely hardy and is best used as a winter substitute for lettuce. Watercress (*Rorippa nasturtium-aquaticum*), too, is at its best in winter and can be persuaded to grow without running water, though it is not quite as succulent. It is packed with iron and vitamins.

Most useful of all is rocket (*Eruca vesicaria*) which, grown in pots or window boxes, makes an ideal salad crop for city dwellers. It runs to seed quickly in hot weather, so is best sown frequently in small quantities. The deeply lobed leaves should be picked while still very young, and have a piquant, spicy taste that quickly wakes up a bland gathering of lettuce.

These are only a few of the most popular leaves that you might use in a mixed salad. Other possibilities include nasturtium, sorrel (both broad-leaved and buckler-leaved), orach, amaranth and texel greens.

RECOMMENDED CULTIVARS
- **Rocket** 'Sky Rocket': has deeply lobed leaves and is slow to bolt. 'Wild Rocket': has a more intense flavour than salad rockets such as 'Sky Rocket'.
- **Mustard and Cress** 'Sprint': an exceptionally fast cress, though still not as fast to sprout as a mustard such as 'Fine White'. Rape seed (*Brassica napus*) is often substituted for true mustard.
- **Purslane** Both 'Green' and 'Golden' types are available, and are said to reduce levels of cholesterol. Winter purslane (claytonia or miners' lettuce) is rich in Vitamin C.
- **Corn salad** 'Verte de Cambrai': an old French variety with a smallish leaf but excellent flavour. 'Vit': the most vigorous variety, producing masses of glossy leaves with a faint hint of mint.

Cultivation
However smoothly you try with paper and pencil to plan the production of these salad crops, sowings either catch up with each other or else dawdle like recalcitrant runners to widen the gap between themselves and the crop in front. Little and often is the key to sowing. These are extras, rather than staples. There are two golden rules in growing salad crops: look after the soil, which has to work hard to support crops for almost twelve months of the year and, secondly, match crop to season. Rocket, for instance, is less likely to be chewed by flea beetle when sown in late summer. It grows so fast you will need several patches growing at once: one to cut, one to cultivate and one to come on behind.

SITE AND SOIL CONDITIONS

You would not want to give over your best ground to these crops. They must make the best of what they are given. Watercress, however, will only succeed in a moist, shady bed and is happiest of all growing in a stream.

SOWING

Watercress is best grown from rooted cuttings rather than seed (stems readily produce roots in a jar of water). Take out a narrow trench, 5cm (2in) deep, with a hoe and fill it with water until really soggy. Dribble sand along it about 2cm (1in) deep and then, using a dibber, make small holes about 15cm (6in) apart. Drop in the cuttings and keep well watered.

Summer purslane can be sown outdoors in early summer. Broadcast seed for a cut-and-come-again crop.

Sow corn salad in late summer for leaves to cut in winter. Sow seed thinly, just under 1cm (1/2in) deep, in a drill if you want to transplant seedlings. Broadcast seed over a wide drill or bed for a cut-and-come-again crop. Corn salad is slow to resprout, so is often better transplanted to grow to maturity, when whole plants can be cut. Set out young plants 10cm (4in) apart, in rows 30cm (12in) apart.

Sow small quantities of mustard and cress at weekly intervals for a continuous supply. You can sow outside in drills, barely covering the seed with soil, but it is often more convenient to sow in small pots or boxes on the kitchen windowsill. If you are growing this crop inside, sow the cress first, and then two days later sprinkle the mustard on top. Then they will germinate together.

Rocket is a relatively hardy annual that can stand a mild winter and will germinate at low temperatures. Seed can be broadcast (or sown in big pots) from early spring to late summer. Late summer sowings will give leaves unpeppered by flea beetle holes. In hot weather, plants quickly run up to seed.

To make things easier, you can think of sowing salad crops in three main periods. If you have a greenhouse or cold frame, the first sowing can be in late January under cover, when you might start off lettuce in modules to plant out from mid- to late March and to crop from late April to early July. Early sowings of spinach and sorrel are worth trying too. The second sowing might be in mid-May, outside of course, when you could include more lettuce, purslane and basil to crop from late June to late August. The third sowing might be in mid-July, when you would include lettuce, endive, rocket and oriental salads to crop in September and October.

THINNING

Thin corn salad to about 10cm (4in) apart. Summer purslane will not need thinning if harvested as seedlings; nor will mustard and cress, or watercress if planted at the spacing given above.

ROUTINE CARE

Watering and weeding are all that is required.

Rocket, squash and Greek cheese salad

Serves 4
1 small butternut squash, peeled, cubed and roasted
4 handfuls rocket
1 handful mint
100g (4oz) feta cheese, crumbled
pumpkin seeds, roasted
For the dressing:
100ml (3 fl oz) apple juice
100ml (3 fl oz) balsamic vinegar
2 tbsp sunflower oil

1. Make the dressing by mixing the apple juice with the vinegar and reducing it by at least half. Add the oil and mix well.
2. Assemble the squash, rocket, mint and cheese in a bowl, dress with the dressing and scatter over the pumpkin seeds.

YIELD AND HARVESTING
Yield depends on time of year and the stage at which you cut the crop. You can gather individual leaves from rocket, watercress and summer purslane, or cut down the whole plant. Snip mustard and cress with scissors.

PESTS AND DISEASES
These crops are generally free from trouble, apart from the flea beetle, which attacks mid-summer crops of rocket. Time sowings to avoid the most troublesome period.

	SOW	HARVEST
ROCKET	Apr–Aug (outdoors), Sep–March (under cover)	Year round
MUSTARD AND CRESS	Apr–Aug (outdoors), Sep–March (under cover)	Year round
PURSLANE	Apr–June (summer), Aug–Sep (winter)	June–Aug (summer) Oct–Dec (winter)
CORN SALAD	Aug–Sep	Oct–Jan

CHICORY AND ENDIVE
Cichorium intybus and *C. endivia*

These are designer vegetables *par excellence*; you could fill a whole potager with decorative combinations of this one group. The names are muddling. In France curly endive is called *chicorée frisée* and Belgian chicory, which looks like a small cream bomb, is called endive. Sugar loaf chicory, which is not blanched, grows like a cos lettuce. Endives can be blanched or not, depending on your taste, but you do not need to choose special blanching varieties, as you do with chicory. The French use chic little caps, like berets, which they put over the hearts of the endives to blanch them. An upturned plate does the same thing, though less stylishly. In growing terms, the major difference between the two is that endive is an annual. Chicory is not, and in its second year produces tall sheaves of blue flowers, which are extremely attractive.

RECOMMENDED CULTIVARS
- **Belgian/blanched chicory** 'Lightning': best for mid-late forcing. 'Witloof': the traditional finely textured variety for forcing.
- **Chicory (unblanched)** 'Pain di Zucchero': quick growing, large headed. 'Bianca di Milano': forms crisp, elongated heads which you can use small as a cut-and-come-again crop. 'Biondissima di Trieste': green, smooth, round leaved.
- **Chicory (red)/raddichio** 'Palla Rossa': neat wine-red leaves for winter salads. 'Rossa di Treviso': non-hearting, extremely hardy. 'Variegata di Castelfranco': wonderfully decorative old variety with green and red leaves surrounding an inner head of white and red; known in northern Italy since the eighteenth century.
- **Endive** 'Fine Maraichere': small, compact, frizzy and extremely decorative, though not hardy. 'Pancaliere': makes masses of self-blanching growth, good for cut-and-come again. 'Wallonne': traditional hardy French curled variety which makes a large, tightly packed head.

Cultivation
To blanch or not to blanch, that is the question. Blanching alleviates the bitterness that is a characteristic of both these salad crops. With Belgian chicory, of course, it is essential. With others you can experiment, blanching hearts with an upturned plate or saucer, or entire plants with an upturned bucket or plant pot.
SITE AND SOIL
Both crops need fertile, well-drained soil, preferably in full sun, though summer crops of endive will tolerate light shade.
SOWING
Sow seed of Belgian chicory (for blanching) in early to mid-summer, dribbling the seed as thinly as possible 1cm (1/2in) deep, in rows 30cm (12in) apart.

Seed of unblanched (sugar loaf) types should be sown at the same depth and spacing. Sow in mid-summer or else plants may run to seed. Red chicory/radicchio can be sown from mid-spring to mid-summer, using early or late maturing cultivars. Sow 1cm (^{1}/2in) deep in rows 25–30cm (10–12in) apart. Seed of 'Rossa di Treviso' can also be broadcast over a raised bed for cut-and-come-again crops. Sow curly endive from late spring to mid-summer (earlier sowings often run to seed). You can also sow under glass for a useful winter crop. Sow 1cm (^{1}/2in) deep in rows 25–38cm (10–15in) apart.

THINNING
Thin Belgian chicory to 23cm (9in) apart in the rows and unblanched and red chicory/radicchio to 25–30cm (10–12in) apart. This spacing will also suit most endives but the large, broad-leaved types need to be 30–38cm (12–15in) apart.

ROUTINE CARE
Keep the plants well weeded and watered during the three months between sowing and harvesting.

FORCING
Witloof chicory can be forced outdoors or inside, but outside forcing is only feasible where the soil is not too heavy and cold. In early winter cut any remaining leaves about 3cm (1in) above the neck of the plant. Cover the stumps with at least 15cm (6in) of soil and then fix cloches over the ridge. To force chicons inside (which gives quicker results) lift the roots in November and discard any that are very thin. Trim the leaves back to about 23cm (9in) and pack the roots in a box of sand.

Take out roots to force a few at a time. Trim off side shoots and shorten the main roots to about 15cm (6in). Pack the roots in moist soil. You can fit about six in a 23cm (9in) flowerpot. Invert another pot over the first and store them in a suitable forcing place. In the warmth of an airing cupboard, chicons will develop in about three weeks. In a cooler cellar (though the temperature should not be below 10°C/50°F) forcing will take longer. Some red chicories such as 'Red Treviso' can be forced in the same way. Blanch curly endive when it is nearly full grown by putting a plate over the middle to whiten the centre. The leaves must be dry or they may rot. Cover the plant with a cloche to keep off rain.

YIELD AND HARVESTING
Expect about 3kg (6lb) of forcing chicory, or 10–15 heads of unblanched chicory and endive from a 3m (10ft) row. Cut forced chicons when they are about 13–15cm (5–6in) long. Use them immediately before they become green and bitter. Make the cut 3cm (1in) above the neck of each plant, as the root will sometimes sprout again to give a second, smaller chicon. After that, you have to throw them away. Treat unforced chicory and endive as you might lettuce (though endive is hardier, which makes it a useful crop) and gather leaves or whole heads as necessary. If you cut a whole head, leave 3cm (1in) or so of the neck, which will then resprout.

PESTS AND DISEASES

Chicory and endive are robust vegetables. The chief difficulty is likely to be rot, which sets in if you blanch vegetables when the foliage is wet.

Witloof chicory with ham and cheese

Serves 6
6 heads of Witloof (Belgian) chicory, trimmed
lemon juice
sugar
Dijon mustard
6 thinnish slices of ham
Parmesan cheese and breadcrumbs for topping
For the cheese sauce:

2 tbsp butter — salt, black pepper and grated nutmeg
1 small onion, chopped — 2 tbsp grated Gruyère cheese
2 tbsp flour — 2 tbsp grated Parmesan cheese
300ml (½ pint) milk
300ml (½ pint) stock (stock from cooking a ham is ideal here)

1. Make the sauce by melting the butter and softening the onion in it. Stir in the flour and gradually add the milk and stock, stirring vigorously so that the sauce does not get lumpy. Season with salt, pepper and nutmeg and stir in the two cheeses.
2. Blanch the chicory for 10 minutes in boiling water with a little lemon juice and sugar. Drain it thoroughly.
3. Spread mustard on the slices of ham and wrap each slice round a head of chicory.
4. Butter a shallow dish and pack in the wrapped chicons. Pour over the sauce and top with breadcrumbs and more Parmesan. Bake for about 20 minutes at 190–220°C/375–425°F/gas mark 5–7.

	SPRING			SUMMER			AUTUMN			WINTER		
	EARLY	MID	LATE	EARLY	MID	LATE	EARLY	MID	LATE	EARLY	MID	LATE
RADICCHIO/ RED CHICORY		✿	✿	✂	✿ ✂	✿ ✂	✂	✂	✂			
BELGIAN ENDIVE		✿	✿					✂	✂			
CURLY ENDIVE		✿	✿	✂	✿ ✂	✿ ✂	✂	✂	✂			
ESCAROLE		✿	✿	✂	✿ ✂	✿ ✂	✂	✂	✂			

FRUITING AND FLOWERING VEGETABLES

Cauliflowers and broccoli apart, this group is mostly made up of plants that hate frost. In cold areas they cannot go out until early summer, but once planted they grow rapidly and peak in a rich harvest of gold, green, orange and red in autumn. Courgettes and marrows, pumpkins and squashes can all be used to great effect, trailing over the ground between upright blocks of sweetcorn or tall pillars of cordon tomatoes securely tied in to their supports. In this respect, they are natural companions, one needing vertical space, the other horizontal. Both like the same growing conditions, with plenty of sun to ripen their crops. Pumpkins and squashes are dramatically varied: striped, spotted, shiny pewter-grey or vivid as a setting sun. Using this family alone, you could make a splendidly decorative summer bed. Cauliflowers and sprouting broccoli tie up space for a long time and in a small garden will scarcely earn their keep. All the vegetables suggested below, though, are handsome as well as delicious.

Looking like a smooth scallop-edged apple pie, the summer 'patty pan' squash may be almost pure white or striped and speckled with yellow or green. Winter squashes include blue-grey Hubbard types, decorative Turk's turbans of all colours and the huge golden pumpkins that flicker with candles at Hallowe'en. The long trailing growths of pumpkins and squashes can easily be trained over arches or supports such as a wigwam of bamboo canes. For this purpose, use cultivars with reasonably small fruit. No wigwam will be able to support an 'Atlantic Giant' once the bit is between its teeth.

If you have room, you could plant a whole avenue of globe artichokes to line a path in the kitchen garden or to fill a narrow border. These are spectacular plants at their peak and their sculpted, arching foliage leaves little room for other plants around them. In a smaller space, use a single plant as a centrepiece for a potager or herb garden.

Few plants can boast of fruit so glossily polished as the aubergine, which in cool areas will succeed best in a greenhouse border. In warm areas, you can grow aubergines in tubs and group them with pots of chillies and trailing cascades of cherry tomatoes. Although the flowers are attractive, they tend to be overwhelmed by the foliage and fruit.

The smooth curds of an unblemished cauliflower have the strange texture of an underwater sponge, the heart protected by great winged leaves of dark, contrasting green. But cauliflower is not an easy crop to grow well and, like many other brassicas, needs a long growing period before coming to fruition.

CAULIFLOWER, CALABRESE AND BROCCOLI
Brassica oleracea Botrytis and Italica Groups

If you can grow a good cauliflower, you can award yourself maximum merit stars. They are not easy vegetables to bring to crisp perfection, and will produce only small, misshapen heads if their growth is checked in any way. Cauliflowers are generally creamy white, the heads surrounded by a crisp green frill of leaves, but there are also lime-green, orange and purple types. With a careful choice of cultivars, you could be harvesting cauliflowers during most months of the year, but then you would tie up a great deal of ground for long periods. In a small garden, fast-maturing mini-cauliflowers are probably the most useful.

If cauliflower, as Mark Twain wrote, 'is nothing but cabbage with a college education', then calabrese and broccoli have the PhDs of the family. The names are both Italian, but it is likely that the broccolis came into that country originally from the Eastern Mediterranean some time during the seventeenth century. Philip Miller, who wrote one of the first gardening dictionaries in 1724, called it 'Italian asparagus' and if you eat the first of the broccoli crop with some hollandaise sauce on the side, you will be pushed to decide which is the more ambrosial.

The colour range is similar to that of the cauliflower family: lime green, white and deep purple. In form, the prettiest are the 'Romanesco' types with cone-shaped clusters of miniature flowers grouped together in a pointed head. But that is a calabrese, not a broccoli. Calabrese is a summer vegetable with one heavy central head, while the sprouting broccolis, which provide ambrosial suppers when there is very little else to pick in the vegetable garden, have masses of small florets, purple or white, which are produced over a long season.

The stems wilt quickly, and the season is short. That makes sprouting broccoli unpopular with supermarkets. And, though it tastes as good as asparagus, it has never, thank goodness, commanded the lunatic prices that you have to pay for fresh asparagus. Like calabrese, it can acquire a bitter taste if it is left hanging about too long. As the great French gourmet Vilmorin-Andrieux wrote, 'Everyone who can should grow their own and cut it an hour before dinner.'

But grown from seed, the spring-sprouting broccolis take a whole year to produce a crop. In a small garden, this laid-back attitude to production may be difficult to accommodate. You need to be creative in the way you use space. Market gardeners at the turn of the century grew broccoli crops in rows under their apple trees. Others lined out young plants between their early potatoes. Once the potatoes are cleared off the ground, the broccolis can have it all to themselves.

Cauliflower cheese

Cauliflower cheese is a simple dish, but well cooked (that means not overcooked) it is always comforting, especially with a few rashers of good farm bacon laid alongside.

Serves 4
1 cauliflower
2 tbsp butter
2 tbsp flour
300ml (½ pint) stock (to include some of the water in which you have cooked the cauliflower)
300ml (½ pint) milk and cream mixed
2 tbsp each grated Gruyère and Parmesan cheese
salt and black pepper
For the topping:
2 tbsp breadcrumbs
1 tbsp each Gruyère and Parmesan cheese, grated

1. Trim the cauliflower and cut it into four. Put it into a pan of boiling, salted water and cook until it is just yielding to a knife point.
2. Make the sauce by melting the butter, stirring in the flour, letting the mixture bubble slightly before adding the stock and milk/cream mixture. Start by adding the liquid slowly, so that the sauce does not get lumpy, and stir vigorously. As you go on, the liquid can be sloshed in more liberally as the sauce is beyond the point at which it can be troublesome. Add the cheese and stir until it is melted. If necessary, Cheddar cheese can be substituted for the Gruyère and Parmesan.
3. Put the cauliflower quarters in a buttered dish, pour the sauce over them and sprinkle the breadcrumbs and extra cheese on the top. Bake at 190°C/375°F/gas mark 5 until the sauce is bubbling again and the top is brown. Do not overcook. The cauliflower must still have an echo of crunch.

The potato trick is an easy one to copy. If you time the two crops perfectly, you may even have the potatoes out of the ground before the broccoli needs to be transplanted in its place. But timing in a vegetable garden is easier to bring off on paper than it is in reality.

Broccoli is a more ancient vegetable than the beefy cauliflower, but both must have been bred over centuries from a wild kind of cabbage, selected for its flowering shoots rather than its leaves. For years, sprouting broccoli had no specific names. It was either purple or white, late or early. Now several named cultivars have been introduced, but the purple remains hardier and more prolific than the white.

RECOMMENDED CULTIVARS
- **Cauliflowers** 'All the Year Round': tolerant of less-than-ideal growing conditions. 'Limelight': autumn cropping, with bright green heads, easy to grow. 'Purple Cape': to crop in April with rich purple heads. 'Snowball': a mini-cauliflower to harvest in autumn from a spring sowing. 'Violet Queen': produces deep purple heads to cut in early autumn.
- **Calabrese and broccoli** 'De Cicco' (calabrese): an old Italian variety that does not crop all at the same time as so many cauliflowers and calabrese do. 'Early Purple': (broccoli) heavy crops available to pick from March onwards. 'Fiesta' (calabrese): a tolerant type that produces heads from June to October. 'Romanesco' (calabrese): cone-shaped clusters build into geometric, lime-green heads to cut from summer to early autumn. 'Rudolph' (broccoli): the earliest of all, producing spears to cut in January.

Cultivation
Cauliflower cultivars have been bred to be ready for harvesting at different times of year but some, such as the spring varieties, take almost twelve months to reach maturity. Late summer and autumn cauliflowers are better suited to most gardens. 'Violet Queen', to be sown in late May or early June for cropping in early autumn, is a good-looking cauliflower with deep purple heads. Mini-cauliflowers such as 'Snowball' are the most useful for filling small beds in a potager.

As for calabrese and broccoli, the two plants are very different in character. Calabrese goes in for one big extrovert gesture and, having shot its bolt, has very little capacity to follow on. Broccoli twitters into life with a shower of possibilities, but has the greater staying power. Eventually by late spring its sprigs will be only matchstick sized, but by then other crops will have come into production. In late winter when sprouting broccoli's season starts, there is little else to beat it in the vegetable garden.

SITE AND SOIL
Cauliflowers prefer a more alkaline soil than most of the other members of the brassica family. Acid soils, even when they are limed, may not produce worthwhile crops. Cauliflowers must have soil that is deeply dug and fertile, with sufficient moisture to enable them to grow smoothly and productively. Calabrese will cope with less luscious soil than cauliflowers, although the best crops come from well-dug, well-fed ground. Both calabrese and broccoli thrive in warm, well-drained sites.

SOWING
Sow cauliflower seed thinly in drills in a seedbed outside, 1cm ($\frac{1}{2}$in) deep. Sow late summer varieties in early or mid-spring and autumn cauliflowers in late spring. Small quantities of calabrese can be sown in succession from spring to mid-summer for crops from summer until autumn. Sow two or

three seeds 'at stations' 15cm (6in) apart to avoid the need for transplanting. Broccoli should be sown thinly in drills in mid-spring.

TRANSPLANTING/THINNING

After 6–8 weeks, cauliflowers should be transplanted to their final growing positions. Water the seedlings well beforehand and keep as much earth as possible around the roots. Allow at least 60cm (24in) between plants in the row and space the rows 60cm (24in) apart. Mini-cauliflowers can be grown much closer. Plant them about 15cm (6in) apart each way. Thin calabrese seedlings to leave one strong plant at each station. Transplant broccoli in the same way as cauliflower from early to mid-summer, setting the plants at least 60cm (24in) apart in rows that are also 60cm (24in) apart.

ROUTINE CARE

Water frequently throughout the growing season and keep well weeded. Mulch to conserve moisture in the soil. Broccoli may need earthing up or staking as it develops. If plants grow well they can become dangerously top heavy.

YIELD AND HARVESTING

You will get about six cauliflowers from a 3m (10ft) row, but the size of each may vary greatly. Cut while the heads are still firm, before the florets start to grow away from the core. Expect 3–4kg (6–8lb) of calabrese or broccoli from a 3m (10ft) row. Calabrese is ready from summer to autumn, broccoli from late winter to spring.

PESTS AND DISEASES

As with cabbages, cabbage root fly and clubroot are the worst problems. Nets will probably be necessary to protect the crop from winter attack by pigeons. Green caterpillars are a nuisance on calabrese, as they are well camouflaged. Nothing puts you off a vegetable so much as the sight of a small boiled corpse entombed within it. Soak the heads in salt water before you cook.

	SPRING			SUMMER			AUTUMN			WINTER		
	EARLY	MID	LATE	EARLY	MID	LATE	EARLY	MID	LATE	EARLY	MID	LATE
CAULIFLOWER		✳ (sow)	⁖ (plant) →		✂	✂	✂					
HEADING BROCCOLI	✳ (sow)	✳ (sow)	→	⁖ (plant)	→	✂	✂	✂				
SPROUTING BROCCOLI	⁖ (plant)	⁖ (plant)			✂	✂	✂	✂				

COURGETTES AND MARROWS Cucurbita pepo

Courgettes are zucchini under a different name and they have the frightening capacity to metamorphose into marrows if you go on holiday at the wrong time. Marrows have heroic status among gardeners who are also showmen – there is always a class for the heaviest marrow at a British horticultural show. But in the kitchen garden (and even more so in the kitchen) there is not much to recommend them, unless you want to camouflage a chain-link fence or some other unsightly boundary. For growing on the flat in confined spaces, bush courgettes are the easiest to manage. The golden flowers glow richly among the sober foliage and yellow-fruited varieties make an even greater impact (though they are not as prolific). Trailing varieties of marrow can be used to cover a compost heap.

RECOMMENDED CULTIVARS
- **Courgette** 'Defender': an early variety with good resistance to cucumber mosaic virus. 'Parador': produces bright yellow courgettes, though it does not fruit as freely as green types. 'Striato d'Italia': a classic Italian variety bearing striped fruit. 'Tuscany': makes a compact, upright plant, ideal for containers.
- **Marrow** 'Long Green Trailing': large dark green fruits with paler stripes.

Cultivation
Marrows and courgettes are thirsty beasts, so any device you can think of to conserve water around the plants will be a great advantage. The traditional method is to build a shallow circular wall of earth about 60cm (24in) in diameter around each plant. When you water, the water stays where you want it. Mulching is also very beneficial: it suppresses weeds as well as conserving moisture.

SITE AND SOIL
Rich, moisture-retentive soil will give the best results. Plants can cope with partial shade if necessary.

SOWING
Seed will not germinate at temperatures lower than 13°C/56°F, so you have two choices. Either sow inside, one seed to a 7cm (3in) pot, and grow on in the pot until late spring/early summer; after hardening off, plants can be set outside. Or be patient and sow directly outside in late spring or early summer, setting the seed 2cm (1in) deep and 1–1.2m (3–4ft) apart each way. Set upside-down jam jars over the seeds to protect them from mice and to act as mini-greenhouses.

TRANSPLANTING
If you have sown seed inside, set the plants out when they have three or

Courgettes with pasta

Courgettes, though not strong in flavour, are wonderfully adaptable. They are, of course, one of the standard ingredients in ratatouille, but you can also make soups with them (try courgette with Boursin) or grate them into soufflés. Combined with crème fraiche they make an excellent sauce for pasta.

Serves 4

6 small courgettes, sliced
salt
1 onion, finely chopped
2 cloves garlic, chopped
30g (1oz) butter
2 tbsp olive oil

150ml crème fraiche or sour cream
salt and black pepper
350g (12oz) pasta, such as farfalle
a smallish bunch of dill, chopped
Parmesan cheese, grated

1. Put the sliced courgettes in a colander, sprinkle salt over them and let them drain.
2. Cook the onion and garlic in the butter and oil until they are soft.
3. Add the courgettes and cook for about 5 minutes. Add the crème fraiche and season.
4. While all this is going on, cook the pasta in a large pan (it usually takes 10–12 minutes) and then drain it.
5. Quickly stir the dill into the sauce and tip it over the pasta. Stir in plenty of Parmesan.

Culinary notes
* For the most intense flavour, pick courgettes when they are still small. Slice them lengthways and chargrill them.
* The flowers have little taste, but you can pick them just as they are fully open and use them as little packages to stuff with a rice and meat filling, well flavoured with herbs. Bake them with a covering of home-made tomato sauce.

four proper leaves and danger of frost has passed. Leave plenty of room for them to develop. Bush courgettes will need 1–1.2m (3–4ft) each way, trailing marrows slightly more.

ROUTINE CARE
Courgettes and marrows must be fed and well watered. There are two critical periods: when the plants are first set out and when they are first flowering and setting fruit. Once they have become established, their huge leaves will smother any weeds. They will also smother other crops. Do not plant less competitive plants, like carrots, too close.

YIELD AND HARVESTING
Expect about four marrows and four times as many courgettes from each plant. If you want a monster marrow, pick off all fruits except one. Courgettes need to be picked regularly to keep the plants cropping. The advantage of

growing your own is that you can pick them when they are only finger sized. This is when they are at their most ambrosial.

PESTS AND DISEASES
If fruits wither rather than develop, attend more carefully to watering and feeding. The plants will soon respond. Slugs may eat young plants if they are not protected. Cucumber mosaic virus can mottle the foliage, but some cultivars such as 'Defender' are resistant.

	SPRING			SUMMER			AUTUMN			WINTER		
	EARLY	MID	LATE	EARLY	MID	LATE	EARLY	MID	LATE	EARLY	MID	LATE
COURGETTES AND MARROWS		✳	♣ ➡	♣ ➡	✄	✄	✄	✄				

PUMPKINS AND SQUASH
Cucurbita maxima, C. moschata, C. pepo

'Squash never fail to reach maturity. You can spray them with acid, beat them with sticks and burn them; they love it,' wrote the American humorist S.J. Perelman. So, secure in the knowledge that you will have to work hard to prevent them from growing, you can think instead about which of the staggering variety of pumpkins and squashes you would like to have in the garden. In a small plot, the modest fruits of cultivars such as scalloped 'Custard White', creamy 'Butternut' or the fast and reliable 'Uchiki Kuri' will be easier to accommodate than 'Atlantic Giant', a pumpkin big enough to have taken Cinderella to the ball. The smaller cultivars can be grown trailing over fences and strongly constructed arches, which could scarcely be expected to bear the weight of a fully seasoned giant. There are two main kinds: summer squash, which are eaten as soon as they are ready, and winter squash and pumpkins, which need to be 'cured' in the sun to harden their skins if they are to store successfully under cover through the winter.

In North and South America, the home of the pumpkins and squashes, the fruits are traditionally grown in conjunction with sweetcorn, the long trailing growths winding their way through the strong tall stems of the corn. This is an economical way to use ground and the combination looks good too.

RECOMMENDED CULTIVARS
- **Pumpkins** 'Rouge Vif d'Etamps': heavily ribbed with a bright orange-red skin. 'Baby Bear': small pumpkins (harvest them at about 4–5kg/8–10lb) which produce the best seeds for toasting.
- **Summer squash** 'Custard White': pale scallop-edged fruit, which can be cut

Stuffed butternut squash

Serves 4
1 butternut squash, not too big
olive oil
1 tsp ground cumin (grind your own for a more vital flavour)
salt and black pepper
4 rashers of smoked bacon
3 tbsp sour cream or crème fraiche
3 tbsp finely chopped chives
2 tbsp grated Parmesan cheese

1. Cut the squash in half lengthways and scoop out the seeds. Scatter olive oil, cumin, salt and pepper over the top and bake the squash, cut side upwards, for about 45 minutes at 200°C/400°F/gas mark 6.
2. Cook the bacon and cut the rashers into strips.
3. Scoop out the flesh in chunks and, when it has cooled a bit, mix it with the bacon, sour cream or crème fraiche and most of the chives. Spoon the mixture back into the squash cases.
4. Top off with Parmesan and bake at 180°C/350°F/gas mark 4 for 15 minutes or so. Scatter the rest of the chives on top before serving.

Culinary notes
* Do not waste the seeds when you prepare pumpkins for cooking. Spread them out on a baking sheet and roast them for five minutes at 180°C/350°F/gas mark 4. Then sprinkle over them a couple of tablespoons of water in which you have dissolved a teaspoon of salt. Return them to the oven to dry out.

in half and stuffed. 'Sunburst': productive, bright yellow patty pan squash.
• Winter squash 'Buttercup': firm sweet flesh in a dark green skin. 'Crown Prince': steel-grey skin, orange flesh and superb flavour. 'Little Gem': apple-sized fruit which ripen from green to rich gold. 'Uchiki Kuri': big tear-drop-shaped fruit ripening to bright orange.

Cultivation

In essence, you raise pumpkins and squash in the same way as courgettes and marrows, which are members of the same family, the cucurbits. They are no hardier and the plants cannot be set out in the open until all danger of frost has passed.

SITE AND SOIL

Choose an open, sunny site in ground that is rich and well fed but also well drained. Pumpkins and squash grow most happily where the soil is slightly acid to neutral.

SOWING
Sow indoors from mid-spring onward, pressing the seeds on edge 2cm (1in) deep into individual 7cm (3in) pots of compost. Cover with cling film and keep at a temperature of 15–18°C/60–65°F until the seeds have germinated. This should take no more than a week.

TRANSPLANTING
In early summer, once the soil outside has warmed up, set out the hardened-off plants, raising ridged circles of soil around them to retain water. Set them at least 1.2m (4ft) apart and far away from less robust crops, which they may smother. Sweetcorn, with its upright growth, will not be bothered by the territorial habits of squash.

ROUTINE CARE
These are hungry and thirsty plants. Food is best supplied by incorporating plenty of compost or manure into the ground before planting. Drink must be lavishly provided. The smothering foliage of pumpkins and squash will take care of any weeds.

YIELD AND HARVESTING
The yield depends entirely on the type of pumpkin or squash that you are growing. The little pancake-shaped scallopinis should be cut when they are just 7cm (3in) across. Cut the summer squash as you need them. Dry off the winter squash and pumpkins until the skins are hard and the fruit sounds hollow when tapped. Then store them in a frost-free, cool shed.

PESTS AND DISEASES
These are generally trouble-free crops, though slugs may be tempted by young plants when they are first set out in early summer. Take precautions.

	SPRING			SUMMER			AUTUMN			WINTER		
	EARLY	MID	LATE	EARLY	MID	LATE	EARLY	MID	LATE	EARLY	MID	LATE
PUMPKINS AND SQUASH		✸	✸	✸ ➡	➡	✂	✂					

AUBERGINES, PEPPERS AND CHILLIES
Solanum melongena and Capsicum spp.

Nothing looks quite so unreal in a vegetable garden as a waxy aubergine, smooth, glossy and enigmatic. The standard type is deep purple, almost black, but the white-skinned kind is more likely to have given the aubergine its common name of eggplant. There are also very pretty striped varieties – streaked with cream and maroon – which have more recently come to us from France and Italy. Set the dark, lustrous fruits of aubergines close to the brilliant red of peppers or chillies. All three crops do well in containers or grow bags but are unlikely to succeed outside in cold areas. Try them in a greenhouse, or cold frame. In late spring, you can buy young plants of peppers, chillies and aubergines, which saves the bother of raising them from seed. They need no complicated staking and, as long as you take care over the watering and feeding, look their best grouped in mellow clay pots.

RECOMMENDED CULTIVARS
- **Pepper** 'Ferrari': gives a heavy crop of chunky red peppers. 'Marconi Rossa': a productive variety with long, thin pale green fruits that turn red as they ripen. 'New Ace': early, dependable and heavy cropping, green fruits turning to red.
- **Chilli** 'Early Jalapeno': smooth, bullet-shaped fruit on upright plants, excellent in pots. 'Habenero': greenish-orange fruit, extremely hot, only for masochists. 'Hungarian Hot Wax': gets hot only as it ages, used young tastes like a sweet pepper. 'Tricolour Variegata': purplish stem and leaves with fruits that may be white, green or purple.
- **Aubergine** 'Black Beauty': well-flavoured fruit, early, pear shaped. 'Moneymaker': long fruits, prolific and well flavoured. 'Rosa Bianca': globe-shaped fruit, striped in pink and white.

Cultivation
If you can grow tomatoes, you should be able to grow aubergines, peppers and chillies. And like tomatoes, especially the cherry types, they are particularly well suited to patio gardening. Plants are most vulnerable when they are young, but you may find you can persuade them to grow outdoors if you wrap them up at night with polythene or fleece for the first couple of weeks. Aubergines have a longer growing season than peppers and need about five months to complete the full cycle from seed to fruit. They are also less hardy than peppers or chillies.

SITE AND SOIL
Shelter is all important, especially if you are growing plants in open ground. If you are using grow bags outside, push them up against a sunny wall for extra warmth. Cloches, polytunnels, frames and greenhouses provide their own protection.

SOWING
Sow seed in trays or pots indoors 1–2cm (½–1in) deep, in a heat of about 21°C/70°F in early March. For aubergines you need to maintain a growing temperature for the seedlings of 15–18°C/60–65°F. Pepper and chilli seedlings need to be kept at 12–15°C/55–60°F.

TRANSPLANTING
Prick out the seedlings when they are about 5cm (2in) high, into separate 7cm (3in) pots to grow on. Gradually lower the growing temperature, harden off the seedlings and plant them in their permanent positions in late spring or

early summer when the first flowers appear, spacing them about 45cm (18in) apart. Alternatively, move them into larger containers, setting each plant in a pot at least 25cm (10in) wide.

ROUTINE CARE

Keep the plants well watered, particularly when the fruit has begun to set. Tomato feed is a good booster for plants growing in containers. Pinch out the growing tips of aubergines, peppers and chillies when the plants are about 20–25cm (8–10in) high.

YIELD AND HARVEST

Aubergines do not do well in poor light, so in overcast summers a good crop is unlikely. In decent summers, expect about four aubergines on each plant, slightly more from the peppers and about twenty chillies on a plant. Green peppers will ripen and turn red if they get enough warmth in early autumn.

Stuffed aubergines

Serves 4
4 aubergines
salt and pepper
100ml (3fl oz) olive oil
2 onions, diced
500g (18oz) tomatoes, skinned and quartered (or a tin)
4 rashers smoked streaky bacon (or pancetta), chopped and fried till crisp
200g (7oz) risotto rice
300ml (1/2 pint) chicken stock
Parmesan cheese, grated
toasted pine nuts
parsley

1. Halve the aubergines and scoop out the flesh. Chop it into cubes. Sprinkle the insides with salt and let them stand for 30 minutes before rinsing them under the tap.
2. Brush the insides of the shells with olive oil and roast them in the oven at 175°C/ gas mark 3–4 until they begin to soften.
3. In a saucepan, fry the onion in the remainder of the olive oil. Add the cubed aubergine flesh and cook for 10 minutes or so until the vegetables are soft and beginning to colour.
4. Add the tomatoes (fresh or tinned), and the bacon (or pancetta). Season to taste.
5. Add the rice and the stock and cook gently in the saucepan with the lid on for about 20 minutes, or until the rice is cooked.
6. Pile the mixture into the aubergine shells, top with Parmesan cheese and roast in the oven at 175°C/gas mark 3–4 until the cheese melts. Serve with toasted pine nuts and chopped parsley scattered on top.

PESTS AND DISEASES

Whitefly and red spider mite are the chief pests if you are growing under glass. Keep the atmosphere as damp as possible. A car vacuum cleaner quickly disposes of whitefly when they are on the wing. In an enclosed area, a natural predator such as *Encarsia formosa* may be effective.

	SPRING			SUMMER			AUTUMN			WINTER		
	EARLY	MID	LATE	EARLY	MID	LATE	EARLY	MID	LATE	EARLY	MID	LATE
AUBERGINES, PEPPERS AND CHILLIES	✳	✳	➡	➡		✂	✂	✂				

CUCUMBERS *Cucumis sativus*

There are two types of cucumber, beauty and the beast, although Japanese breeders have worked hard to make the warty, outdoor beast as attractive as the smooth-skinned, indoor-raised beauty. Outdoor cultivars can be trained over arbours or tripods to make centrepieces or fruitful arches in the decorative kitchen garden. Or you can allow plants to sprawl around the feet of a tall crop of sweetcorn.

Cucumbers, like melons, used to be one of the crops that old-fashioned gardeners of the Victorian age minded about to quite an extraordinary degree. A kinked cucumber was a dangerous sign of moral slackness, and gardeners fixed long glass tubes over newly set fruit to ensure that their cucumbers grew as straight as rulers.

RECOMMENDED CULTIVARS

- **Outdoor** 'Masterpiece': a reliable type producing heavy crops of dark-skinned fruit about 20cm (8in) long. 'Crystal Apple': a pretty novelty, pale lemon-sized fruit. 'La Diva': mini cucumbers 15cm (6in) long, sweet tasting and resistant to mildew.
- **Indoor** 'Rocky': an F1 hybrid from Israel, very prolific with its crunchy mini-fruit. 'Tiffany': a vigorous, all-female variety with well-flavoured fruit.

Cultivation

Outdoor 'ridge' cucumbers (so called because they were planted on ridges to ensure good drainage for the roots) are hardier, easier to grow and less prone to attack by pest and disease than the greenhouse types. Greenhouse cucumbers will only do well if you can keep both heat and humidity at almost tropical levels.

SITE AND SOIL

Cucumbers like a very rich soil, well larded with plenty of manure or compost. They lap up water faster than camels and must never be allowed to dry out.

Tzatziki

Serves 4

$^1/_2$ cucumber
a little salt
200g (7fl oz) natural yoghurt

a small bunch of mint, chopped
2 cloves garlic, crushed
1 tbsp olive oil

1. Grate the cucumber and let it drain, sprinkled with salt, in a sieve set over a bowl.
2. Mix it with the yoghurt, mint, garlic and olive oil. Add a little water if it seems too stiff.

In sheltered sites, they will grow in dappled shade.

SOWING

Sow seed indoors from early spring onwards, setting them on edge in individual 7cm (3in) pots. Water them and cover them with polythene until they germinate. They respond to high temperatures, 21°C/70°F at least. Keep plants growing well, repotting if necessary, to put outside after the last frost. Seed can also be sown directly outside in early summer. Cover with upturned jam jars for protection and set the seeds no deeper than 2cm (1in) and 60cm (24in) apart.

TRANSPLANTING

Harden off indoor-raised plants and set them out in early summer, leaving at least 60cm (24in) between each transplant.

ROUTINE CARE

Water frequently, especially once the fruits have set. Lack of water is the most usual reason for fruits failing to develop.

YIELD AND HARVESTING

An outdoor cucumber may produce about ten fruits, an indoor one probably twice as many. As with courgettes, you must pick fruit regularly to keep the production line in business.

PESTS AND DISEASES

Aphids may attack plants in the open; under glass, plants are prey to red spider mite. Cucumber mosaic virus is the most serious disease. Leaves may become so mottled and misshapen that plants die. There is no cure. Bacterial rot of root or stem may cause sudden and dramatic wilting. Heap compost round the base of the plant and water it well to encourage it to make new roots.

	SPRING			SUMMER			AUTUMN			WINTER		
	EARLY	MID	LATE	EARLY	MID	LATE	EARLY	MID	LATE	EARLY	MID	LATE
CUCUMBERS		✿	✿	✿ ➡	✄	✄	✄	✄				

SWEETCORN *Zea mays*

Tall sheaves of sweetcorn provide an authentic hint of harvest in the late summer garden. They are stately plants and anciently cultivated ones: husks found in caves in Peru and Mexico where the plant is a native suggest that people were growing and eating it by 3500 BC. Breeders have been working hard to persuade sweetcorn to be as happy in cool northern climates as it is in its Latin American home. Whereas a traditional variety might take more than eighty days to reach maturity, a modern cultivar will ripen in under sixty. Growth in cooler climates may be slower than this. Interplant sweetcorn with low-growing courgettes or squash to make the best use of limited space.

RECOMMENDED CULTIVARS
• 'Sweet Nugget': an F1 hybrid that is reliable and superbly flavoured. 'Minipop': an FI hybrid that produces mini cobs, ideal for stir-fries; excellent where space is short as the plants can be set only 20cm (8in) apart.

Cultivation
Pollination is the key to fat, well-filled cobs and since sweetcorn is wind-pollinated, it is best planted in blocks rather than rows. The pollen from the male tassels at the top of the plant then has the best possible chance of reaching the silky tassels of the female flowers. New 'supersweet' varieties have been bred for extra succulence but are slightly tender. You must grow these on their own so that they do not cross-pollinate with unimproved varieties, which would make them lose some of their sweetness.

SITE AND SOIL
Sweetcorn needs a warm, sheltered site and grows best on deep, well-drained, fertile and slightly acid soils.

SOWING
Climate dictates how you should proceed. In warm areas, sow seed direct into the soil in late spring, setting them in a block pattern about 2cm (1in) deep. Set a few seeds together at each growing point, about 35cm (14in) apart and thin out the weaker seedlings after germination. Seed will not germinate in soil temperatures below 10°C/50°F, but you can use a floating plastic mulch to warm up the ground beforehand or set jam jars over the seeds to act as mini-greenhouses. In cold areas, sow seed inside in mid-spring in gentle heat, setting them no more than 2cm (1in) deep in individual 7cm (3in) pots. Make sure that seedlings are thoroughly hardened off before transplanting.

TRANSPLANTING
Set out the plants when all danger of frost has passed, spacing them in a block about 35cm (14in) apart in each direction. For baby corn, use cultivars such as 'Minipop' and set the plants no more than 20cm (8in) apart.

Sweetcorn and potato pottage

Serves 4

4 corn cobs
750g (1.5lb) potatoes, cooked
30g (1oz) butter
1 large onion, finely chopped
2 tsp mustard

900ml (1 ½ pints) chicken stock
2 tbs chopped parsley
2 tbs chopped thyme
2 hard-boiled eggs, chopped
180g (6oz) Edam or Cheddar cheese, diced

1. Scrape the corn from the cobs. It comes away more easily than you might think.
2. Mash the potatoes while still warm.
3. Melt the butter in a big saucepan, add the chopped onion and cook gently for 10 minutes.
4. Take the pan from the heat and mix the potatoes and mustard with the onion.
5. Gradually stir in the stock, and then the kernels of corn and the herbs.
6. Simmer the soup for another 10 minutes before adding the eggs and cheese.

Culinary notes
* A fat, home-grown corn on the cob needs only lashings of butter and an unselfconscious air of abandon. Don't think about that dribble of butter down your chin. Everyone else will have one too. The fresher the cobs, the quicker they will cook. Five minutes will probably be enough. Add salt while you eat, not while you cook, as it toughens the kernels.

ROUTINE CARE
Little water will be needed until the cobs start to swell. Sweetcorn is usually sturdily self-supporting, but in exposed areas you may need to earth up the plants when they are about 30cm (12in) high.

YIELD AND HARVESTING
Expect no more than one or two cobs from each plant. Do not leave them toughening on the stem. Pick them when the silky tassels begin to turn brown and the juice that oozes from the kernels is milky. If you pick too soon, the juice will be watery. If you pick too late, it will be thick and starchy. Use as soon as possible after picking. Sugar in the cobs turns rapidly to starch after they have been picked, although the conversion process is slower in new supersweet cultivars.

PESTS AND DISEASES
Mice are the most troublesome pests, feasting daintily on seed that has been sown direct in the ground. Upturned jam jars placed over the seeds provide useful protection.

	SPRING			SUMMER			AUTUMN			WINTER		
	EARLY	MID	LATE	EARLY	MID	LATE	EARLY	MID	LATE	EARLY	MID	LATE
SWEETCORN		❂	⁂ ➡	⁂ ➡		✂	✂	✂				

GLOBE ARTICHOKES AND CARDOONS
Cynara scolymus and C. cardunculus

A globe artichoke has the right dramatic credentials to be the star and centrepiece of a decorative scheme in the kitchen garden. With its jagged, greyish-green leaves and showy, fat flower buds – the edible part – it looks as though it has been sculpted by one of the builders of the Parthenon. It certainly makes a cheaper centrepiece than an arbour in a planting scheme, but unfortunately it is an all-or-nothing plant. It will look stunning from late May to October, when it will spread at least 1m (4ft) in all directions, but once it is reduced to nothing, sheared down by the first frosts, it is a big nothing. Cardoons are equally handsome, but it is the fleshy leaf bases, tied up and blanched, that you eat, not the flower buds.

RECOMMENDED CULTIVARS
- **Artichokes** 'Green Globe': has a flattish rounded head with blunt-ended scales. 'Gros Vert de Laon': one of the many French varieties with a big, fleshy heart and excellent flavour; like 'Purple Roscoff', it is grown in vast quantities in Brittany. 'Romanesco': a handsome purple-headed variety that matures slightly later than the green.
- **Cardoons** 'Gigante di Romagna': an Italian favourite, excellent for blanching. 'Plein Blanc Enorme': a French selection that produces succulent leaf bases.

Cultivation
Seed-raised plants are very variable, so globe artichokes are generally grown from rooted offsets, propagated from types that are known to have good flower heads. If you leave the buds too long before picking, they open into spectacular great thistle heads of bluish purple. These dry well for winter flower arrangements. Cardoons can be raised from seed or offsets. They are generally available from garden centres but are usually to be found among the ornamental plants. They have smaller, more prickly flower heads that also look superb dried.

SITE AND SOIL
In the great artichoke-growing areas of France (Brittany) and Italy (the coastal plain around Brindisi), the soil is light and the climate mild. A combination of heavy soils and cold winters is likely to be too much for these plants. In

---

Cooking globe artichokes

Culinary notes

* You need little more than a large pan and some good butter. Cook the artichokes in boiling water. Timing depends on size; allow somewhere between thirty and forty minutes. Drain them well and serve them with plenty of melted butter.

---

very hot areas, artichokes will tolerate shade. Elsewhere they should have sun, as should cardoons.

PLANTING

Young offsets of both artichokes and cardoons should be planted shallowly, with only as much of the base below ground as is needed to keep them upright. New offsets quickly develop a sustaining root system. Set them out in late spring, about 1.2m (4ft) each way, and keep them well watered until they are established.

ROUTINE CARE

Offsets may produce small flower heads late in the season of their first year. Pick these off to encourage the plant to develop more side shoots. Where winters are hard, protect established plants by packing them with straw. Mulch thickly with manure in spring. Plants are not long lived. After 3–4 years replace old clumps with the new offsets that they produce. Begin blanching cardoons in late spring when they are about 45cm (18in) high. Tie the leaves in a bundle with soft string, and wrap them in newspaper and then black polythene.

YIELD AND HARVESTING

Expect about ten artichokes from an established plant. Cut the terminal 'king' bud first, with 5cm (2in) of stem attached. The head should be large but the scales not yet opening away from the centre. While the artichokes are still young, the inside of the stem is very succulent. Peel back the stringy outside and nibble out the innards.

PESTS AND DISEASES

Artichokes and cardoons are relatively disease free, although blackfly can be a problem on developing flower heads. More problematic than any pest or disease is the question of winter wet which, combined with cold, may rot the plants entirely.

TOMATOES *Lycopersicon esculentum*

For the decorative vegetable garden, outdoor tomatoes, of either the cordon or the bush type, will be your first choice. They are simplicity itself to manage and the flavour of the new cultivars, especially when buffed up by hours of sunshine, is outstanding. Once planted – in tubs, grow bags or even hanging baskets – the bush varieties can be left to their own devices. You do not have to pinch out side shoots or tie any stems in to canes. The plants start to sag gently as they grow and then sprawl around on the ground, popping out fruit as fast as children with bubble gum. Crops are generous, but last only a month or so.

The cordon types of tomato, trained up tall canes, make good centrepieces for decorative schemes, especially if you contrast a yellow-fruited cultivar such as 'Yellow Perfection' with the stripy 'Tigerella'. For extra decorative effect, you can add golden canary creeper scrambling over a neighbouring support. Cordon tomatoes crop over a much longer period than bush types. You need both.

RECOMMENDED CULTIVARS

- **Best under glass** 'Brandywine' (cordon): Beefsteak type, known since 1885, and superbly flavoured but needs good weather to fruit well. 'Costoluto Fiorentino' (cordon): vivid red, ribbed fruit of the beefsteak type. 'Gardeners' Delight' (cordon): a reliable favourite producing large crops of small fruit over a long season. 'Sungold' (cordon): voted by many gardeners as the best and sweetest tomato of all, golden, cherry-type tomatoes borne over a long period.
- **Outdoor** 'Ferline' (cordon): a good outdoor tomato, as it is resistant (but not immune) to blight, medium-sized fruit. 'Principe Borghese da Appendere' (cordon): a prolific plum tomato, much used in Italy for drying, fruit the size of bantam eggs. 'Red Alert' (bush): excellent outdoors, if you can keep slugs at bay, early and prolific with its medium-sized fruit. 'Tumbling Tom Red' (bush): small, sweet, juicy fruits, ideal for tubs, also available in yellow.

Cultivation

Not all tomatoes are suitable for growing outside in colder areas. Check before you buy that you have got the right variety for your purpose. In frost-free greenhouses plants can be started into growth sooner than plants that you plan to use outside.

SITE AND SOIL

For growing outdoors, choose a sheltered site which gets plenty of sun. If you are growing tall cordon types of tomato in grow bags or containers, try to arrange them so that they are backed by a protecting wall. As for all vegetables and fruits, soil should be fertile and well drained. The best results come from ground that has been well manured.

In greenhouses, soil diseases and detrimental salts can build up quickly if tomatoes are grown too often in the same borders. Use grow bags, or rotate the tomatoes round different parts of the greenhouse.

SOWING

In a greenhouse, you can get tomatoes off to an early start, but with outdoor plants nothing is gained by sowing seed too soon, since plants cannot go outside until all danger of frost is past. Scatter seed thinly on the surface of a 12cm (5in) pot of compost and cover lightly with more compost or vermiculite. Cover with cling film to retain moisture during germination and keep at a temperature of 15–18°C/60–65°F. When the seedlings develop their first true leaves, prick them out into individual 7cm (3in) pots. Alternatively sow two or three seeds direct into a series of small pots, thinning out the weaker seedlings as they develop. Germination takes 8–10 days.

TRANSPLANTING

The plants will be ready to set outside roughly two months after you have sown the seed, but they must be thoroughly hardened off. If they catch cold, their leaves go blue. If you do not want to raise your own, buy named varieties of tomato and plant them out when the soil has warmed up to about 10°C/50°F. You should be able to see the first flower truss. Set tall cordon tomatoes 38–45cm (15–18in) apart, bush tomatoes 45–60cm (18–24in) apart.

ROUTINE CARE

Bush tomatoes need little attention, but with cordon varieties the side shoots that start to grow in the leaf axils need to be nipped out regularly. Cordon varieties will also need to be staked and the plants regularly tied in. 'Stop' cordon varieties by nipping out the tip of the stem in late summer. In cold areas, this may be after about three trusses have set fruit. In warmer areas, five to six trusses will have developed. Overwatering and overfeeding have a detrimental effect on the flavour of tomatoes. An initial drench and a mulch are often enough for crops growing outdoors. Irregular watering gives the plants hiccups and is the most common cause of blossom end rot, which shows as brownish-black sunken patches on the fruit. In open ground, no extra feeding should be necessary. When grown in containers, tomatoes will need plenty to eat and drink. Use a liquid feed. In a hot dry summer, you will need to feed and water tomato plants in containers perhaps as often as twice a day. Use only one plant in a 35cm (14in) basket, choosing one that is as deep as possible.

YIELD AND HARVESTING

Expect 2–4kg (4–8lb) of fruit per plant, more from cordon than from bush types. Plants in greenhouses and plants growing in warm areas will obviously have a longer cropping period and heavier yields than plants grown outdoors in cold areas. For the best flavour, leave the fruit to ripen fully on the plant.

PESTS AND DISEASES

In greenhouses, whitefly are the chief irritation around tomatoes. With outdoor bush types, small black slugs are a nuisance, for they come out in the evenings like winetasters – a nibble here, a nibble there, nothing properly consumed but a good deal started. Beware. Watch out too for grey mould (*Botrytis*), stem rot and potato blight. Blight is the worst problem on outdoor-grown tomatoes, especially in a dull, sunless summer. Once it has descended, it can't be got rid of, but you can ward it off by regular spraying with a fungicide based on mancozeb.

Stuffed tomatoes

Serves 4

4 large beefsteak tomatoes	parsley, finely chopped
salt and black pepper	4 eggs
4 rashers streaky bacon	30g (1oz) butter
125g (4oz) mushrooms, finely chopped	4 slices toast

1. Preheat the oven to 180°C/350°F/gas mark 4. Cut the tops off the tomatoes and scoop out the seeds and flesh. Season the insides with salt and pepper.
2. Fry the bacon rashers until crisp, then chop them finely and set aside. Brown the mushrooms in the bacon fat, and then mix them with the bacon and parsley.
3. Spoon the mixture into the tomatoes and break an egg into the top of each one. Dot with butter and bake in the oven for 15 minutes until the eggs are set. Serve with toast.

Culinary notes

* Tomatoes will sit happily on the plant for two weeks or more. They are certainly better there than in the refrigerator, which does them no good at all. Late leftovers may be ripened on a windowsill indoors, but the green fruit of autumn makes very good chutney.
* Tomatoes are one of the few crops that you can scarcely have too much of. They freeze well and although the texture of the fruit disintegrates in the process, the taste remains very good. The easiest way to prepare them is to do nothing. Just bag them as they are. They stay whole and separate, like marbles rolling round in a bag. This is a huge advantage when you want to use them. You do not have to hack away at a solid frozen mass to extract your half pound. When you run each frozen tomato under the tap, the skin slips off like a silk camisole. This is much easier than peeling tomatoes before freezing.
* Some recipes instruct you to get rid of the seeds before you use tomatoes for cooking. A high concentration of vitamins lies in the jelly coating of these seeds. It seems a pity to waste them.
* Home-grown tomatoes make superb salads, sliced and scattered with finely chopped basil or chives, and then dressed with a vinaigrette. Tossed with some black olives and feta cheese, they recreate the authentic taste of a Greek island holiday.

	SPRING			SUMMER			AUTUMN			WINTER		
	EARLY	MID	LATE	EARLY	MID	LATE	EARLY	MID	LATE	EARLY	MID	LATE
	✿	✿	✿	➡	✂	✂	✂	✂				

PODDED VEGETABLES

The scrambling habit of some peas and beans can be used to good effect in the decorative kitchen garden, whether trained over a tunnel made from hazel sticks or up a tripod to form the centrepiece of a bed. Runner beans hold on to their supports by twining; peas have exploratory tendrils that grasp as tightly as a baby's fist on to any useful prop. All the podded vegetables are attractive in bloom, but not all are as showy as the runner bean, with its blazing red flowers. The broad bean, though a beefy-looking plant, has a delicate flower beautifully marked with black on white. Bean pods may be purple, green, cream, waxy yellow or striped. Among the low-growing French beans is a wonderful strain of plants with cream pods streaked and splashed with bright pink, such as 'Rob Roy'. 'Rob Splash' is a climbing French bean with cream pods splashed with deep purple.

Try planting two different runner beans, such as 'Painted Lady' and 'White Apollo', to train over a hazel tunnel, straddling a path through the vegetable garden. Set tall purple-flowered *Allium hollandicum* 'Purple Sensation' and the striped roses *Rosa gallica* 'Versicolor' and 'Ferdinand Pichard' together with catmint to jostle at their feet. Red-flowered runner beans can be combined with purple everlasting pea on a decorative tripod, perhaps rising from a sea of Florence fennel and the tall flowering stems of red orach, *Atriplex hortensis* var. *rubra*. The orach is a fast-growing annual, which self-seeds vigorously. Rows of broad beans and peas scrambling up a support of chicken wire can be backed by decorative tripods of pink-flowered sweet peas. For scent, these are unparalleled, but if you bend your nose to the more workaday broad bean you will find that this too has sweet-smelling flowers.

The dark purple colour that suffuses the foliage of climbing French beans such as 'Blauhilde' or 'Purple Teepee' is intensified in the pods and flowers. The colour disappears when you cook the beans, but you can use the plants to decorative effect with purple verbena, dark red dahlias such as 'Bishop of Llandaff' and feathery clumps of bronze fennel. The runner bean 'Painted Lady' with its distinctive red and white flowers was being grown in kitchen gardens more than 150 years ago. It is a decorative climber, but it also produces a heavy crop of well-flavoured beans. Mix it with white-flowered 'White Lady' and clematis on an arbour or arch.

PEAS & MANGETOUT *Pisum sativum*

Early visitors to Troy, where Heinrich Schliemann excavated Priam's fabled palace, were said to have been fed on peas from the great king's larder. One huge storage jar contained more than 180kg (400lb) of peas that had remained perfectly preserved for 3,000 years. Clarence Birdseye, who brought us frozen peas, had a hard act to follow.

Priam's peas would have been tall-growing types. In the decorative kitchen garden, low-growing cultivars – such as the mangetout 'Sugar Ann', which grows up to 75cm (30in), or 'Dwarf Sugar Sweet', which is even smaller (about 45cm/18in) – can be used to make informal low hedges around plots. Tall-growing cultivars such as the superb mangetout 'Carouby de Maussane', which has pretty purple flowers, will scramble up a support to about 1.5m (5ft) to make a tall screen or centrepiece. 'Alderman' is another tall-growing type that has survived from the Victorian era and is still worth growing for its fine flavour. Wrinkle-seeded peas provide the sweetest crop, but round-seeded ones the hardiest. You need both.

RECOMMENDED CULTIVARS

- **Peas to shell** 'Feltham First' (round-seeded): an old variety, but still one of the first to mature with sweet, dark green peas. 'Hurst Green Shaft' (wrinkled): superb sweet peas which mature over a long period, 'Onward' (round seeded): early maincrop variety which produces heavy crops.
- **Mangetout** 'Carouby de Maussane': purple flowers produce large, succulent pods. 'Oregon Sugar Pod': excellently flavoured pods on a plant that grows to 1m (3ft) tall. 'Sugar Snap': fleshy pods with long season of use.

Cultivation

All seed sowing is a kind of horticultural futures market and gamblers will not mind risking a row of winter-sown peas in the hope of a succulent and particularly early crop the following spring. Peas for winter sowing must be the round-seeded, not the wrinkle-seeded kind. From spring on, you can then sow any type of pea at 3–4-week intervals until mid-summer.

If you grow one of the so-called leafless peas, in which many of the leaves have been modified into tendrils, you will need to do less staking. The tendrils wind round their neighbours and the whole mass becomes almost self-supporting: group therapy in the vegetable garden.

SITE AND SOIL

Peas positively like cool, damp summers. Soil should be fertile and well dug. Provided there is plenty of moisture, peas do not mind some shade.

SOWING

Sow seed 3–5cm (1.5–2in) deep and 5–7cm (2–3in) apart. If you are growing a straight row, as in a low pea hedge, take out a wide drill about 5cm (2in) deep and the width of your spade. Taking out a drill always sounds daunting, but with peas it is not. Relatively little soil needs to be moved. Sow the seeds so that they lie roughly 5cm (2in) apart. Cover the row with the excavated soil and tread it down firmly. Use wire netting to protect against birds.

Peas and cucumber

If you have a small garden with room for only a short row of peas, you will have difficulty gathering enough of them for a main course serving. Use them instead as a first course, braised in the French way with a few finely shredded lettuce leaves and a little finely chopped carrot and spring onion. If you have plenty, experiment with ways of combining them with other vegetables.

Serves 4

1 cucumber, peeled	sprig of mint, chopped
1–1.5kg (2–3lb) peas, shelled	salt and black pepper
60g (2oz) butter	1 tsp sugar

1. Cut the cucumber into 3cm (1½in) chunks, and then into batons. Sprinkle with salt in a colander, leave to drain for 30 minutes, rinse and pat dry.
2. Bring 1cm (½in) of water to the boil. Add the cucumber, peas, butter and mint. Season, add sugar and cook gently until the peas are tender – for 5 minutes at most.

ROUTINE CARE

Provide some form of support for tall-growing cultivars: either netting or hazel pea sticks which, when woven together at the tops, make a very decorative feature in the vegetable garden. If you have used wire netting to protect the seed, you can draw this up into a V-shaped ridge to support low-growing cultivars rising through it.

If you are using peas to fill a bed in a potager, you can grow them mixed with broad beans, so that as the peas grow they use the sturdier beans for support. For this to work satisfactorily, you need one of the old, tall kinds of pea. The beans do not suffer, as cottage gardeners of the nineteenth century, who invented the technique, soon discovered.

YIELD AND HARVESTING

Expect 5kg (10lb) from a 3m (10ft) row. Pick peas regularly to encourage the vines to produce more. Pick mangetout while the peas are visible only as tiny swellings. When the pea crop has finished, chop off the stems at the base, working along the rows with a Dutch hoe. In this way you can remove the vines withering on their supports while retaining the roots with their nitrogen-bearing nodules to enrich your ground for another, different crop the following season.

PESTS AND DISEASES

Birds and mice are the most serious pests. Soaking seed in paraffin is said to deter mice. Otherwise, harden your heart and use traps.

Peas spiced with cumin

3 tbs vegetable oil
1 1/2 tsp whole cumin seeds
2 dried hot red chillies
175g (6oz) onions, chopped
175g (6oz) carrots, diced

175g (6oz) peas, shelled
175g (6oz) potatoes, cooked and diced
salt
1 spring onion, finely sliced

1. Heat the oil in a large frying pan and sizzle the cumin and chillies for a few seconds before adding the onion. When this is limp and translucent, add the carrots and peas and cook for 5 minutes until the vegetables are tender.
2. Add the potatoes and salt and cook for a few minutes until the potato is heated through. Remove the chillies before serving and garnish with the spring onion.

	SPRING			SUMMER			AUTUMN			WINTER		
	EARLY	MID	LATE	EARLY	MID	LATE	EARLY	MID	LATE	EARLY	MID	LATE
SHELLING PEAS		✿	✿	✂	✿ ✂	✿	✂	✂				
SNOW PEAS		✿	✿	✂	✿ ✂	✿	✂	✂				
SNAP PEAS		✿	✿	✂	✿ ✂	✿	✂	✂				

RUNNER BEANS *Phaseolus coccineus*

In the wild, runner beans grow in the Mexican mountains together with dahlias, begonias and lobelias. There is no reason why you should not make your own beans feel comfortably at home by providing similar companions. When the runner bean was first introduced into England by Charles I's gardener, John Tradescant, in the seventeenth century, it was used as an ornamental climber rather than a food plant. The hummingbirds that pollinate the beans in Mexico will be in short supply in most gardens. Fortunately bumblebees have learned the trick of opening the flowers and provide an efficient pod-setting service.

Use runner beans scrambling up a taut net to make a quick summer screen in the garden. They will grow up to 3m (10ft). Grow them up tripods in a flower border, or use them to cover an arbour, where they can twine happily among clematis or late summer-flowering nasturtiums and the flame-coloured climber *Eccremocarpus scaber*.

Runner beans with cream and herbs

The most important thing is to use only young, tender beans. When pods start to toughen, runner beans are disgusting. Serve them with butter and a hint of garlic, or tossed in bacon fat, with the bacon cut into strips and scattered on top. For a fancier dish, combine them with cream and a herb such as savory or thyme.

Serves 4

450g (1lb) runner beans
150ml (¼ pint) double cream
1 clove garlic, peeled

1 tbsp summer savory or thyme, chopped
salt and black pepper
Parmesan cheese, grated

1. Slice the beans and cook them until just tender.
2. Heat the cream, garlic, savory or thyme, salt and pepper together in a saucepan and simmer for a few minutes.
3. Add the beans and allow them to heat through. Dish up with the Parmesan and more herbs scattered on top.

RECOMMENDED CULTIVARS

'Hestia': a dwarf variety (30–45cm/12–18in tall), which can be grown in containers. 'Lady Di': has long, tender pods, generously produced. 'Painted Lady': very pretty, with red and white flowers producing good-quality beans. 'Polestar': grows to about 2m (6½ft) with well-flavoured, stringless pods.

Cultivation

Runner beans are not difficult to grow, but in some seasons they seem reluctant to set fruit. Spraying the flowers with water does not help as much as keeping the roots well supplied with water. Less easy to cope with are pollen beetles, which move on to runner beans (and sweet peas) when oil seed rape has finished flowering. Sitting in the keel of the flower, they discourage visiting bumblebees and the flowers are left unpollinated.

SITE AND SOIL

Start thinking about the site six months before you sow, and dig masses of well-rotted farmyard manure or compost into the soil. Runner beans are deep-rooted and their roots like to feel the journey has been worthwhile. Some shade is beneficial, provided the ground is fertile.

SOWING

Do not be in a hurry to sow direct into the ground, as the soil temperature must be at least 10°C/50°F for the seeds to germinate. This is usually not until the very end of spring. Set seed 15cm(6in) apart, or sow one seed at the base of each cane in a wigwam. You can push on the crop by sowing seed inside in big boxes or individual 7cm (3in) pots and setting out plants from late spring.

TRANSPLANTING

Runner beans are tender, so do not transplant indoor-sown beans while there is any danger of frost. Set out plants 15cm (6in) apart or space them regularly around a wigwam or some other support that they can climb.

ROUTINE CARE

Water liberally, especially as the plants come into flower. Mulching will help to conserve moisture in the soil and keep down weeds.

YIELD AND HARVESTING

Expect about 1kg (2lb) of beans from each plant. Pick the pods before the beans have started to swell inside. If you leave mature pods on the plants, they will not feel they have to produce more.

PESTS AND DISEASES

Diseases are uncommon, but flowers may be unwilling to set. If so, pay attention to the watering. Nothing, however, will deter pollen beetles.

	SPRING			SUMMER			AUTUMN			WINTER		
	EARLY	MID	LATE	EARLY	MID	LATE	EARLY	MID	LATE	EARLY	MID	LATE
RUNNER BEANS			✿	✿ ➡	✂	✂	✂	✂				

FRENCH & HARICOT BEANS *Phaseolus vulgaris*

French beans are not really French. Like runners, they are New World beans, brought back to Europe by the Spanish conquistadores. These beans, wrote the early herbalist John Gerard, 'boiled together before they be ripe, and buttered, and so eaten with their cods, are exceeding delicate meat, and do not ingender wind as the other pulses do'. French beans may climb or they may grow as bushes. They may have flat pods, or rounded. They may be green, purple, cream, yellow or wonderfully speckled and spotted, as in the old Dutch variety 'Dragon Tongue', which has cream pods flecked with purple. 'Tongues of Fire', which may have originally come from Tierra del Fuego, has the same pale pods, dramatically splashed with red. The beans of some types can be eaten either green (when they are known as flageolets) or dried (when they are known as haricots).

RECOMMENDED CULTIVARS

- Green-podded 'Masterpiece Stringless': easy and productive. 'Slenderette': excellent green bean cropping over a long period. 'The Prince': produces long, straight pods of good flavour.
- Purple-podded 'Purple Teepee': productive and quick to mature; turns green when cooked but the flavour of the purple cultivars is unparalleled.

- **Yellow-podded** 'Mont d'Or': black seed inside golden waxpod beans, superbly flavoured. 'Rocquencourt': dark yellow round pods contrasting with dark green foliage. 'Sonesta': waxy, yellow beans, ready 60–70 days after sowing, good in cold areas.
- **Climbing** 'Blauhilde': pretty purple flowers and beans. 'Blue Lake': similar, with fat, tender pods. 'Helda': flat-podded beans, giving an early though short harvest. 'Neckargold': yellow beans borne on vigorous plants. 'Purple Podded Climbing': prolific and finely flavoured.
- **Dry beans** 'Borlotto Lingua di Fuoco': can be used as a French bean or left to mature. 'Chevrier Vert': a classic French flageolet, known since the 1880s. 'Marengo': has yellow pods with pale green beans inside.

Cultivation

By nature these are fast-growing annuals and it is a waste of seed to sow it in cold, dank ground. Compact bush varieties will crop successfully in pots and grow bags; climbing types will need canes or some other support.

SITE AND SOIL

French beans like rich, light soil, which can be neutral or slightly acid. They do best in a sheltered position.

SOWING

For early crops sow seed indoors in deep boxes or individual 7cm (3in) pots so that plants can be set out after the last frost. When the soil temperature has reached 13°C/56°F, sow outside at regular intervals from late spring until mid-summer. Set seed 3cm (1 1/4in) deep, in staggered rows, so that the plants grow about 23cm (9in) apart in the rows. They germinate in 1–2 weeks.

TRANSPLANTING

The shock to the system holds back transplants, and plants set out from seed sown indoors may crop no sooner than a later sowing outside. Water transplants well.

ROUTINE CARE

Earth up the stems of young plants as they grow to give them extra support. Provide canes for climbers and short twiggy sticks to prop up bush varieties, which tend to get top heavy when laden with beans. Keep the soil moist throughout the growing period, but especially when the plants come into flower.

YIELD AND HARVESTING

Expect 4kg (8lb) of beans from a 3m (10ft) row. For fresh beans, pick the pods frequently while they are still succulent. For dry haricot beans, leave the pods on the plant until the end of the growing season. Hang the stems under cover until the pods have dried off. Then shell the beans and store them in airtight jars.

PESTS AND DISEASES

As for runner beans, page 107.

Haricot bean salad

Serves 4

225g (8oz) small white haricot beans
125ml (4fl oz) good olive oil
2 cloves garlic, crushed
1 bay leaf
1 sprig thyme

1 dessertspoon tomato concentrate
lemon juice
salt and pepper
finely sliced raw onion rings

1. Cover the beans generously with water in a saucepan, bring them slowly to the boil, and then pull them off the heat and leave them to soak for 3 hours before draining them.
2. Heat the oil in a separate pan, add the beans and cook gently for about 10 minutes with garlic, herbs and tomato concentrate.
3. Add water, sufficient to cover the beans by about 2cm (1in), and cook gently for 2–3 hours until the beans are softish and the sauce has substantially reduced.
4. Add lemon juice, salt and pepper to taste and serve cold with finely sliced onion rings scattered on top.

	SPRING			SUMMER			AUTUMN			WINTER		
	EARLY	MID	LATE	EARLY	MID	LATE	EARLY	MID	LATE	EARLY	MID	LATE
FRENCH AND HARICOT BEANS			✿	✿ ➡	✿ ✂	✂	✂	✂				

BROAD BEANS Vicia faba

Before potatoes came sailing with Raleigh from the New World to the Old, beans, including broad beans, had long provided the staple carbohydrate for those living in the cooler parts of Europe. Primitive broad beans have been unearthed in Iron Age settlements at Glastonbury in Somerset and blackened seeds of broad bean were also discovered in Schliemann's excavations at Troy. In the Middle Ages they were such an important source of food that anyone caught stealing them from the fields where they grew was immediately sentenced to death. Once supplanted, the broad bean quickly fell out of favour. Dr Venner, Doctor of Physick in Bath in 1637, warned that they would 'fill the brain with grosse melancholic fumes' but grudgingly added that the dire effects could be eased if the beans were dressed with butter and parsley.

Broad beans are useful in a decorative vegetable garden because from winter-sown seeds you will get an early summer crop. This can then be cleared away to make room for another crop such as ornamental kale or sprouting broccoli, which will benefit from the nodules of nitrogen left in the soil by the beans' obliging root system.

The plants themselves can be tall or short, depending on variety. All have pleasant glaucous foliage and black and white lipped flowers that have a surprisingly sweet smell. 'Red Flowered' has showier red flowers, which set to produce bronze-red beans in a green pod.

RECOMMENDED CULTIVARS
'Aquadulce Claudia': early, hardy old variety grown since the 1930s, about 1m (3ft) tall with white seeds. 'Express': fast (can mature in about 70 days given good growing conditions) and hardy. 'Imperial Green Longpod': plants 105–120cm (3½–4ft) tall with pods that may be 37cm (15in) long, containing up to nine green beans. 'Red Flowered': the most decorative of the broad beans with red flowers and beans. 'Stereo': produces slim, succulent pods, which can be eaten whole, before the beans are fully mature. 'The Sutton': compact, dwarf, rarely more than 30cm (1ft) high, needs little support and is of excellent flavour.

Cultivation
Broad beans are the hardiest of the whole bean family and can survive a winter outside, if mice, slugs and birds will let them. An autumn sowing gives the earliest crop, but you may find it safer to sow seed in boxes and keep them in a frame or greenhouse before planting out in late winter. Long-podded types are the most suitable for forcing in this way. Short-podded beans such as 'Green Windsor' should be used for spring plantings. Some think these have the better flavour.

SITE AND SOIL
Deep, heavy soils produce the best crops, though the ground must not be waterlogged. Broad beans do best on a soil that is neutral or very slightly acid (pH 6.0–6.5). Do not grow them in the same place two years running or else you will run the risk of encouraging the build-up of pea cyst eelworm in the soil.

SOWING
The seeds are large and can be planted with a trowel or dibber. Set them about 3cm (1¼in) deep, at intervals of 23cm (9in) in rows that are 23cm (9in) apart. You can also space the seed out over the bed of a potager, setting them 23cm (9in) apart each way. The beans germinate well at low temperatures, but overwintering crops will succeed better under a floating mulch or cloches. Sow a few extra seeds at the end of the line to fill in any gaps.

ROUTINE CARE
This is an easy crop and the plants are so vigorous that they deter all but the most pernicious perennial weeds. Support will be necessary, especially for the tall forms. Posts at either end of a row with strings stretched between provides a simple method of keeping the plants on their feet. Dwarf cultivars such as 'The Sutton' can be propped up with short lengths of twiggy hazel.

Broad bean dip

Broad beans, especially the ones that have chased away from you and are a little larger and older than they should be, can be turned into a tasty dip, particularly good with toasted garlic bread.

Serves 4
150g (5oz) shelled broad beans (you'll need at least 500g (18oz) of beans to release this amount when podded)
3 tbs good olive oil
1 lemon, juice and zest
finely chopped mint, to taste
salt and black pepper
pecorino cheese, sliced

1. Cook the broad beans until tender (they should not take more than 5 minutes).
2. If they are very tough, pop them out of their skins.
3. Purée them with the olive oil, lemon juice and zest, mint, salt and pepper.
4. Pile on to toast with a sliver of pecorino cheese on top.

YIELD AND HARVESTING
Expect about 9kg (20lb) of beans from a 3m (10ft) row, or less if you eat them when they are at their best, before the skins have become tough and leathery and when the scar on the bean's edge is still white or green, rather than black. Broad beans can also be picked and eaten whole, pod and all. Pick them when they are no bigger than your little finger.

PESTS AND DISEASES
The worst pest is the black bean aphid, which clusters on the growing tips of plants from mid-summer after overwintering as eggs, usually on spindle trees (*Euonymus europaeus*). Nip out the growing shoot with its colony of aphids and get rid of it (and them). If you sow in late autumn or early spring, the plant will be well enough advanced by mid-summer to take this treatment. Chocolate leaf spot is a rarer problem that is more likely to occur where winter sowings coincide with unusually wet conditions. Leaves, stems and pods show brown spotting and in the worst cases the plants collapse completely.

	SPRING			SUMMER			AUTUMN			WINTER		
	EARLY	MID	LATE	EARLY	MID	LATE	EARLY	MID	LATE	EARLY	MID	LATE
BROAD BEANS	🌸	🌸		✂	✂	✂	✂	🌸	🌸			

STEM, BULB AND ROOT VEGETABLES

This group is largely composed of plants whose important edible parts are hidden underground. What you see is not what you eat. Among these vegetables, your greatest allies in arranging decorative combinations will be onions, leeks, fennel, kohl rabi, carrots, beetroot and parsnips. Asparagus is very ornamental when in mid-summer you allow the spears that you have been cutting to grow up into fine filmy clouds of foliage, but you need a lot of space for a proper asparagus bed and once in, it cannot be moved. Put some plants in the herbaceous border instead, or grow them among your roses for an instant buttonhole. Rhubarb is a handsome plant, but it also ties up ground on a permanent basis. Onions and leeks are stars because both have foliage that is strong, upright and entire. The leek is the better of the two and its tall sheaves of leaves contrast well with lacy foliage such as that of carrot, or the dumpy shapes of soft butterhead lettuce.

Potatoes do not have great decorative merit but can be an important crop in a traditional walled kitchen garden, where they can be surrounded with roses. Low Floribundas and Hybrid Teas may grow in a side border, while a central path can be swagged with climbers trained on ropes between tall supports.

The swollen lower stem of kohl rabi rests on the earth like a strange egg from which a baby dinosaur might suddenly emerge. The leaves sprout at odd angles and in themselves these are not especially decorative, but the curious form of the whole construction makes kohl rabi a good choice for a potager.

Use marigolds to provide bright strokes of colour among vegetables such as beetroot. They are as useful as they are beautiful. They attract hoverflies, which hoover up aphid pests faster than any other predator in the garden. As well as being a visual delight, companion planting such as this has sound practical advantages. Other flowers you can use include cornflowers, which you might plant in a thick swathe to fence in a rectangular patch of Florence fennel, cool as a pool of water at the centre of a jostling patch of mixed fruit and vegetables. Despite its self-seeding habit, tall *Verbena bonariensis* will look at home in a vegetable patch, particularly if you combine it with purple-leaved beet and aquilegias. Nasturtiums can be sown direct into the ground and will quickly spread to make a colourful, weed-suppressing carpet.

ONIONS *Allium cepa*

'Kitchen garden gods' said Juvenal, the Roman satirist, about the pungent family of onions. It is true. There are few savoury dishes that do not require a hint of

Soupe a l'oignon gratinée

The onion may be the most frequently used vegetable in the kitchen, but it rarely has a chance to star alone. This soup warms the foulest winter day. Treat it as a main course rather than a starter.

Serves 6
60g (2oz) butter
1 tbs olive oil
750g (1¹/₂ lb) onions, thinly sliced
60g (2oz) flour
2 litres (3¹/₂ pints) good beef stock (shin of beef makes the best)
150ml (¹/₄ pint) dry white wine
salt and black pepper
1 thickish slice of bread per person
1 clove garlic, halved
2 tbs grated raw onion
175g (6oz) grated cheese, preferably Gruyère for the authentic sticky finish

1. Heat the butter and oil in a large, heavy-bottomed pan and gently braise the onions for 15 minutes. Stir in the flour and cook for another 2–3 minutes. Add the stock and wine and simmer gently for 45 minutes. Season to taste.
2. Rub the slices of bread with the clove of garlic and bake them in the oven until they are crisp and dry.
3. Pour the soup into individual ovenproof bowls or a large tureen. Stir the grated onion into the soup and float the toasted bread on top. Sprinkle the grated cheese on the bread and brown under the grill or at the top of a hot oven.

Culinary notes
* For less of a meal, miss out the bread and cheese and add a couple of tablespoons of flamed brandy to the soup. (Heat in a ladle and put a lighted match to it to burn off the alcohol quickly.)
* For more of a meal, ladle the soup into bowls and add a very lightly poached egg to each. Top with bread and cheese and brown as before.

onion, a smudge of garlic or a discreet touch of shallot. When they first swept into the West from the East, the onion tribe were considered luxury items. An onion may have been useful to disguise the flagging appeal of a rich man's meat but it provided little to fill a poor man's stomach. The bean remained top of the list of survival food, until the potato gradually took its place.

In the garden, the leaves are tubular and sturdily upright, a bluish kind of green, contrasting well with the feathery foliage of carrots. There is also a practical reason for combining these two crops: the scent of the growing onions is said to mask the smell of the carrots and so deter the carrot fly from laying its eggs.

RECOMMENDED CULTIVARS
- **Yellow-skinned** 'Sturon': widely available globe-shaped onion to grow from sets. 'Turbo': long-necked onion, easy from sets.
- **Red-skinned** 'Long Red Florence' ('Rossa Lunga di Firenze'): traditional torpedo-shaped onion from Italy. 'Red Baron': early, prolific, flat-bottomed onion.
- **Spring onions** 'Ramrod': a mild-flavoured spring onion with stiffly upright leaves. 'White Lisbon': popular salad onion with a fine, fresh flavour.

Cultivation
The first task for gardeners is to choose between seed or sets. Sets, though more expensive, have many advantages. You skip stage one of the growing process and move swiftly on to stage two. There are disadvantages, though. The range of varieties is more limited and onions grown from sets are more likely to bolt than those grown from seed. 'Heat-treated' sets should be used if possible. The heat treatment destroys the flower bud inside the set and so makes it less likely to run up to seed. If size is important, grow yellow-skinned onions, which tend to be larger (and better behaved) than red-skinned varieties.

SITE AND SOIL
Well-drained, fertile soil that has been well manured the previous autumn is ideal. The growing site should be sunny, so that bulbs will ripen satisfactorily at the end of the growing season.

SOWING
Sow seed indoors in mid-winter and prick the seedlings out into trays to grow on. Sets can be sown in the first half of spring. Push them gently into the soil so that the tops just show above the surface of the earth. Plant them 10cm (4in) apart in rows 25cm (10in) apart. Spring onions can be sown direct in drills outside every 3 weeks from early spring to mid-summer for a continuous supply.

TRANSPLANTING
After hardening off, seed-grown onions will be ready to plant out in early spring when they have two proper leaves. Set them 10cm (4in) apart in rows 25cm (10in) apart.

ROUTINE CARE
Onions hate competition from weeds, especially in the first half of the growing season. They are not hungry for nitrogen, like leafier crops; nor are they particularly thirsty. Give them light, air and clean ground.

YIELD AND HARVESTING
Expect 3.5kg (7lb) of onions from a 3m (10ft) row. They will be ready to pull

up and dry off when the foliage starts to wither. Thorough drying is essential if onions are to be stored successfully through the winter. Lay them on some wire netting in the sun or spread them out in a greenhouse. Any bulbs with thick necks should be used immediately, as they will not keep.

PESTS AND DISEASES

Onion fly is the worst pest, laying its eggs in young onion bulbs. The maggots eat the bulbs and can quickly decimate a crop. Parsley, planted in rows between the onions, is a traditional deterrent. Downy mildew may be a problem in damp, humid summers and can be controlled with a proprietary fungicide.

	SPRING			SUMMER			AUTUMN			WINTER		
	EARLY	MID	LATE	EARLY	MID	LATE	EARLY	MID	LATE	EARLY	MID	LATE
ONIONS FROM SEED	✽	➡			✂	✂					✽	✽
SCALLIONS		✿			✂	✂						
ONION SETS		✿	✿	✂	✿ ✂	✿	✂	✂				

GARLIC & SHALLOTS
Allium sativum & A. cepa Aggregatum Group

Garlic has long been supposed to have magical properties. A single whiff is considered enough to see off even the most bloodthirsty vampire. Courtiers at the birth of Henry IV in Pau, France, brushed a clove of garlic over the baby's lips to keep evil at bay. Shallots have a more prosaic reputation – nobody carries them in their pockets on a dark winter's night – but both are invaluable in the kitchen, and in the garden equally easy to grow if given the right conditions. Their upright foliage, like that of onions, provides a welcome contrast to the dumpy, rounded shapes of lettuce.

RECOMMENDED CULTIVARS
- **Garlic** 'Early Wight' (hardneck): early variety produced on the Isle of Wight and selected for British conditions. 'Elephant Garlic': huge cloves with a very mild flavour. 'Germidour' (softneck): purplish bulbs with a soft flavour. 'Oswego White' (softneck): big, white-skinned bulbs, not strong. 'Spanish Roja' (hardneck): strong-flavoured, thin-skinned bulb.
- **Shallots** 'Ambition': a reddish-brown bulb to grow from seed. 'Banana Shallot': a curiosity with long, pinkish bulbs and a mild flavour. 'Delicato': a pretty red-skinned shallot, sweet flavoured. 'Picasso': mild-tasting, pinkish bulbs, slow to bolt. 'Red Sun': reddish-brown bulbs to grow from sets.

Roasted garlic and shallots

Roasted whole, both shallots and garlic dissolve into delicious sweet mouthfuls, though the garlic has a much creamier texture than the shallot. In this recipe, both are roasted with new carrots and potatoes. You can produce equally delicious one-dish meals by throwing them into the oven with red peppers and aubergines.

Serves 8

1kg (2lb) new carrots	some sprigs of thyme
600g (1lb 5oz) new potatoes	grated zest of 1 lemon
400g (14oz) shallots	1 tsp caraway seed
2 tbs olive oil	salt and black pepper
1 head garlic	

1. Scrub the carrots and potatoes. Peel the shallots.
2. Heat the olive oil in a pan and shake all the ingredients except the garlic into it.
3. Add the garlic, broken into cloves. You do not need to peel them.
4. Cook in an oven at 180°C/350°F/gas mark 4 for about 45 minutes. Season with salt, pepper and a sprinkling of extra thyme.

Cultivation

Shallots, which grow in small bunches (if you sow from sets) or as singletons (if you sow from seed), can be harvested earlier than onions, which is useful in a small garden, where the space they occupy can then be used for another catch crop. Shallots, especially the yellow-skinned types, last in store better than onions, and are an invaluable asset in the kitchen. Garlic will only develop a good head if the dormant clove undergoes a period of cold (0–10°C/32–50°F) lasting 1–2 months. If you plant in autumn, this period will occur naturally through winter. Garlic leaves grow best in cool conditions. When foliage growth stops, the underground bulb begins to swell, and this usually happens in the lengthening days of early summer. When choosing what to grow, remember that hardneck and softneck garlic behave in different ways: softnecks produce more but smaller cloves in each head, while hardnecks have the stronger flavour.

SITE AND SOIL

Light, well-drained soil suits garlic, though shallots can cope with something heavier. Both need an open situation, but the ground, though it should be fertile, does not need to be heavily manured.

SOWING

Sow both garlic and shallot sets as if you were sowing onion sets, pressing them into the ground so that only the tip of the clove shows above the surface of the soil. Heads of garlic should be broken up into individual cloves before planting. Set them about 15cm (6in) apart in rows 30cm (12in) apart. Elephant garlic needs more space: set the cloves 30cm (12in) apart in rows 30cm apart. Shallots can also be grown from seed spaced at intervals of 1cm (about 1/2in).

ROUTINE CARE

Weeding is the only imperative, but hardneck garlic develops more satisfactorily if you remember to cut off the flowering stem when it emerges in mid-spring.

YIELD AND HARVESTING

Expect about twenty heads of garlic and 3.5kg (7lb) of shallots from a 3m (10ft) row. Pull up and dry off shallots in the same manner as onions when the foliage begins to die down. Garlic should be lifted as soon as the foliage turns yellowish. When it has dried off, it can be plaited into strings for storage.

PESTS AND DISEASES

These are generally trouble-free crops, though both may occasionally suffer from the same pests and diseases as onions.

	SPRING			SUMMER			AUTUMN			WINTER		
	EARLY	MID	LATE	EARLY	MID	LATE	EARLY	MID	LATE	EARLY	MID	LATE
GARLIC						✄	✿					
SHALLOTS	✿				✄	✄		✿				

LEEKS *Allium porrum*

The only good thing known about the Roman emperor Nero is that he liked a bowl of leek soup as often as possible. Was vichyssoise born in the steamy cookhouses of first-century Rome? Leeks are easy to grow and the steel-blue ribbons of foliage are surprisingly good set among tall waving heads of purple *Verbena bonariensis*. Once young leek plants are set out in early or mid-summer, they will furnish the ground through to the following spring and need very little attention. Edge your leek bed with violas. Plant rows of leeks to pierce through a ferny blanket of the yellow daisy *Bidens aurea*. Use them to paint stripes of blue across a golden patch of marigolds.

RECOMMENDED CULTIVARS

• 'Autumn Mammoth' (strains such as 'Goliath and 'Toledo'): matures in mid-autumn yet will stand in the ground until late spring. 'Hannibal' thick white stems and dark green leaves. 'King Richard': an early variety that needs to be harvested before frost sets in. 'Musselburgh': short and hardy, an old and reliable variety. 'Oarsman': a vigorous grower for harvesting in December. 'Porvite': high yielding, slow to bolt and best between October and January. 'St Victor': the best-looking spring leek with attractive blue-grey leaves.

Cultivation

If you are lucky, some other grower will take on the responsibility of raising young plants from seed and you can buy bundles of them to plant in summer. If not, take heart: leeks are not difficult to raise from seed.

SITE AND SOIL

Leeks need rich, well-drained ground that has been liberally fed with manure or compost. Dig thoroughly before you plant. If you want long, well-blanched stems, the leeks must go in deep holes.

Leek tart

Leeks, gentler in taste than other members of the onion family, make superb soups. Sliced and sautéed briefly in butter, they also combine with bacon to make an excellent filling for a tart. This one can be eaten hot or cold. It is best somewhere in between the two, just warm enough to slide succulently over the tongue.

Serves 6 as a starter, 4 as a main course
For the pastry:
90g (3oz) butter
175g (6oz) flour
pinch of salt
a little cold water
For the filling:
90g (3oz) butter
500g (1lb) leeks, washed, trimmed and finely sliced
125g (4oz) smoked streaky bacon
2 eggs
175ml (6fl oz) milk or single cream (or a mixture of the two)
salt and pepper

1. Make the pastry by rubbing the butter into the flour and salt to form fine crumbs. Bind with a little water to form a dough and leave to rest for 30 minutes.
2. To make the filling, melt the butter and cook the leeks gently for 3–4 minutes. Season with black pepper and allow to cool. Grill the bacon and cut into small pieces.
3. Line a 23cm (9in) flan dish with the pastry and bake blind in a hot oven (200°C/400°F/gas mark 6) for about 10 minutes until the pastry is lightly cooked.
4. Mix the bacon with the leeks and tip into the pastry case. Beat the eggs with the milk or cream. Add a little salt and pour over the top.
5. Bake in a cooler oven (180°C/350°F/gas mark 4) for about 30 minutes, until the egg is just set.

SOWING

There are early, mid-season and late varieties, the early ones tending to be tall and thin, the late ones squat and fat. For the earliest crops, sow an early variety under cover in late winter. Main sowings can be made in a seedbed outside during spring. Sow seed as thinly as possible, 1cm (1/2in) deep.

TRANSPLANTING

Leeks can be thinned and left to grow in the drills in which they were sown, but the best results come from transplanting. Water the seedbed well before lifting young leeks in early or mid-summer. By this time they should be about 2–23cm (8–9in) tall. With a dibber, make holes 15cm (6in) deep and 15cm (6in) apart in rows that are 30cm (12in) apart. Drop a leek into each hole and then fill up the holes with water so that soil is washed over the roots of the leeks. Traditionally, leaves and roots were shortened before transplanting, but this practice is not necessary.

ROUTINE CARE

Extra watering will be needed only in the driest summers. Apart from this, the crop will need very little attention.

YIELD AND HARVESTING

Expect 5kg (10lb) from a 3m (10ft) row. Leeks can be lifted as needed, though they are extremely difficult to extract when the ground is frozen hard: the stem snaps, leaving the best part of the vegetable in the earth. Where this is likely to be a problem, lift a supply before the ground freezes, trim the leaves (generally called flags) and wrap the leeks in newspaper to store in a cool place.

PESTS AND DISEASES

Rust is the biggest problem and breeders are increasingly turning their attention towards producing cultivars that are resistant to the disease. It shows as orange spots and blotches on the leaves, but is disfiguring rather than fatal. Plants overfed on high-nitrogen fertilizers are worst affected. Rotate leek crops to prevent build-ups of the disease in the same spots in the garden. Burn leaves that are badly affected. There is no cure.

	SPRING			SUMMER			AUTUMN			WINTER		
	EARLY	MID	LATE	EARLY	MID	LATE	EARLY	MID	LATE	EARLY	MID	LATE
LEEKS	✿	➡	➡				✂	✂	✂	✂	✂	✿

FLORENCE FENNEL *Foeniculum vulgare* var. *dulce*

With its fine feathery foliage and neatly interleaved white bulb, Florence fennel is an extremely decorative vegetable but, like a highly bred horse, it tends to bolt if it is faced with anything that it does not understand. It is widely grown in the warm countries around the Mediterranean where, well watered, it will grow unchecked to produce a succulent crop. In chillier climates it may leap up into flower before the base has swollen into anything even remotely edible.

Although this fennel has been known in England since the eighteenth century, when the nurseryman Stephen Switzer included it in his vegetable seed list, it is still an unfamiliar sight with us. It is much happier in Italy, where selected forms of the wild fennel were developed to produce the succulent swollen bulbs we are now used to. In 1824 it went from Italy to the US, when the American consul at Livorno sent seeds to Thomas Jefferson for his garden at Montecello, Virginia.

RECOMMENDED CULTIVARS

- 'Finale': can be sown before 'Romanesco' to crop from July to October. 'Fino': a good variety, reasonably resistant to bolting. 'Romanesco': has the potential to produce the biggest bulbs of all. 'Rondo': fast-growing and productive.

Cultivation

The earliest sowings are the ones that are most likely to bolt, if plants are checked by unaccustomed chills. The best results in cool climates come from a mid-summer sowing for an autumn crop. Though a variety such as 'Finale' can be sown in late May, 'Romanesco' is much better left until mid-June or early July. Allow fifteen weeks between sowing and harvesting. Fennel will withstand light frost, but is not generally hardy.

SITE AND SOIL

The best soil for this crop is light, sandy and well drained, though the bulbs must never be allowed to dry out.

SOWING

Do not be tempted to sow too early. Florence fennel is one of many plants that adapts its behaviour to day length. Sow after the longest day to minimize the possibility of bolting. Scatter the seed thinly in drills outside, 1cm (1/2in) deep in rows 30cm (12in) apart. Water the drill first if the ground is very dry.

THINNING

Thinning is much better than transplanting, as fennel rarely recovers from the shock of being transplanted and bolts into flower instead of swelling to produce a bulb. Thin the plants in the rows to leave about 30cm (1ft) between each one.

ROUTINE CARE

Fennel must never be starved or thirsty. Keep the plants growing smoothly by watering and feeding them well. Mulch to conserve moisture and to keep down weeds. Fennel does not like competition. Once the bulbs start to swell, earth them up to keep the plants stable and to blanch the stems.

Fennel soup

The aniseed flavour of fennel is strongest if you slice the bulb finely and use it raw in a mixed salad. Braised, the flavour is gentler, excellent when fennel is mixed with tomato and topped with cheese to make a bubbling gratin. Of course, with a proper stock, Florence fennel also makes an exquisite soup.

Serves 4

butter and olive oil	2 tbsp Pastis or Pernod
1 onion, chopped	100ml (3fl oz) white wine
400g (14oz) fennel, chopped	400ml (14fl oz) chicken stock (home made if possible)
4 cloves garlic, peeled	150ml (1/4 pint) single cream

1. Heat the butter and olive oil and gently stew the onion and fennel until they are soft but not brown. This will take about 30 minutes.
2. Add the garlic and cook for another 4–5 minutes.
3. Turn up the heat and add the Pastis or Pernod and set fire to it. Extinguish the flames with the wine before lowering the heat and adding the chicken stock.
4. Simmer for about 30 minutes before liquidizing. Reheat gently and add the cream.

YIELD AND HARVESTING

Expect about nine bulbs of fennel from a 3m (10ft) row. Cut the bulbs just below ground level three weeks or so after you have earthed them up. The stump may throw up some feathery shoots, which you can use as you do the herb fennel.

PESTS AND DISEASES

The vagaries of climate have a far greater effect on fennel than any pest or disease. Chewing pests are perhaps put off by the strong aniseed flavour of the stems and foliage.

	SPRING			SUMMER			AUTUMN			WINTER		
	EARLY	MID	LATE	EARLY	MID	LATE	EARLY	MID	LATE	EARLY	MID	LATE
FLORENCE FENNEL			❀	❀	❀	✄	✄	✄				

CELERY *Apium graveolens*

Wild celery is a marsh plant, growing widely all over Europe and Asia, but it is very pungent. That is fine if you are taking it as a medicine, which is how it was first used, but not so good if you want to eat it for pleasure. Hundreds of years of selection has produced the succulent pale-stemmed celery that we now crunch noisily at table.

There are three different kinds, some more hardy than others, some more easily grown than others. The hardiest are the old-fashioned trench varieties, which you need to blanch or earth up as they grow. Self-blanching varieties require less effort on the part of the gardener but mature in late summer and do not stand through hard winters. American green varieties have long, pale green stems and a better flavour than other self-blanching types. The best flavour, nutty, aromatic and unforgettable, comes from a well-grown trench celery, such as 'Clayworth Pink', which matures in mid-winter.

RECOMMENDED CULTIVARS
- **Trench celery** 'Clayworth Pink' superb flavour, and long pale pink stems, at their best after a frost.
- **Self-blanching celery** 'Golden Self Blanching': tall, yellowish stems to harvest between August and November. 'Lathom Self Blanching' ('Galaxy'): compact, pale yellow sticks, well flavoured but one of the least hardy.
- **Green celery** 'Green Utah': long, green, self-blanching stems. 'Victoria': tall, strong upright variety with slightly ribbed stems.

Cultivation
Celery is rated by the size and succulence of its leaf stalks. For these to be good, plants have to grow fast with a non-stop supply of water. Self-blanching and green types are ready by late summer, trench celery by mid-winter. The foliage is fresh and green and the leaves pleasantly cut. They contrast well with the solid foliage of cabbages or the simple blue-green ribbons of leek leaves.

SITE AND SOIL
Deep, well-drained ground is an absolute necessity for the best crops. Plenty of organic matter should be worked into the soil and the pH should be somewhere between 6.5 and 7.5. Celery will not grow well on an acid soil.

SOWING
Celery seed may take a long time to germinate, as it has a complicated pattern of dormancy. The seed contains unusually high levels of a hormone that can stop the seed sprouting, especially if it is too warm. Aim for a temperature around 10–15°C/50–60°F and sow seed on the surface of the compost without covering it. It needs light to germinate. Prick out the seedlings into trays as soon as possible. Or take the easy route and order young plants, which will be delivered in May.

TRANSPLANTING
When the seedlings have five or six proper leaves, usually by early summer, harden them off and transplant them to their growing quarters. For trench celery dig a trench 30cm (12in) deep, half fill it with manure and top it with 5cm (2in) of soil so that the final level is about 10cm (4in) below the

Celery and stilton soup

Unfortunately most bought celery is self-blanching, hydroponically grown stuff with practically no flavour. If you are lucky enough to find the real thing, trench-grown celery with the dirt still clinging to its roots, eat it raw and relish the tough nuttiness of its winter stems. The green, self-blanching stuff can be braised or turned into soup.

Serves 4

3 sticks celery, chopped
1 medium-sized onion, chopped
38g (1¹/₃oz butter)
25g (1oz) flour
300ml (10fl oz) milk

850ml (30fl oz) chicken stock
150ml (5fl oz) wine
150ml (5fl oz) cream
75–100g (3–4oz) Stilton cheese

1. Soften the celery and onion in the butter, stir in the flour and allow to cook for about a minute.
2. Gradually add the milk and stock and cook until the liquid thickens slightly.
3. Add the wine, cream and cheese.

surrounding soil. Leave the soil to settle. Space the plants 30–45cm (12–18in) apart. Self-blanching and green kinds can be planted in a block 15–30cm (6–12in) apart, depending on the size of plant you want to grow.

ROUTINE CARE

Water generously through the whole growing period, and mulch to conserve moisture. On hungry soils, a liquid feed given a month or so after transplanting may be beneficial. Start blanching trench celery when the plants are about 30cm (12in) high, first by filling in the trench and then by earthing up more soil around them.

YIELD AND HARVESTING

Expect 6kg (14lb) of celery from a 3m (10ft) row.

PESTS AND DISEASES

Slugs are connoisseurs of celery and settle comfortably into hearts to feast on the best bits. Take preventative measures. Celery fly is the other great enemy. White maggots inside the leaves cause serious brown blistering of the foliage. This slows down growth and makes the stalks stringy.

	SPRING			SUMMER			AUTUMN			WINTER		
	EARLY	MID	LATE	EARLY	MID	LATE	EARLY	MID	LATE	EARLY	MID	LATE
CELERY	✳		➡			✂	✂					

CELERIAC AND KOHL RABI *Apium graveolens* var. *rapaceum* & *Brassica oleracea* Gongylodes Group

The bulbous edible parts of celeriac and kohl rabi are not roots, such as a carrot has, but swollen parts of the lower stem. Though home-grown celeriac rarely swells to the impressive size of shop-bought specimens, it has crisp cut foliage, which you can use to good effect in a potager. It is a rugged vegetable and after a long growing season shows a marked reluctance to leave the cradle: lifting requires a crane rather than a fork, and the roots cover the whole of the manically uneven globe and spread horizontally like kedge anchors. Initial cleaning is best done outside, to save precious topsoil.

Kohl rabi is a member of the cabbage family and its bulbous, smooth globes in purple or pale whitish-green can also be a decorative addition to the vegetable garden. It grows fast and is more tolerant of drought than most brassicas. Eat it when it is no larger than a tennis ball.

RECOMMENDED CULTIVARS
- **Celeriac** 'Giant Prague': a strong growing, well-flavoured type. 'Monarch': one of the most widely grown varieties with smooth skin and tender flesh. 'Prinz': has similar qualities and is slow to bolt.
- **Kohl rabi** 'Delikatess Witte' ('White Delicacy'): produces early white roots. 'Delikatess Blauer' ('Purple Delicacy'): will give a later crop of purple roots. 'Superschmelz': is a giant but does not go woody even when harvested at the end of the year.

Cultivation
The most critical period in raising celeriac is the time immediately following its being set out. The whole operation should be as smooth as a butler's bicycle ride. It has a long growing season. Kohl rabi, in contrast, may be ready to pull only seven or eight weeks after sowing and is more tolerant of drought than most brassicas. Eat it when it is no larger than a tennis ball, as some cultivars quickly turn woody. It is a useful catch crop in bare ground.

SITE AND SOIL
By nature, celeriac is a plant of marshland and likes rich, damp soil. It will tolerate some shade, provided the other two conditions are met. Kohl rabi is a different animal, tolerant of drier conditions and doing best in a fertile, light, sandy soil. The pale types mature faster than the purple ones.

SOWING
Sow seed of celeriac in a pot inside in early spring, roughly ten weeks before planting out time. Germination takes about three weeks. If you are sowing in modules, set several seeds in each one and thin out the weaker, surplus seedlings after germination. If you are pricking out into trays, give the

Gratin of celeriac

If you grow a modern variety of celeriac, you escape the palaver of using lemon juice to stop the flesh turning brown as you prepare it. Natural anthocyanins regulate the amount of discolouring in this vegetable and seed breeders have learned how to adjust the dose so that celeriac stays white without help.

Serves 4
1 large or 2 small celeriac
6 tbsp Parmesan cheese, freshly grated
30g (1oz) butter
30g (1oz) breadcrumbs
For the tomato sauce:
3 large cloves garlic, finely chopped
1 large onion, finely chopped
125g (4oz) streaky bacon (or Italian coppa) chopped
3 tbsp olive oil
1 large carrot, diced
1kg (2lb) tomatoes, skinned and chopped
150ml (5fl oz) dry white wine
salt and black pepper
oregano
fresh basil, chopped

1. Make the tomato sauce by softening the garlic, onion and bacon in the oil. Add the carrot, tomatoes and wine and cook hard for 15 minutes. Then add the seasoning and herbs to taste.
2. Peel the celeriac, cut it into chunks and cook it in boiling, salted water for about 15 minutes or until just tender.
3. Drain and arrange the celeriac in layers in a shallow gratin dish, adding some grated Parmesan and a few knobs of butter between each of the layers.
4. Pour over the tomato sauce. Then top with breadcrumbs and the remaining Parmesan and butter. Bake for 25–30 minutes at 190°C/375°F/gas mark 5.

seedlings plenty of room, about 7cm (3in) each way. Sow kohl rabi outdoors in drills, little and often, setting the seed 1cm (1/2in) deep in rows 30cm (12in) apart.

TRANSPLANTING
By the time of planting out, the baby celeriacs should be about 7cm (3in) tall and hardened off. Set them 30–40cm (12–16in) apart in the ground. Do not plant them too deep. The point where the leaves join the root should be level with the surface of the soil. Thin kohl rabi as it develops, leaving the plants about 15–23cm (6–9in) apart.

ROUTINE CARE

Keep celeriac plants liberally supplied with water. You can try mulching between the plants to keep the ground moist. As the plants develop, gently pull off the leaves that splay out from the globe. Do not allow secondary growing points to develop. Kohl rabi needs little attention apart from weeding.

YIELD AND HARVESTING

You should get 8–10 celeriac and 15–20 kohl rabi from a 3m (10ft) row. Both crops are best left in the ground until needed.

PESTS AND DISEASES

Celeriac may suffer from the same problems as celery. Clubroot is the most likely disease to attack kohl rabi, but crops may also be spoiled by either flea beetle or cabbage root fly.

	SPRING			SUMMER			AUTUMN			WINTER		
	EARLY	MID	LATE	EARLY	MID	LATE	EARLY	MID	LATE	EARLY	MID	LATE
CELERIAC	✵		➡				✂	✂				
KOHL RABI		✿	✿	✂	✿ ✂	✿	✂	✂				

ASPARAGUS Asparagus officinalis

As a crop, asparagus is quite difficult to fit into a decorative kitchen garden. You need a lot of it to be able to pick a decent meal at any one time and the bed, once made, should remain undisturbed for at least twenty years. On the other hand, few vegetables are so ambrosial, and asparagus is always expensive to buy. It also deteriorates fast; even if you take out a bank loan and clear the greengrocer's shelves to produce an asparagus feast, you will be tasting the vegetable at third best. 'Asparagus is not fresh when it is gathered in the morning for the evening's dinner,' warned Edward Bunyard sternly in his *Epicure's Companion*, published in 1937. The asparagus basket must be steaming on the stove even before you cut the spears.

Left to itself, asparagus produces both male and female plants. The female ones carry small red berries among the fern which grows when you finish cutting the spears in mid-summer. You can now buy 'all-male' asparagus, which produces the fatter spears. To have more than a single spear at a sitting, you will need at least thirty crowns (roots).

RECOMMENDED CULTIVARS

- 'Connover's Colossal': an early and heavy cropper. 'Dariana': a newish French hybrid that produces both male and female spears. 'Franklin': all-male, high-quality spears. 'Guelph Millenium': a Canadian cultivar good for cold areas and colder soils. 'Pacific Purple': purple only before it is cooked, when it turns green, but exceptionally tender.

Cultivation

'There is only one secret to obtain large sticks, and that is to have the plants wide enough apart – four feet square, say the French growers, for each plant.' That is Bunyard again. He was evidently used to having a muscleman around to produce his epicurean crops, for his second recommendation is that good stable manure should be buried 60cm (24in) down under the asparagus bed. The least you can do is eradicate perennial weeds from the ground. Traditional asparagus beds are 1.2m (4ft) wide, giving room for two rows of plants and allowing for easy weeding and cutting. Leave 1m (3ft) between beds.

SITE AND SOIL

Asparagus grows best in well-drained sandy soils, but not hungry ones. Time spent making a good, rich home for your asparagus will be amply repaid by the crop. Incorporate plenty of well-rotted manure, and grit if the soil is heavy. On really heavy soil, make a raised bed to ensure that water drains away from the crowns. If they are permanently soggy, they rot. Acid soils will need to be treated to achieve a pH between 6.5 to 7.5.

PLANTING

Asparagus can be raised from seed – the cheapest method – but is usually sold ready grown as crowns, which may be from one to three years old. The younger crowns transplant more easily, though you will have to wait longer before picking a decent crop. If you plant one-year-old crowns, you can start cutting in the second year after planting. Plant them in early spring about 45cm (18in) apart in rows that are also 45cm (18in) apart. You can fit two long rows in a raised bed, 1.2m (4ft) wide. First take out a trench and then make a raised saddle down the middle of each trench. Soak the crowns for two hours in a bucket of water and then plant them astride the saddle, with the roots draped down either side of the ridge. Make sure that when the trenches are filled in, the crowns are no more than 10cm (4in) below the surface of the soil.

ROUTINE CARE

Asparagus does not like competition, so the bed must be kept free of weeds at all times. In some European countries, white asparagus is preferred to green and the shoots are blanched by earthing them up like chicory. Traditionally beds were dressed with salt in summer and though modern research can find no good reason for doing this, the salt may help to discourage weeds and slugs. Mulch the beds thickly with manure or mushroom compost in the late winter. Cut down the fern only when it has yellowed and died back in autumn.

YIELD AND HARVESTING

Expect 8–10 spears from each crown, when the asparagus is properly

Hollandaise sauce

Given the shortness of the season, there is little time to tire of asparagus simply steamed and served with butter. If you want something posher for a first course at a dinner party, try serving the asparagus with a hollandaise sauce, or with a warm cream sauce, flavoured with herbs. The easiest way to cook asparagus is to tie it in bundles, with the stalks all cut to roughly the same length. Then you can stand the bundles upright in a saucepan and steam them with the asparagus heads out of the boiling water. Fix a domed cap of aluminium foil over the saucepan instead of its lid, which will probably not fit. If you have a double boiler, cook the asparagus in the bottom half with the top half turned over on top of it.

Serves 4 as a starter

2 tbs white wine vinegar
4 tbs water
4 crushed peppercorns
4 egg yolks

175g (6oz) butter, melted
salt and black pepper
lemon juice, to taste

1. Put the vinegar, water and peppercorns in a pan and boil until the volume is reduced by a third. Strain into a basin set on top of a pan of hot water (or into a double saucepan).
2. Over a gentle heat, whisk the egg yolks into the mixture until it begins to thicken. Add the butter in a slow stream, whisking furiously the whole while. As with mayonnaise, you need to go carefully at the beginning but can increase the rate at which you add the butter as you continue the whisking.
3. Season with salt, pepper and lemon juice and keep the sauce warm in its basin over hot water. Serve as soon as possible.

established. The proper way to cut is with an asparagus knife, which has a curious semicircular flattened blade with saw teeth on the end of a long stem. A sharp knife suffices. Cut just beneath the surface of the soil when the spears are 12–18cm (5–7in) high. The cutting season should last no more than 6–8 weeks, ending in early summer. Cut sparingly in the first season.

PESTS AND DISEASES

Moles are great connoisseurs of asparagus and crunch on the shoots underground before they ever see the light of day. Slugs can also inflict great damage. The asparagus beetle overwinters on or near asparagus beds and lays its black eggs on the emerging shoots. Both the larvae and the adult beetle feed on asparagus foliage. Violet root rot is a soil-borne fungus that infects asparagus roots. They become covered with violet-purple strands of mycelium, which feeds on the roots and eventually kills the plant. Control is impossible. Move the bed and burn the infected stock.

Cream sauce

Serves 4 as a starter
300ml (^{1}/2 pint) single cream
2 tbsp chopped herbs (try tarragon, chives and parsley)
salt, and black and cayenne pepper

1. Gently heat the cream, stir in the herbs and season to taste with the salt and pepper.
2. Serve warm. If you prefer, this sauce is also good served slightly chilled as a dressing for cold spears of asparagus. You need not heat the cream for this.

RHUBARB *Rheum* x *cultorum*

Rhubarb is a misfit. It is the vegetable that wants to be a fruit and nobody quite knows which category to put it in. There is a fine ornamental rhubarb (*Rheum palmatum*) which you could grow as a centrepiece in a decorative kitchen garden if you have room. The variety 'Atrosanguineum' has large deeply cut leaves, brilliant red when they first emerge, though changing to bronze with red reverse as they age. The flower spike is 2m (6ft) tall, half knobbly, half fluffy, the whole a rich deep crimson.

Culinary rhubarb is not so showy. Though the leaves are large, they are not so well coloured or cut as those of its ornamental cousin. The edible stalks may be green, pink or deep red. Left to themselves they are short and stubby, but they can be forced to grow longer if you cover the plant with a forcing pot. These stalks can be extremely decorative extras in a kitchen garden. An upturned bucket does the same job less fancily.

Rhubarb was used for medicine long before it found its way into the kitchen. The ground root was used as a laxative, and later as a treatment for venereal disease. Old gardeners believe that a slice of rhubarb put at the bottom of the planting hole prevents clubroot in brassicas.

RECOMMENDED CULTIVARS
'Glaskin's Perpetual': an early variety producing long bright red stalks of good flavour. 'Timperley Early': an early variety raised before 1945, red skinned but green fleshed. 'Victoria': a reliable late variety.

Cultivation
Like asparagus, rhubarb, once settled, does not like to be moved and will tie up ground in the kitchen garden over a long period. But you can pick it from early spring until summer and, if you plant it in the right situation, it is little trouble.

Rhubarb mousse

Rhubarb makes surprisingly good mousse, syllabub and ice cream. Freeze any leftovers of this mousse and serve it up later as ice cream.

Serves 6

700g (1½lb) rhubarb, chopped	4 eggs
1 orange, zest and juice	150g (5oz) caster sugar
about 2cm (1in) root ginger, grated	250ml (9fl oz) double cream
3 star anise	2 sachets gelatine

1. Cook the rhubarb till just tender with the orange juice, zest, ginger and star anise.
2. Separate the eggs and whisk the yolks with the sugar until the mixture is pale and fluffy. Then whip the cream.
3. Strain the rhubarb and dissolve the gelatine in the warm juice. Whisk up the egg whites.
4. Fold the cream into the strained rhubarb, and then the whipped egg whites.

Its great blankets of leaves suppress all but the most troublesome weeds.

SITE AND SOIL

Rhubarb will grow on any kind of soil, including an acid one, provided that it is well fed and well drained. The site needs to be open, away from shade cast by overhanging trees. Dig plenty of manure or compost into the soil before planting.

PLANTING

Like asparagus, rhubarb can be grown from seed, but is usually planted as a dormant 'set'. Each set should have a plump bud sitting on top of the rootstock with plenty of fibrous root underneath. You must start with stock that is certified virus free. Plant in the dormant season between mid-autumn and early spring, setting the plants 1m (3ft) apart. The buds should be covered by no more than 2cm (1in) of soil.

ROUTINE CARE

The best plants are those that can be kept damp in summer and dry in winter. Water liberally if necessary and mulch round the stems with manure or grass cuttings to retain moisture in the soil. Tall creamy flowering stems are produced on mature plants. These are decorative and can be left without harming the plant. About every five years, the plants will need dividing. The most vigorous offshoots are generally those round the edges of a clump.

FORCING

Forcing lengthens the stems of rhubarb and brings it into production several weeks earlier than normal. To force a plant, cover the crown with straw in late winter and then put a special terracotta rhubarb forcer or upturned bucket over the whole thing. Remove the forcer when you have pulled the first forced stems. If you pack fresh manure around the forcing pot, this will heat up and accelerate the process even more, but you will lose the decorative value of the pots themselves.

YIELD AND HARVESTING

Expect 2.5kg (5lb) of sticks from each plant. Pull the stems rather than cutting them and always leave at least four stems on each plant. Do not pull any stems after mid-summer, in order to give the plant a chance to replenish itself.

PESTS AND DISEASES

Pests leave rhubarb alone. The most likely problems are untreatable: honey fungus, which attacks the roots, and various virus problems that either cause stunted growth or an unhealthy mottling on the leaves. Dig up affected sets and burn them. Plant new stock on a fresh site.

CARROTS *Daucus carota*

Modern carrots are all descended from purple and yellow types that came into Europe from Arabia in the fourteenth century. Selection by Dutch growers in the seventeenth century produced the forerunners of the varieties we grow today. For decades breeders have been in pursuit of the perfect carrot. Unfortunately the carrot fly, *Psila rosae*, whose larvae snuffle greedily through carrot roots, has the same objective. There is some evidence that intercropping carrots with onions or with annual flowers such as love-in-a-mist discourages attack.

Choosing the right time to sow also limits damage. If you use a fast-maturing Nantes type of carrot and sow seed in mid-summer you will avoid the peak egg-laying period of the first generation of carrot flies. The roots will be ready to harvest in mid-autumn.

The ferny upright foliage of carrots contrasts well with the smooth, rounded shapes of lettuce leaves or the strappy green ribbons of garlic foliage. You can also mix carrot seed with faster-maturing radish to get two crops from the same patch of ground.

RECOMMENDED CULTIVARS

- 'Adelaide': early, smooth-skinned cylindral roots. 'Amini': early, quick and a good choice if you like baby carrots. 'Amsterdam Forcing': early, long and thin. 'Bangor': medium-sized, cylindrical, smooth-skinned roots, ready late winter/early spring. 'Berlicum': a high-yielding maincrop carrot. 'Carson': a Chantenay hybrid with a particularly sweet taste. 'Early Nantes': early, round-ended carrot of excellent quality. 'Flyaway': British-bred carrot with partial resistance to carrot fly. 'Parabell': short, rounded carrots, good in heavy soil. 'Parmex': tiny globe-shaped roots, very sweet and ideal for

---

Summer carrots with cream sauce

Serves 4
375–500g (12oz–1lb) summer carrots, scrubbed and cut into chunks
300ml (1/2 pint) chicken stock
1/2 to 1 tsp puréed garlic (see below)
150ml (1/4 pint) single cream
1 tsp chopped chervil to garnish

1. Simmer the carrots in the chicken stock for about 8 minutes or until just tender.
2. Stir in the puréed garlic (see below) to taste. The sauce should be quite thick. Add the cream and sprinkle the chervil over the top.

Culinary notes
* This recipe calls for puréed garlic. A small supply is very easy to make. Cover several heads of peeled cloves with boiling water and blanch them for 2–3 minutes. Drain and repeat the blanching process twice more, using fresh water, until the cloves are really soft. Then purée them. The purée will keep for several weeks in the refrigerator if you pack it in a pot and top it with a thin layer of olive oil.
* Home-grown carrots have a much sweeter, more pronounced flavour than shop-bought ones. Do not overcook them. If you steam them, you may feel that they need nothing more than to be finished off with some melted butter and finely chopped parsley.
* Hot steamed carrots are delicious sprinkled with grated Stilton cheese and browned under the grill.
* If you like carrots raw, try Madhur Jaffrey's Indian carrot salad. Heap some grated carrot on to a large dish and sprinkle fresh lemon juice over it to taste. Heat together in a pan 2 tbsp of oil with 1 tbsp of mustard seed until the seeds begin to pop. Pour the mixture over the grated carrot.

---

container growing. 'Primo': for baby carrots, early, quick and sweet. 'Sytan': has partial resistance to carrot fly.

Cultivation
By sowing seed of different varieties at regular intervals, you can have fresh carrots for much of the season. The Nantes and globe types mature from mid- to late summer; Chantenay types crop from late autumn to early winter and Berlicum from late winter to spring.

SITE AND SOIL
The ideal soil is light and friable, well drained, loose and deep so that roots can swell without constraint. In heavy soil, leaves tend to grow at the expense of root and the roots themselves are sometimes misshapen.

SOWING

Sow seed as thinly as possible, no more than 1cm (1/2in) deep in rows 15cm (6in) apart. Seed germinates poorly at temperatures below 8°C/45°F, so for early sowings warm up the soil beforehand with cloches or polythene film. Using different varieties, seed can be sown from early spring until mid-summer.

THINNING

Thinning carrots is bad practice. It releases a smell that the carrot fly finds irresistible and the little crevices left in the soil provide ready-made entry holes for the adults to lay their eggs in. Sow thinly and you will avoid the need for thinning.

ROUTINE CARE

Weed carefully while the seedlings are still small. Do not overwater.

YIELD AND HARVESTING

Expect 4–5kg (8–10lb) from a 3m (10ft) row. The maincrop varieties will produce heavier roots than the early ones. On light soils, leave carrots in the ground and pull them as required. On heavy soils, winter crops can be lifted and stored in boxes of sand.

PESTS AND DISEASES

Carrot fly is the most persistent nuisance, as the larvae burrow deep into the roots. Some cultivars have a greater resistance to it than others. This seems to be associated with the level of chlorogenic acid contained in the roots. The fly's larvae need the acids to further their own development and stay away from carrots that have a low level of this particular fix.

	SPRING			SUMMER			AUTUMN			WINTER		
	EARLY	MID	LATE	EARLY	MID	LATE	EARLY	MID	LATE	EARLY	MID	LATE
CARROTS	❀	❀	❀ ✂	❀ ✂	❀ ✂	❀ ✂	✂	✂	✂	✂	✂	✂

BEETROOT *Beta vulgaris*

You can use shining beetroot leaves to telling effect among the lighter, lacier foliage of carrots or coriander. They also look sumptuous with bright pot marigolds. For the greatest impact, choose a variety such as 'Bull's Blood', which has dark burgundy-coloured leaves, narrow and shining. 'Globe 2' is also handsome, producing sheaves of dark leaves with a bright crimson midrib. Cut while they are still young and tender, leaves of both these beetroot are excellent in mixed salads. The roots are easy to grow and store well for winter use. Since its early wedding to vinegar, beetroot has had problems shedding its drear pickle image. Try instead cooking fresh beetroot with butter and orange juice.

RECOMMENDED CULTIVARS

• 'Alto': long, thin, cylindrical beetroot, easy to slice. 'Boltardy': can be sown earlier than other beetroot. 'Burpees Golden': an old variety, popular in Victorian times with very sweet, golden-yellow flesh. 'Chiogga': an Italian variety prettily striped in pink and white, though the colours melt together when the root is cooked. 'Detroit 6': very slow to bolt and generally earlier to crop than 'Boltardy'. 'Forono': slow to go woody, good flavour and texture. 'Pablo': uniform, round, smooth-skinned roots ideal for a container, to pull as baby beet. 'Pronto': easy, smooth-skinned variety that can be left in the ground without getting woody. 'Solo': a monogerm variety producing only one seedling from a cluster – no need to thin.

Cultivation

Besides the traditional deep red varieties, there are many 'novelty' beetroots that are worth experimenting with, both yellow and white forms and a very pretty old cultivar called 'Chioggia' (see above). Young leaves are good in salads and an old root left in the ground over winter will often produce an unexpectedly good crop of leaves to pick for an early spring salad.

SITE AND SOIL

The best soil is rich, light and fertile, but not freshly manured.

SOWING

Start sowing in mid-spring. Choose a bolt-resistant cultivar for early sowings, to stop plants running to seed, and sow as thinly as possible in drills 1.5cm (1/2in) deep in rows 20cm (8in) apart or 30cm (12in) for later sowings. Seed contains a natural germination inhibitor and it may help to soak it for half an hour before sowing. The seed is usually gathered in small clusters, but monogerm varieties produce only one plant from each seed, so reducing the need for thinning.

THINNING

Thin as soon as the seedlings start to touch each other, leaving them about 15cm (6in) apart.

ROUTINE CARE

Mulch around the crop to conserve moisture and suppress weeds.

YIELD AND HARVESTING

Expect 5–8kg (10–18lb) from a 3m (10ft) row. Long varieties crop more heavily than globe types. Use as required direct from the ground, before the roots have got too big. If necessary, beetroot can be stored in boxes of sand through the winter. Twist off the foliage first.

PESTS AND DISEASES

Beetroot is an easy crop to grow and is generally free from pests and diseases.

Beetroots and shallots in a white sauce

However you decide to cook beetroot, baked whole in the oven or boiled, leave the root intact and just trim the leaves down to 2cm (1in). If you don't cut into it, it won't bleed. Skin the roots after you have cooked them: at this stage, they slip off easily. With good vegetables, the simplest ways are often the best. This dish simply combines beetroots with shallots in a white sauce.

Serves 4

1 beetroot (not too big) per person	1 tbsp flour
2 shallots per person	300–400ml (10–14 fl oz) milk, warmed
olive oil	salt and black pepper
30g (1oz) butter	

1. Cook the beetroot until tender, either by boiling or baking in tin foil. Skin them and cut them into quarters.
2. Peel the shallots and, after blanching them in boiling water for about 5 minutes, cook them gently in olive oil until they are just beginning to soften.
3. Make the white sauce by melting the butter and stirring the flour into it. Let this mixture cook gently for a minute or so before adding the warmed milk. Season to taste with salt and black pepper.
4. Pour the sauce over the vegetables and leave the dish in a warm place to let the flavours meld together.

	SPRING			SUMMER			AUTUMN			WINTER		
	EARLY	MID	LATE	EARLY	MID	LATE	EARLY	MID	LATE	EARLY	MID	LATE
BEETS		❀	❀	❀ ✂	❀ ✂	✂	✂	✂				

POTATOES *Solanum tuberosum*

Digging potatoes is always an adventure. The haulm (stems and leaves) gives no indication of the extent of the treasure buried underneath. Sometimes the potatoes cluster together as neatly as a clutch of goose eggs, smooth and palely shining in the nest of the earth. At other times you dig wildly down a row to find that slugs or blight or eelworm have beaten you to the prize.

Even their best friends would not call potatoes decorative, but what they lack in looks they make up for in comfort. A baked potato straight from the oven, or a thick soup of potato blended with leek, makes even the dreariest winter doldrum more bearable. Thanks to potato connoisseurs who have rescued many old varieties from the edge of oblivion, seed suppliers now offer

---

Onion, bacon and potato hotpot

'That which was heretofore reckon'd a food fit only for Irishmen and clowns is now become the diet of the most luxuriously polite,' wrote the London nurseryman Stephen Switzer in 1733, when potatoes were just emerging from a long period when they were viewed with suspicion by Europeans after their introduction from the New World.

To taste potatoes at their most luxuriously polite, you need to choose the right kinds for the right dish. Some, like 'Désirée', bake well; some, such as 'Maris Piper', make excellent chips; some, like 'Pink Fir Apple', are supreme used in cold potato salads; some, like 'Catriona', are best roasted. No one potato does everything equally well.

The proportions of the three main ingredients here can be varied to taste.

Serves 4
a little butter
500g (1lb) onions, thinly sliced
250g (8oz) bacon, chopped
750g (1½lb) potatoes, thinly sliced

For the sauce:
60g (2oz) butter
60g (2oz) flour
600ml (1 pint) milk
125g (4oz) strong Cheddar cheese, grated
salt and black pepper, to taste

1. Preheat the oven to 190°C/375°F/gas mark 5. (Use a slightly lower temperature if the dish you are using is shallow and wide rather than deep.)
2. Butter a deep ovenproof dish (with a lid if possible), and put in the onion, bacon and potato in layers, finishing with a potato layer.
3. Make the sauce by combining the butter and flour in a saucepan over a low heat. Slowly add the milk, stirring all the time to avoid lumps. Add the cheese and stir until it has melted. Taste the sauce, adding salt and pepper if necessary, and then pour it over the potato dish.
4. Cover the dish (with foil if there is no lid) and bake for about an hour, or until the potatoes are cooked. Uncover the dish for the final 10 minutes so that the top becomes nicely crisp and brown.

---

masses of different kinds. Try a few different novelties each year. There are three types from which to choose: first earlies, second earlies and maincrop, which you lift in their appropriate seasons from mid-summer until autumn.

RECOMMENDED CULTIVARS
- **First earlies** 'Dunluce': crops heavily without compromising on flavour. 'Epicure': nearly 100 years old, good resistance to frost but susceptible to blight. 'Swift': as its name suggests matures exceptionally fast. 'Winston': gives big crops of waxy potatoes.
- **Second earlies** 'Charlotte': a French variety not high yielding but superbly

flavoured. 'Estima': resistant to slugs, blight and drought, yellow, slightly waxy flesh that cooks well. 'International Kidney' (Jersey Royal): produces potatoes with a waxy texture, good for salads. 'Wilja': blight resistant, high-yielding variety good for baking.

- **Maincrop** 'Désirée': oval, red-skinned potato good for chips and for baking. 'Pink Fir Apple': not ready until mid-autumn, but has the flavour of a new potato, superb in salads. 'Remarka': one of the best for baking.

Cultivation

Early potatoes mature in about 14–16 weeks, second earlies in 16–17 weeks and maincrop potatoes in 18–20 weeks. The heaviest crops, of course, come from the later liftings. Choose a succession of varieties, bearing in mind that in a small garden early varieties are the most valuable (and the least likely to be affected by blight). You can grow potatoes in pots, but you should not try to fit more than two plants in a container less than 30cm (12in) wide and deep.

SITE AND SOIL

Although they prefer slightly acid ground (pH 5–6), potatoes grow in a wide range of soils, doing best in deep, fertile and moisture-retentive ground. Dig in plenty of manure or compost the autumn before planting and rotate crops so that eelworm does not build up in the soil.

SOWING

Before planting, potatoes are usually 'chitted' or sprouted. Do this by setting them in a single layer in trays or boxes indoors, the end with the most 'eyes' uppermost, so that shoots start to grow. This generally takes about six weeks. Do not plant early potatoes until a month before the last frost is expected. Set them about 10–12cm (4–5in) deep and 30cm (12in) apart in rows 60cm (24in) apart. Plant second earlies and maincrop potatoes from mid-spring, setting them at slightly wider spacings, 38cm (15in) apart in rows 75cm (30in) apart. You can also use a no-dig method, laying the potatoes in shallow depressions on top of the soil and then mulching them thickly with compost, grass cuttings or leaf mould. It sounds lazy, but it works.

ROUTINE CARE

Earth up the potatoes as they grow to prevent the greening of any that push their way up to the surface of the soil. Green potatoes are poisonous. The easiest way is to earth up just once, when the plants are about 30cm (12in) high. With the no-dig method, top up the mulch as necessary. For high yields, water thoroughly once every two weeks.

YIELD AND HARVESTING

Expect 6–10kg (14–23lb) from a 3m (10ft) row, the heaviest crop coming from the later varieties. The earliest crops can be lifted when the flowers on the haulm begin to open, the latest when the haulm has completely died down. Store in a frost-free shed in the dark to stop the potatoes turning green.

PESTS AND DISEASES
Eelworm is the worst pest and rotating crops is one way to dissuade it from attack. Blight can be a problem in cool, damp summers. Where this is prevalent, stick to faster maturing first earlies or seek out blight-resistant cultivars.

PARSNIPS *Pastinaca sativa*

Nobody writes poems about parsnips. Nor do you find chefs clucking and fussing over them in expensive restaurants, as they do with courgettes and fennel. Courgettes have all the fun, primped out in a hundred different ways. Parsnips rarely crawl out from their traditional berth, tucked under a joint of roast beef.

It was the cookery writer Jane Grigson who first pointed out that the Russian for parsnip was *pasternak*. Would we feel the same way about *Dr Zhivago* if we knew it had been written by Boris Parsnip? That just shows how low the vegetable has sunk in our esteem. Before the potato came waltzing in from the New World, the parsnip was highly valued for its sweetness, its hardiness and its ability to overwinter in the ground. It is now unfairly neglected, for it is a trouble-free crop and seed is still available of the old, superbly flavoured varieties.

RECOMMENDED CULTIVARS
• 'Avonresister': a stumpy-rooted type, ideal for heavy soils. 'Countess': smooth, pale-skinned, white-fleshed roots. 'Gladiator': a vigorous F1 hybrid with good resistance to canker. 'Tender and True': a traditional variety with very long roots, little hard core and a gorgeous flavour. 'White Gem': a reliable, superbly sweet variety.

Cultivation
By nature, the parsnip is a biennial, producing a root in its first year and an airy, branching, yellow flower head in its second, by which time the root is woodily inedible. Cold intensifies the flavour of parsnips and converts some of their starch into sugar, so that they are sweeter in cold winters than they are in mild ones.

SITE AND SOIL
Grow parsnips in an open situation on soil that is deep and light with a pH of around 6.5. Acid soils make the roots more prone to canker. Recently manured ground has traditionally been avoided for this crop, as it was thought to promote forking in the root, but recent research has not borne this out. On shallow soil, use a short, bulbous variety such as 'Avonresister'.

SOWING
Seed must be fresh. Some vegetable seed can be kept from year to year with no appreciable effect on germination rates; not parsnip. Sow seed in spring in drills

Parsnip and apple bake

Traditionally roasted with a joint of meat, parsnips have many other roles to play in the kitchen. They make delicious purées and, having a rich sweetness themselves, combine particularly well with sharp fruit such as apple.

Serves 6
1.5kg (3lb) parsnip, peeled and cubed
a little butter, for greasing
2 large cooking apples, peeled, cored and thinly sliced
juice of a lemon
4 tsp soft brown sugar

1. Boil the parsnips for 5–10 minutes or until tender, drain and then purée in a food processor or blender. Spread half the purée in a buttered gratin dish and cover it with half the apple slices.
2. Repeat with the remaining purée, arranging the second batch of apple slices neatly on top of the parsnip. Sprinkle the lemon juice and sugar over the top.
3. Bake in a moderate oven (180°C/350°F/gas mark 4) for 30–40 minutes until the apples have softened.

Culinary notes
- Try glazing parsnips with melted butter mixed with a little fresh orange juice to serve as a side dish.
- You can make parsnip chips to eat as a snack or a side dish. Parboil them first, and then cut them up and deep fry in hot oil.
- If you intend to roast parsnips, parboil them for a couple of minutes before putting them in the roasting pan. This will make them succulent and crisp.
- Parboiled parsnips are delicious finished off under the grill with a sprinkling of Parmesan cheese.

about 1cm (½in) deep in rows 30cm (12in) apart. If the soil is cold, germination will be slow and erratic. You can warm it up with a floating mulch a month before sowing. Crops raised from later sowings seem to be less prone to canker.

THINNING
Thin the seedlings once they are well established. For large roots, leave 15cm (6in) between plants; for smaller ones, leave 7cm (3in).

ROUTINE CARE
This is minimal, as parsnips are neither particularly hungry nor thirsty. Roots are liable to split if they are watered after a prolonged dry spell. Water regularly or not at all.

HARVESTING AND YIELD
Expect 4kg (8lb) of parsnips from a 3m (10ft) row. Roots can be lifted from

mid-autumn if the ground is not frozen. Where winters are severe, a layer of straw over the crop will make lifting easier.

PESTS AND DISEASES

Canker is the main enemy, showing as reddish-brown or sometimes black patches on the roots, especially at the shoulders. Occasionally it spreads through the whole of the parsnip, but usually the patches are small enough to cut away when you are preparing the roots. There is no effective remedy. Choose a canker-resistant variety and sow seed later rather than earlier.

	SPRING			SUMMER			AUTUMN			WINTER		
	EARLY	MID	LATE	EARLY	MID	LATE	EARLY	MID	LATE	EARLY	MID	LATE
PARSNIPS	⁂	⁂	⁂					✁	✁	✁	✁	✁

TURNIPS AND SWEDES
Brassica rapa rapa & *B. napus napobrassica*

It has usually been the turnip's misfortune to be lumped together with the swede, a vegetable of much less charm. The swede arrived in England from Sweden in around 1775, when it was used as a winter vegetable, large, usually yellow fleshed, fodder rather than food. However you cooked it, it seemed to smack more of the farmyard than the dinner table. The turnip – especially since the arrival of the small, summer-maturing Japanese types – is an altogether more succulent proposition, though it is less hardy and does not yield so heavily. There are two important rules to bear in mind with turnips: never let them get too big and never eat them when they are too old. Neither vegetable is very decorative, but if you grow your own turnips, you can enjoy the bonus of cooking and eating the young, green tops.

RECOMMENDED CULTIVARS

- **Turnip** 'Blanc de Croissy': an old French variety with long, thin tapering roots. 'Golden Ball': a sturdy turnip to use between October and December. 'Milan Purple Top': reliable, flat-topped roots. 'Oasis': sweet juicy roots, as good raw as cooked. 'Primera': very fast growing, best eaten while small, can be grown in tubs.
- **Swede** 'Brora': a well-flavoured, hardy variety with reddish-purple skin, best harvested between late autumn and the new year. 'Magres': fine-grained yellow flesh, ready to harvest from September onwards, foliage resistant to mildew. 'Marian': resistant to clubroot and mildew, with globe-shaped, yellow-fleshed roots. 'Ruby': deep orange flesh of good flavour.

Mashed neeps

'Mashed neeps is a stalwart of Scottish cookbooks, but much depends on the age of the neeps (whether they are turnips or swedes) and the extras that you add to the mash. This recipe uses ginger and cinammon to spice up a purée of winter roots.

900g (2lb) swede	4 tbsp double cream
4 cloves garlic, crushed	salt and black pepper
2 big tsp root ginger, finely chopped	ground cinnamon, to taste
50g (2oz) butter, melted	

1. Peel the swedes and cut them into chunks before cooking them until tender.
2. Gently cook the crushed garlic and the ginger for a few minutes in the melted butter.
3. Purée the swede in a processor, adding first the garlic/ginger mixture and then the cream. Season with salt, pepper and cinnamon to taste.

Cultivation

The early maturing types of turnip deteriorate quickly. Sow small batches of seed at three-weekly intervals. A cultivar such as 'Primera' may be ready to harvest after only six weeks; hardy autumn types take about twelve weeks to mature.

SITE AND SOIL

Neither crop will thrive in an acid soil (the ideal pH is about 7). Use ground that has been well manured for a previous crop and is cool, fertile and friable. Summer sowings of turnip can be made in light shade, provided the soil is moist.

SOWING

Start sowing turnips in mid-spring for late spring and summer crops, and from mid- to late summer for autumn and winter crops. Sow seed as thinly as possible in drills about 1.5cm (1/2in) deep in rows 30–38cm (12–15in) apart. Start sowing swedes in mid-spring. They can be sown at the same depth, but need a wider spacing of 38–45cm (15–18in) between the rows.

THINNING

Turnips grow fast and thinning should be done while the seedlings are still small. Thin spring and summer plants to 10cm (4in) apart, autumn and winter plants to 15cm (6in) apart. Swedes need more room to develop: thin them to 25cm (10in) apart.

ROUTINE CARE

If necessary water during dry periods.

HARVESTING AND YIELD

Expect 6kg (14lb) of maincrop turnips and 14kg (30lb) of swedes from a 3m (10ft) row. Early sowings of turnip should be pulled when the roots are no bigger than a golf ball. Scratch away some soil from the top of the roots if you want to check the size. Summer-sown maincrop varieties can be left in the ground until needed, as can swedes. Any roots not used by mid-winter should be lifted and stored in a cool, frost-free place.

PESTS AND DISEASES

Turnips and swedes are brassicas and, as with others in the family, their seedlings may be attacked by flea beetle.

	SPRING			SUMMER			AUTUMN			WINTER		
	EARLY	MID	LATE	EARLY	MID	LATE	EARLY	MID	LATE	EARLY	MID	LATE
TURNIPS		✿	✿ ✂	✂	✿ ✂	✿		✂	✂	✂		
SWEDES		✿	✿	✿			✂	✂	✂	✂		

RADISHES *Raphanus sativus*

The radish is taken more seriously in China and Japan than it is in Europe. Chinese chefs carve huge 'China Rose' radishes into intricate flowers to decorate their dishes of food. Japanese gardeners cultivate long white mooli radish, a single root of which can weigh 15kg (33lb). The typical fast-maturing European radish is the size of a marble, usually pink- or red-skinned, though there is a bigger black-rooted Spanish radish that is grown for winter use. When growing, none of the radish family is particularly decorative, but they are good salad vegetables. If you let them run up to flower, the plants produce small, hot seed pods which can be steamed, stir-fried or made into a spicy pickle.

RECOMMENDED CULTIVARS

- **Small red summer** 'Cherry Belle': grows fast to produce perfect, rounded roots. 'Flamboyant Sabina': smooth, cylindrical roots, with a strong flavour. 'French Breakfast': classic cylindrical root, mild and sweet. 'Rudi': dark red, very rounded roots, good for gentle forcing in a greenhouse or cold frame. 'Sparkler': is a round radish, very slow to go woody.
- **Mooli type** 'Minowase': white, tapering roots as much as 60cm (2ft) long. 'Neptune': crisp, mild mooli radish with roots at about 25cm (10in).
- **Winter radish** 'China Rose': long bright red roots with white flesh.
- **Pods** 'Rat's Tail': crisp, tapered seed pods, crunchy and succulent.

Cultivation

Different types of radish need different treatment as regards sowing time. Start in early spring with the small red summer types such as 'French Breakfast'.

As these will be ready to harvest within a few weeks, you can grow them between other slower-maturing vegetables such as parsnips. Delay sowing mooli types until after the longest day of the year, or else they will run to seed, as will winter radishes. These are best sown towards late summer.

SITE AND SOIL
Radishes grow best in a light, sandy soil in an open, sunny situation. Summer crops will tolerate partial shade.

SOWING
Little and often is the key with summer radishes. Sow in short rows 1cm (1/2in) deep and 15cm (6in) apart, at fortnightly intervals. Encourage rapid germination and growth by watering the drills if necessary in dry weather. Sow mooli and winter types 1cm (1/2in) deep in rows 20–25cm (8–10in) apart, watering the drills first if the ground is dry.

THINNING
Thin summer radishes to leave about 2cm (1in) between plants. Leave at least 15cm (6in) between mooli and winter radish.

ROUTINE CARE
This is an easy, carefree crop, requiring no feeding but some watering. Excessive watering makes leaves grow at the expense of the roots.

YIELD AND HARVESTING
Expect about thirty summer radishes and 1.5kg (3lb) winter radishes from a 1m (3ft) row. Summer radishes should mature within a month and need to be eaten as quickly as possible before they become tough or woolly. Mooli and winter radishes have a much longer growing season. Expect to wait three months for a crop.

PESTS AND DISEASES
Flea beetle may attack seedlings, leaving them peppered with characteristic small holes. Slugs may attack roots of large winter radish.

	SPRING			SUMMER			AUTUMN			WINTER		
	EARLY	MID	LATE	EARLY	MID	LATE	EARLY	MID	LATE	EARLY	MID	LATE
DAIKON/ WINTER RADISHES						✿		✂	✂			
GLOBE RADISHES	✿	✿	✿ ✂	✂		✿	✿ ✂	✂				

JERUSALEM ARTICHOKES *Helianthus tuberosus*

Most people know one thing about the Jerusalem artichoke (which is neither an artichoke, nor from Jerusalem). Its salient characteristic was described by

---

Artichoke and potato gratin

'Many vegetables can be quickly turned into gratins and this mixture of Jerusalem artichoke and potato makes a particularly good one, topped with a crust of Parmesan mixed with mature Cheddar.

Serves 4
300g (12oz) Jerusalem artichokes
300g (12oz) potatoes
butter, for greasing
salt, pepper and grated nutmeg, to taste
75g (3oz) pancetta or chopped bacon
570ml (1 pint) chicken stock
50–100g (2–4oz) grated Parmesan and Cheddar cheese

1. Peel the artichokes and potatoes and slice them thinly.
2. Butter an ovenproof dish and put a layer of potato and artichoke at the bottom. Season well and scatter some of the pancetta or chopped bacon on top, and then a sprinkling of cheese.
3. Repeat the layers until all the vegetables are used up. Pour the stock over the top and finish off with a layer of cheese.
4. Bake in the oven for about an hour at 180°C/350°F/gas mark 4.

---

the seventeenth-century botanist John Goodyer, soon after the vegetable arrived in England. 'In my judgement,' he wrote, 'which way soever they be drest and eaten they stirre and cause a filthie loathsome wind within the bodie.' Being tall, however, sometimes topping 3m (10ft), they make useful summer screens in a kitchen garden and will filter wind on an exposed site. This artichoke is a member of the sunflower family and some cultivars bear large yellow daisy flowers.

RECOMMENDED CULTIVARS
'Fuseau': has long, relatively smooth tubers, easier to peel than the knobby kinds. 'Gerard': well-flavoured, reddish-coloured tubers.

Cultivation
Jerusalem artichokes are tough, hardy plants. Like potatoes, they are a useful first crop to plant in rough, heavy ground, where their roots will help to break up the soil.
SITE AND SOIL
No plant could be less fussy, but the best tubers come from non-flowering cultivars grown in rich, cool soil. Once suited, they spread rapidly and may become invasive.

PLANTING
Plant the knobby tubers 10–15cm (4–6in) deep and 30cm (12in) apart in spring.
ROUTINE CARE
In very exposed positions it may be necessary to earth up or stake the thick stems of the artichokes to prevent them blowing over. The top growth dies back naturally in late autumn. Cut the withered stalks to within 7cm (3in) of the ground.
YIELD AND HARVESTING
Each plant should yield about 1.5kg (3lb) of tubers. These can be left in the ground over winter and lifted as needed. Clear them away completely before spring or else you will find the tubers sprouting where you may not want them.
PESTS AND DISEASES
Underground slugs may attack the tubers. The stems may be attacked by *Sclerotinia*, a fluffy white mould that appears on the base of the plant. This fungus can last for years in soil. The only answer is to replant sound tubers in a fresh site.

SALSIFY/SCORZONERA
Tragopogon porrifolius & *Scorzonera hispanica*

These two vegetables grow in a similar fashion, producing long, thin, thong-like roots that are fiddly to prepare. It is easiest to skin them after cooking, like new potatoes. Salsify is a biennial and has narrower, grassier foliage than scorzonera. In its second year it produces long conical flower buds, which open to produce pink-purple flowers. They are delicious picked just before they open and used in omelettes.

Whereas salsify produces a thin, white root, scorzonera is black skinned and the foliage is less glaucous. Its name comes from the Spanish word for a viper, for the root was traditionally used to cure snakebite. Scorzonera is a perennial and after its first year of growth produces the same succulent flower buds as salsify. Its flowers are bright yellow.

RECOMMENDED CULTIVARS
Breeders have paid little attention to these crops. Few selected cultivars have been named.
- **Salsify** 'Giant': produces especially long roots. 'Mammoth Sandwich Island': long, straight, sweet-flavoured roots.
- **Scorzonera** 'Hoffman's Long Black': good resistance to bolting. 'Maxima' well-flavoured long black roots.

Cultivation

If you can persuade the roots to swell thicker than your little finger, you will be doing well. You also need to prevent the roots forking, which they will do (like carrots) if the ground has been too recently manured. The flowers of mature plants are very decorative, but as the plants age the roots become woody.

SITE AND SOIL

Because the roots are so long, both salsify and scorzonera need deep, light, friable soil. They grow best in an open, sunny situation.

SOWING

Sow seed thinly in mid-spring, 1cm (1/2in) deep, in drills that are at least 15cm (6in) apart.

THINNING

Thin the plants to 10cm (4in) apart.

ROUTINE CARE

Neither is troublesome, provided seed is sown in suitable soil.

YIELD AND HARVESTING

You should get about twenty roots (2kg/4lb) from a (3m) 10ft row. They can be left in the ground until needed. In very cold areas where the ground is likely to freeze, lift roots, trim the tops and keep them in a store, loosely wrapped in newspaper. Take care when lifting roots, for they are brittle and snap off easily.

PESTS AND DISEASES

White blister occasionally develops as glistening white pustules on the foliage. Cut off and destroy affected leaves.

	SPRING			SUMMER			AUTUMN			WINTER		
	EARLY	MID	LATE	EARLY	MID	LATE	EARLY	MID	LATE	EARLY	MID	LATE
SALSIFY & SCORZONERA		✿						✂	✂	✂	✂	

HERBS & EDIBLE FLOWERS

You are as likely to find thyme on a rockery as in a herb garden, or to use different kinds of sage to bolster up a herbaceous planting of misty blue and purple, as you are to pen them off in a kitchen garden. The decorative possibilities of herbs were recognized long ago: clipped pyramids of bay to flank a front door, feathery stands of fennel to bring variety to a foliage border. Nothing sets off lemon or orange tulips better in late spring than young plants of bronze fennel. Collecting herbs all together in one place has an academic kind of charm, but you may find you can create better plant groups by combining herbs with annual flowers or other perennials. Set your chives free to edge a rose bed or let them fraternize in a window box with ivy and golden feverfew. Be careful, though, about liberating rampant herbs such as mint: only the pretty golden variegated mint *Mentha × gentilis* 'Variegata' can be trusted to behave well away from the herb bed.

Basil is one of the most rewarding of herbs to grow, either in beds outside or in pots on a kitchen windowsill. Most common is the plain green-leaved basil, but there are types with richly luxuriant purple leaves and others, such as Greek basil, that grow as neatly as pieces of topiary. Chives, often used as edging, can be combined with frilly lettuce to fill the box-edged bed of a potager. The purple flowers echo the tone set by the dark leaves of a lettuce such as 'Lollo Rossa'; the clumps, sheared down when they begin to look scruffy, will quickly sprout again with fresh new foliage.

Fennel, both the green and the bronze-leaved kinds, can have an important part to play in a herbaceous border, particularly in late spring before the fennel's big flat heads of yellow flowers emerge. Try setting it in front of the glowing leaves of a golden hop; the feathery foliage also contrasts well with plain-leaved perennials such as brunnera. Sage is another excellent foliage plant, a perfect foil for crisply curled heads of parsley. As well as contrasts of texture, there are strong differences in tone and form between these two plants. In this respect, flat-leaved parsley, which is not such a bright green, is a less successful partner. Though borage foliage is somewhat coarse, the fine hairs on the stems and flower heads give it a shimmering quality, especially when seen against the light. In mixed plantings, it associates well with foxgloves; or it can be used to fill a bed in a formal herb garden, where it will seed itself about with abandon.

ANNUAL & BIENNIAL HERBS

These herbs need to be sown each spring, so use their relative impermanence to your advantage by growing them in different places each year where they can bring variety to the decorative kitchen garden. The plan for a herb garden on pages 52–3 mixes annual with perennial herbs in a formal design, but you can grow annual herbs in rows among vegetables to add colour and contrast to a productive plot.

DILL *Anethum graveolens*

Dill is grown for the aniseed flavour of its leaves and seeds, the seeds having the stronger taste. Like fennel, it has thread-like leaves and flat heads of yellow flowers from mid- to late summer but is smaller in all its parts. 'Fernleaf' is a special strain producing plants no more than 45cm (18in) tall; 'Hera' has a stiff, upright habit and is slow to bolt; 'Mammoth' is the best variety for seed.

CULTIVATION

Height 1m (3ft). Sow in drills or broadcast seed in a sunny spot from spring to mid-summer. Sow by mid-spring if you want to harvest the seeds, to be sure of them ripening in time. Cut the heads as the seeds turn brown and shake them upside down over a sheet of paper. Pick out insects and stray bits of stem before storing the seed in an airtight jar.

ANGELICA *Angelica archangelica*

A statuesque biennial, producing umbels of pale green flowers on tall, stout stems. *Angelica gigas* has dramatic purple stems.

CULTIVATION

Height 1.8m (6ft). Thrives in moist soil, in sun or partial shade. It will self-seed enthusiastically. Sow outside in mid-spring and thin to 30cm (12in). Lift and plant in permanent positions in late summer.

CHERVIL *Anthriscus cerefolium*

Fresh chervil is a revelation to anyone used only to the dried kind. It has ferny leaves and hollow stems, and white flowers too, if it is allowed to grow on for a second year. When it has flowered it dies. It grows quickly and useful quantities of leaves can be picked only six weeks after sowing.

CULTIVATION

Height 30cm (12in). Sown outside, chervil does best in light shade. Sow in drills or broadcast small batches of seed at fortnightly intervals from early spring until late summer. Grown in deep boxes in a greenhouse kept at 8°C/45°F, it will give fresh supplies of leaves throughout winter.

BORAGE *Borago officinalis*

Borage is easy to please and bees love it. The brilliant blue flowers can be sprinkled on salads, while the cucumber-flavoured leaves are traditionally used in Pimm's.

CULTIVATION

Height 60cm (24in). Prefers a sunny site and well-drained soil. Sow in spring in drills 30cm (12in) apart. Thin the seedlings to 30cm (12in) apart.

MARIGOLD *Calendula officinalis*

An enthusiastic self-seeder with bright orange flowers that continue throughout summer. Use the petals instead of saffron to flavour and colour rice, or sprinkle them fresh on top of a green salad.

CULTIVATION

Height 45cm (18in). Likes sun. Broadcast seed in early spring, covering with 5mm (1/4in) of soil. Thin to 15cm (6in) between plants.

CARAWAY *Carum carvi*

The ripe seeds are often used in bread and cakes, but can also be added to soups to give a piquant flavour.

CULTIVATION

Height 60cm (24in). Grow in any fertile, well-drained soil, preferably in full sun. Sow in early spring where the plants are to flower, setting the seed shallowly in drills 30cm (12in) apart. Thin seedlings to 15cm (6in) apart.

CORIANDER *Coriandrum sativum*

The first leaves of coriander are like flat French parsley, but as the plants shoot up the leaves become wispy and develop a different taste. The first leaves and the seeds are what you need for cooking, the leaves being more difficult to get in sufficient quantity. 'Cilantro' and 'Leisure' are the best strains for leaf production, 'Moroccan' for seeds.

CULTIVATION

Height 60cm (2ft). Prefers sun. Seed germinates quickly. For a constant supply of leaves, sow in drills or broadcast seed fortnightly in small batches from early spring. You can also sow quite thickly in a large pot and snip off foliage when you need it. The seeds are ready to harvest in late summer, but you have to be quick to catch them as they drop as soon as they are ripe.

BASIL *Ocimum basilicum*

One of the most rewarding herbs to grow, smelling of heat and holidays. It can be raised very successfully on a windowsill indoors and picked until late winter. Grown outside, its season is shorter, for it is tender. For fat, bushy plants, pinch the tops once they are established. This will force new growth to sprout from the leaf junctions. If you grow Greek basil, the plants will naturally be fat and bushy. 'Dark Red', 'Purple Ruffles' and 'Rubin' are very decorative varieties with large purple leaves. There are many others. All are good.

CULTIVATION

Height 30–45cm (12–18in). Needs warmth and sun. Sow seed indoors in pots and trays in early spring and prick out seedlings into individual pots or containers to keep on the windowsill. Outside, sow seed 1cm (about 1/2in) deep in drills 38cm (15in) apart in late spring or early summer. Thin the seedlings to 30cm (12in) apart. Cover with a floating mulch for extra protection in the early stages.

PARSLEY *Petroselinum crispum*

This is one of the most useful of all culinary herbs. You need two different types: the tightly curled kind for decorative effect, to use among marigolds and red lettuce, and the flat-leaved French kind for the most intense flavour.

CULTIVATION

Height 30–45cm (12–18in). Grow in fertile, well-drained soil in sun or partial shade. Sow seed thinly in drills 25cm (10in) apart from early spring to early summer. It may be slow to germinate but do not give up hope. Thin the seedlings gradually until the plants are 23cm (9in) apart. Cut down plants in early autumn and water them to encourage fresh growth.

NASTURTIUM *Tropaeolum majus*

The colourful flowers make pretty edgings in a potager, but are edible too and can be strewn over salads. The peppery leaves are excellent in salads or sandwiches, while the seeds can be used as a substitute for capers. Bush rather than trailing kinds are easiest to manage in a kitchen garden.

CULTIVATION

Height 23–30cm (9–12in). Best in sun. Sow in situ in mid-spring, setting the seeds 1cm (1/2in) deep. They do not need rich ground.

PERENNIAL HERBS

Although some of these plants reach an impressive height by summer, in winter they disappear from view. In a herb garden, mix them with evergreen herbs for a more permanent effect. Several, notably tarragon, fennel, mint and sorrel, are thuggish in behaviour and your problem will be in controlling rather than growing them. Contain mint by planting it in a bottomless bucket sunk in the ground. Fennel spreads by enthusiastic self-seeding. Be prepared to cut off its head before it starts to shed its seed. Chives are blameless and, if space is limited, should be your first choice in this group.

CHIVES *Allium schoenoprasum*

These are easy to grow and make neat edgings for paths, the delicately onion-flavoured foliage topped with small round heads of purple flowers from early to mid-summer. They also do well in window boxes if well watered. 'Polycross' is early and uniform with dark green foliage. The dramatic giant variety 'Forescate' is twice the normal size. Chinese chives (*Allium tuberosum*) have white, star-like flowers in late summer with leaves tasting mildly of garlic.

CULTIVATION
Height 15–25cm (6–10in). Chives do best in moist, fertile soil. They can be raised from seed, but it is simpler to buy a clump and divide it with a sharp knife in early autumn to make more plants. Set these about 30cm (12in) apart. The foliage dies down completely in the winter, but the leaves are ready for cutting again by late spring.

HORSERADISH *Armoracia rusticana*
Once established, horseradish is difficult to get rid of, so grow it in a corner where it can be left undisturbed out of the way of other crops. The long taproot has a peppery flavour and is grated to flavour sauces.
CULTIVATION
Height 60cm (24in). Plant the thongs (roots) in spring 30cm (12in) apart in a short row, with the top of the root about 5cm (2in) below the surface of the soil. Dig up the roots as you need them.

FRENCH TARRAGON *Artemisia dracunculus*
Tarragon spreads quickly by underground rhizomes, so you are unlikely to need more than one plant. The flavour of the leaves diminishes as the plant gets older. Renew plants every two or three years.
CULTIVATION
Height 45–60cm (18–24in). Plant in a sunny, sheltered site in light, well-drained soil in spring or autumn. Extend the season by planting a few rhizomes in a cold frame. In winter, growth dies back to the ground.

FENNEL *Foeniculum vulgare*
Fennel gives sculptural height in a herb garden, especially the superb bronze-leaved variety called *Foeniculum vulgare* 'Purpureum'. The filigree foliage is topped by flat heads of golden flowers in mid-summer. Although tall, it is not fat, like angelica, which is an advantage.
CULTIVATION
Height 1.5–2.5m (5–8ft). Buy plants or raise them from seed and set them out in well-drained soil in spring or autumn. Cut down stems in autumn. Be ruthless about discarding seedlings emerging in the wrong places; otherwise you will end with a fennel forest.

LOVAGE *Levisticum officinale*
A luxuriant plant, the leaves tasting of celery with a dash of yeast. These are the most commonly used part of the plant, but you can also use the seed, like celery seed, to flavour soup. Lovage takes at least three years to reach full size.
CULTIVATION
Height 1.8m (6ft). Lovage likes rich, moist, well-drained soil in sun or in

Baked eggs with tarragon

'Some herbs have a long-established partnership with particular fish, flesh or fowl: tarragon with chicken, rosemary with lamb, sage with pork. But the cook with a ready supply of fresh herbs will want to experiment. Try sprinkling chopped mint over strawberries or adding thyme to salads of mixed leaves and flowers. In this dish, French tarragon is used as the essential catalyst in a simple dish of baked eggs.

Serves 4

butter	4 tbs water
4 eggs	2 large sprigs of tarragon
4 tbs double cream	salt and pepper

1. Butter four small ramekins and break an egg into each one. Heat the cream gently in a small pan with the water and tarragon. Allow the liquid to reduce slightly, pressing the tarragon with a wooden spoon.
2. Take out the tarragon and pour the creamy mixture over the eggs, dividing it equally between the ramekins. Add a tiny pinch of salt and a flourish of freshly ground pepper on top.
3. Lower the ramekins into a pan with 1cm (¹/₂in) of boiling water in the bottom and cook the eggs gently (for about 4–5 minutes) until the whites are just set. Serve decorated with a few leaves of fresh tarragon sprinkled on the top.

Culinary notes
* For a traditional forcemeat to serve with lamb or use to stuff tomatoes, combine 50g (2oz) breadcrumbs with 25g (1oz) butter, a pinch of mixed herbs, 2 tsps of finely chopped parsley, some grated lemon rind, salt, pepper and enough egg to bind the other ingredients together.
* To make a highly flavoured savoury bread, add some finely chopped sage leaves and some sun-dried tomatoes or stoned black olives to the dough when you are preparing it. Prove and bake in the usual way.

partial shade. You can buy plants or raise them from seed, sowing inside in early spring, pricking out the seedlings and later transplanting them to their final positions in early summer.

MINT *Mentha* spp.

Mints are bullies, inclined to spread and engulf their neighbours. Different types are best grown together in one bed. The common mint (*Mentha spicata*) is very easy to grow. *M. rotundifolia* or apple mint has large, round hairy leaves and heads of pinkish flowers. It is said by connoisseurs to make the best mint sauce. Ginger mint (*M. × gentilis* 'Variegata') has gold variegated leaves and makes excellent ground cover.

CULTIVATION
Height 45cm–1m (18–36in). Mints like rich, moist soil and will grow happily in shade. If foliage becomes shabby in mid-summer, shear it down to encourage fresh growth.

MARJORAM *Origanum* spp.
Pot marjoram (*Origanum vulgare*) has very handsome purple-pink flowers – bliss for bees – but the flavour of the leaves is not as strong as that of sweet marjoram (*O. marjorana*). This does not grow as tall as pot marjoram and has a neat, bushy habit, the leaves greyish green and the flowers white. Both flower in late summer, but sweet marjoram has a longer flowering season. The herb can be used fresh or dried and brings a Mediterranean tang to the bland flavour of chicken. Like basil, it has a natural affinity with tomato.
CULTIVATION
Height 30–45cm (12–18in). Plant in late spring in well-drained soil in full sun. Cut bushes down by two-thirds in late autumn. Both types are reasonably hardy.

SORREL *Rumex* spp.
Sorrel (*Rumex acetosa*) is a large-leaved plant, suspiciously like a dock. The leaves are sharp and acid tasting, becoming more bitter as the season progresses. Use them fresh in small quantities in salad, or blend them, cooked, into a purée. Sorrel also makes good soup. French or buckler-leaved sorrel (*R. scutatus*) has much prettier leaves, like little shields. Rather than shooting strongly upwards as ordinary sorrel does, the buckler-leaved type lolls around on the ground.
CULTIVATION
Height 23–30cm (9–12in). Sorrel succeeds in any well-drained ground in sun or partial shade. Raise it from seed or buy plants to set out in spring or autumn. Pinch out the flowering stems when they appear, to force the plant to produce more leaves.

SWEET VIOLET *Viola odorata*
The flowers of sweet violet, in shades of purple and white, are carried from late winter until mid-spring. They are often crystallized and used to decorate cakes, puddings and ice cream. You can also scatter them fresh over salads or use them to garnish a dish of fruit, tied in a little bunch with some of their own heart-shaped leaves.
CULTIVATION
Height 7cm (3in). Plants of sweet violet are easy to establish in any fertile, moist soil. They will thrive in sun or partial shade and clump up quickly by means of overground runners.

SHRUBBY PERENNIAL HERBS

This group includes herbs with evergreen leaves and woody stems that range from miniature bushes to small trees. They are likely to be permanent fixtures in any planting. All are sun lovers and some, such as thyme, rosemary and sage, may rot if planted in wet, badly drained ground. Bay can be clipped into splendid architectural shapes, but rosemary too lends itself to topiary treatment.

BAY *Laurus nobilis*
Left to its own devices, the sweet bay makes a handsome tall tree, as broad as it is high, the evergreen leaves joined in mid-spring by nobbly little clusters of pale greenish flowers. Trimmed into a geometric shape or grown as a mop-headed standard, it is the perfect plant for a formal herb garden or potager. The seventeenth-century herbalist Nicholas Culpeper said that 'neither witch nor devil, thunder nor lightning, will hurt a man in the place where a bay tree is'. The leaves can be used fresh or dried in cooking; dried, they are an essential ingredient of a *bouquet garni*.
CULTIVATION
Height 3–6m (10–18ft). Plant in mid-spring in a sunny, sheltered position. Bay is not dependably hardy, but will grow well in a pot that can be moved inside in a harsh winter. Clip to shape if necessary during the summer. Bay can sometimes become infested with scale insects.

ROSEMARY *Rosmarinus officinalis*
Most rosemaries have greenish foliage and bluish flowers, both drifting towards grey. 'Miss Jessopp's Upright', which is taller and more upright in growth than the common kind, is useful clipped like topiary to give structure and height in a mixed planting. 'Severn Sea', with bright blue flowers, has the opposite habit and can be planted to sprawl over a step or the edge of a raised bed, or hug a sloping bank. Rosemary can also be trained, fan-like, against a wall. Pillars and pyramids may need to be tied in with fine nylon line.
CULTIVATION
Height 1m (3ft). Plant in spring in a sunny spot in well-drained ground. Some of the cultivars are less hardy than the common type. Overgrown bushes can be cut back hard in mid-spring. This is also the time to trim any unwanted growth from plants that are being trained against a wall, to avoid missing out on the following year's flowers.

SAGE *Salvia officinalis*
The variegated types of sage are just as useful in the kitchen as the ordinary plain green type. There is virtually no difference in flavour. 'Icterina' has rough textured leaves of green and gold. 'Tricolor' is even showier, with leaves

splashed in pink, white and green. The deep purple leaves of 'Purpurascens' look splendid combined with green-leaved herbs or orange pot marigolds. Sage is handsome enough to be used in a herbaceous border, especially when topped by its spikes of bright blue flowers.

CULTIVATION

Height 45cm–1m (18–36in). Sages hate prolonged winter damp and may rot in heavy soils. Plant in spring in light, well-drained soil in a site that gets plenty of sun. Sages quickly become leggy but are easy to propagate from cuttings taken in summer. Pull off side shoots about 7cm (3in) long with a 'heel' attached, and line them out in a cold frame or poke them into pots of sandy compost. When the cuttings are rooted, nip out the tops to encourage bushy growth. Alternatively, try mound layering. Tidy up plants by clipping them over during the summer. You can dry the leaf clippings and store them in airtight jars.

WINTER SAVORY *Satureja montana*

Winter savory is a hardy, almost evergreen dwarf subshrub unlike its cousin, summer savory, which is an annual. Summer savory has the better flavour, but winter savory has, of course, a much longer season. The leaves are peppery in taste, and are often used to flavour salami. Tiny, rather insignificant, whitish-pink flowers appear in summer.

CULTIVATION

Height 30cm (12in). Plant winter savory in spring in any fertile, well-drained soil in full sun. It will need replacing every two or three years as it quickly becomes woody and untractable. Propagate plants by dividing them in spring or autumn. They can also be mound-layered.

THYME *Thymus* spp.

The thyme family contains various species with different habits of growth; some form tiny bushes, others dense, spreading mats of foliage that put down roots as they travel. The creeping kinds, such as *Thymus serpyllum*, are excellent in paths and paving but more difficult to manage in a mixed herb bed. This is the place for upright varieties such as *Thymus vulgaris*, the common thyme, with grey-green leaves and mauve flowers. The bushy 'Silver Posie' has pretty silver variegated leaves and pink flowers. *T.* 'Culinary Lemon' smells of lemons.

CULTIVATION

Height 2–30cm (1–12in). Dry, well-drained chalky soil is best for all the thymes. Plant in spring, incorporating some grit into the soil to improve drainage where necessary. Trim frequently in spring and summer to stop plants getting straggly. The harder they are cut, the more vigorously they grow. New plants are easily propagated by mound layering. As with most of these herbs, wet winters and soggy ground are much more likely to cause problems than any pests or diseases.

FRUIT

While most vegetables are temporary residents in the garden, sown and cropped as the seasons dictate, fruit, once planted, will be with you for many years. Its presence gives a comfortable sense of permanence and continuity. Carrots and parsnips may come and go, but a vine goes on for ever. Careful selection and breeding has brought some fruits such as the apple and the peach a long way from their undomesticated counterparts. Others, such as the blackberry, still have a whiff of the wild about them. Fruit will only set if flowers have been properly pollinated. Some fruit trees are self-fertile; others are not and you must have different types within reach to be sure of a crop. The following pages explain how to achieve the best results.

Tree fruit

These will be the longest-lived elements of your decorative kitchen garden. The type of tree you buy – bush, standard, cordon, fan or espalier – depends on where you want to put it. Bushes start fruiting when they are very young, are easy to pick and spray, but are difficult to mow under. They will never have the satisfying shape of a full-blown tree. Cordons, when planted against wires in parallel diagonals, make an excellent and productive screen. You need to study a pruning handbook carefully to keep them in order and, of course, they will never crop as abundantly as a big tree. However, this is a good way of growing a wide variety of apples in a restricted space. Fans and espaliers are even more elegant. You can make complete outdoor rooms, walled round with trained trees, the branches carefully tied in to long bamboo canes so that they retain their shape as they grow. Half standards and standards are the fruit trees of picture books with tall straight stems breaking into ample rounded heads of branches. Half standards have a clear stem of at least 1.2m (4ft) while full standards go up to 1.8m (6ft) before the branches start. Their height makes spraying and picking slightly more difficult to manage but these trees are infinitely more pleasing to look at than a dwarfed bush. All trees can be grown as standards or half standards, though in cold areas, peaches, nectarines, greengages and apricots are most likely to succeed as fans against a warm wall. Apples are rarely grown as fans, as their spur systems develop more readily on cordons or espaliers.

Soft fruit

Soft fruit is too rarely trained into decorative shapes, though redcurrants make attractive double cordons, shaped like wine glasses, and gooseberries take on quite a different character when grown up on single stems to make round-headed standards. Use the long, exploratory growths of a blackberry to wind in and out of a hedge, or train one of the blackberry/raspberry crosses such as loganberry or tayberry to make a summer screen. Strawberries can be planted as neat edgings to beds.

Vine fruit

In a decorative kitchen garden, you are as likely to plant a vine for its foliage as its fruit, for the leaves have great style and the wayward, exuberant way that a vine grows gives a great sense of generosity in a garden. In a cool climate, serious grape fanciers will probably grow their vines in a greenhouse, training out the rods along the ribs of the roof and assiduously thinning bunches of grapes as they swell. Grown in this way, grapes are ambrosial, but almost a full-time job. Grown outside, the fruit may not be flawless, but the foliage can be allowed its head to a greater extent. Try *Vitis vinifera* 'Fragola', the strawberry vine, which has masses of tiny grapes, ripening in mid-autumn. The outdoor black grape 'Brant' has deep green leaves which colour crimson, orange and pink in autumn. Other vine fruit such as melons, kiwi and passion fruit need warmth to crop successfully.

TREE FRUIT

Trained fruit trees give to the kitchen garden what clipped yew hedges and topiary bring to a flower garden: good structure. With a little help from a patient gardener, apples and pears can both be trained to make living screens between one part of the garden and another or to provide a fruitful backdrop for a border of old-fashioned flowers. Fruit trees pay rent twice a year, first with their spring blossom and then with their autumn harvest. Compared with a Japanese flowering cherry, this is rather generous. And trees such as apples and pears grow old gracefully, welcoming lichens and ferns to their capacious branches. In winter, they assume the gnarled, twisted shapes of avant-garde sculptures. In a small garden, a single tree, grown as a half standard, may be used as a centrepiece in a lawn or splayed in an elegant fan against a warm wall. When the tree itself is well established, use it as a prop for a rose or a late summer clematis.

Old espaliered apples are particularly appealing. The structures on which they were originally trained may long since have rotted away, but such trees, their structure fixed in youth, make strong features wherever they are. In old age, such a tree is easy to maintain, needing little more than a quick mid-winter haircut. You could also use an espaliered apple to reinforce the horizontal lines of stonework or brickwork on a wall. A wall offers protection for blossom against late frosts and its warmth hastens the ripening of fruit in autumn. There may be room for a narrow bed underneath edged with box and filled with white-flowered Chinese chives.

In a greenhouse, different things are possible. Peaches, for instance, blossom long before apples or pears and need a warm situation to thrive outside. They succeed well under glass, where they are not prey to debilitating peach leaf curl. A greenhouse built as a lean-to against a south-facing wall provides ideal growing conditions for peaches, apricots and nectarines. A whitewashed wall inside will reflect light on to a tree, where in comfort you can thin the fruits to regular spacings along the branches. Lemon trees are one of the easiest of the citrus family to grow in pots, but even they will need the shelter of a greenhouse in winter. In summer they can be lined in a row along a terrace, where they give a formal air to a garden scheme. They look equally at ease in an informal courtyard setting grouped with pots of basil and lavender.

APPLES *Malus domestica*

Next time you sink your teeth into a crunchy 'Cox's Orange Pippin', spare a thought for Richard Cox, a retired brewer and besotted gardener who grew the first 'Cox' apple from the pip of a 'Ribston Pippin' in 1826. The new apple would never have been known outside Mr Cox's two acres in Slough, Buckinghamshire, without the help of the Duke of Devonshire's gardener, Joseph Paxton. When Paxton became the first president of the British Pomological Society in the mid-nineteenth century, he promoted the new apple vigorously and, being a man of even more influence than his employer, sent 'Cox' graft wood all over the country. It is still one of the best known of all apples, though not the easiest to grow in your own garden. It is very prone to disease and needs regular doses of medicine to keep on its feet.

The type of apple tree you buy depends on where you want to put it. In grass, bushes will start fruiting when they are very young and be easy to pick, but they will be difficult to mow under and will never have the heart-warming profile and character of a full-blown tree. Cordons, espaliers and fans can be used to make a decorative and productive screen in a garden.

RECOMMENDED CULTIVARS (IN ORDER OF CROPPING)
- **Dessert** 'Discovery': flushed with bright scarlet, fruits on tips and spurs. 'George Cave': crisp, well-flavoured apple, green with an orange flush. 'Ellison's Orange': clean, strongly scented fruit. 'James Grieve': prolific, shiny and handsomely striped. 'Egremont Russet': upright, closely spurred, makes a good cordon. 'Sunset': crisp fruit resistant to scab. 'Elstar': heavy crops of richly flavoured fruit. 'Ribston Pippin': prone to canker in poor soils, but superbly flavoured. 'Orleans Reinette': prolific, hardy, golden-yellow fruit.
- **For cooking** 'Early Victoria': ready by mid-summer, cooks to a pale froth. 'Reverend W. Wilks': huge fruit on a small tree, good resistance to disease. 'Bramley's Seedling': the classic cooking apple, but a vigorous tree, not suitable for training as a cordon or fan.

Cultivation

Apple cultivars are grafted on to rootstocks that largely determine the final size of the tree (see page 235). The question of the best rootstock is bound up with the style of tree that you choose. The modern trend is to graft apples on to extremely dwarfing rootstocks such as M27, so that trees can be fitted into very small gardens and will start bearing fruit after two or three years. Remember, though, that a tree grafted on to M27 will be more difficult to look after, as it needs very good soil and does not like having to share its patch with grass or other plants. MM106 is a good compromise, particularly for bushes and cordons.

SITE AND SOIL

Apples like deep, well-drained ground that does not dry out in summer. On hungry soil, dig in plenty of compost. Choose a planting site that is sunny but not exposed to wind. Apples seldom succeed in coastal situations where they may be damaged by salt-laden spray. Avoid planting at the bottom of a slope where fruit trees may be set back by late spring frosts.

PLANTING

Apples are much better bought as bare-root trees than as container-grown ones. The root system of a tree that has grown in open ground will be far better developed. This means buying and planting in early winter if the weather is kind. If you do this, the roots will be well established before they have to haul up food and drink for the blossom and new leaves in spring. Make a planting hole in which the roots can spread out comfortably and then plant the tree at the same level as it was growing in the nursery. Stake with a short stake.

POLLINATION

Apple crops will be much improved if trees are cross-pollinated. This means that you must have more than one variety in the vicinity. Any variety described as a triploid will not be a good pollinator. 'Jupiter', 'Crispin' and the cooker 'Bramley's Seedling' are all triploids. Trees must be in blossom at the same time if they are to cross-pollinate. Most good catalogues indicate which trees overlap in this respect, though late frosts can play havoc with the most carefully laid plans.

ROUTINE CARE

During the first winter or two firm the ground around young trees that may have been lifted by frost. Water well if the spring season is dry. Once the soil has warmed up in late spring, mulch thickly round the trees with compost or rotted manure. This mulch may provide all that is necessary by way of food. If the tree is not thriving, try a dressing of sulphate of ammonia using 30g/sq m (1oz/sq yd) of ground. If the fruits do not develop well, dress the ground in late winter with sulphate of potash, using 30g/sq m (1oz/sq yd). Keep a circle of ground at least 1.2 (4ft) in diameter clear of grass and weeds round the base of the trunk. Adjust ties on the stake as the stem swells. Thin fruit if necessary.

PRUNING

Specimen trees growing on their own in grass, or as orchard trees, can if necessary be left entirely unpruned. They will still blossom and bear fruit, though perhaps not as heavily as pruned trees, and the shape of the tree will be more beautiful if it is left to its own devices. Trees trained as cordons, espaliers or fans, however, need careful summer pruning if they are to retain their geometric charm. Late summer is the time to take off excess growth and in this context excess means anything that you cannot train in as part of the basic shape. It includes shoots that poke out at the front or the back of the trunk and the new growth that zooms up from the horizontal or obliquely tied in branches. Cut these back, leaving just three pairs of leaves on each shoot. If you start the job too early in summer, you will find the trees sprout again and you have to do the job a second time.

YIELD AND HARVESTING

Yield depends on the style and variety of tree. The earliest apples such as 'Discovery' and 'George Cave' should be picked as soon as the stalk parts easily from the tree and eaten immediately. They do not keep. 'Ellison's Orange' and 'James Grieve' will keep a fortnight or three weeks if stored in a cool place. 'Egremont Russet' and 'Sunset', which ripen in mid-autumn, will keep until early winter. Pick 'Elstar' and 'Ribston Pippin' in mid-autumn. They both ripen in mid- to late autumn but can be kept until the new year. 'Orleans Reinette' should be left on the tree as long as possible before picking and storing. In good conditions it will keep until early spring.

Dorset apple cake

'Like potatoes, apples respond in different ways when they are cooked. Some retain their sliced shapes. Others, like 'Bramley's Seedling', disintegrate into a soft, foamy mass. Any kind can be used in this recipe.

Serves 6

50g (2oz) butter
50g (2oz) lard or other cooking fat
225g (8oz) flour
500g (1lb) apples, peeled, cored and chopped

100g (4oz) sugar
1 egg
2 tsps baking powder
a little milk

1. Preheat the oven to 180°C/350°F/gas mark 4.
2. Rub the fats into the flour, and then add all the other ingredients and mix them together.
3. Pack the mixture into a non-stick cake tin about 20cm (8in) across and 4cm (1½in) deep and bake in the oven for 45 minutes.

PESTS AND DISEASES
Avoid disease where possible by choosing varieties that have some resistance. That means doing without 'Cox', 'Fiesta', 'Gala' and 'Spartan', which are all prone to canker. Canker also attacks apples growing in poor, badly drained ground. Scab is most likely to be a problem in mild, wet seasons. There is no control available. Avoid using the most dwarfing rootstocks, which make a tree fussier about its growing conditions.

PEARS *Pyrus communis*

The pear's natural home is in the warm countries around the Mediterranean and you need to bear this in mind when planting, for it needs more warmth and sunshine than an apple if it is to fruit well. Pears are as ornamental as they are useful but unfortunately it is harder to bring a pear to luscious perfection than it is an apple. The difficulty lies off rather than on the tree. A pear changes more radically than an apple after it has been picked. It does not ripen on the tree. Its flesh, still hard when the fruit is gathered, gradually softens in storage until it has the melting texture of butter. But the point of no return is quickly reached and it is difficult to know when you have got there. Pears are like statesmen: the outside appearance gives little indication of what is going on underneath.

RECOMMENDED CULTIVARS (IN ORDER OF READINESS)
'Jargonelle': an ancient pear with small green and brown tapering fruit, cropping freely when established. 'Marguerite Marillat': upright, small tree with scarlet autumn leaves, enormous golden fruit flushed with bright scarlet on the cheek. 'Beurre Hardy': a strong-growing tree, suitable for orchards with large, russet fruit, resistant to scab. 'Conference': reliable and self-fertile with long, pale green fruit on a tree that is susceptible to wind-damage. 'Josephine de Malines': small green fruit turning yellow when ripe, one of the best flavoured of the winter pears, though the tree is not vigorous.

Cultivation
The wild pear, *Pyrus communis*, is a deep-rooted, slow-maturing tree, able to make the best of soils that are unsuitable for other fruit. Standards and half standards will generally be grafted on to wild pear rootstock. Most other pear trees that you buy will have been grafted on to quince rootstock, which restricts the size of the tree and brings it into fruit more quickly. Quince rootstock (Quince A and the slightly less vigorous Quince C) is not as tolerant of poor soil as the wild pear. It is shallower rooting and needs good soil. If it does not get it, growth slows down, blossom does not set well and fruit

does not mature. Starved pears tend to split. Site and style of tree need to be considered hand in hand. Some of the most aristocratic dessert pears – 'Marie Louise', 'Winter Nelis', 'Glou Morceau' – will do best grown as fans or espaliers against a wall where they can develop their full flavour. Others, such as the well-known 'Conference' and magnificent 'Beurre Hardy', are not so fussy and can be grown as bushes or half standards. Fruiting will depend not only on situation but also on the amount of effort you put into arranging a decent sex life for your pear. 'Conference' can sort out its own, though it will bear more heavily if it is pollinated with help from a neighbouring pear tree. At maturity a decently grown pear tree may be 4.5–6m (15–20ft) or more high.

SITE AND SOIL

Choose a sheltered spot that does not get hit by frost. Pears generally flower two weeks earlier than apples, so the blossom is more prone to frost damage. In exposed gardens, they will need the shelter of a windbreak. Pears are tolerant of a reasonably wide range of soils, though they will struggle and sulk in shallow chalk. Light, sandy soils need bulking up with masses of muck or other humus.

PLANTING

Autumn is the best time to plant, as the trees are dormant and can settle their roots before they have to fuss about flowering. Bushes will need 3.5–4.5m (12–15ft) between them, half standards 6–7.5m (20–25ft), cordons 2–3m (7–10ft), espaliers 2.5–3m (8–10ft). Dig a hole rather larger than you think necessary and spread the roots out comfortably in it before covering them with soil mixed with compost and bonemeal. Tread the soil in round the roots and when the hole is full, water the tree generously. The scion (the joint between rootstock and stem) should be above the soil.

POLLINATION

Cultivars can be sorted into three pollinating groups, depending on the time of flowering. For the most effective cross-pollination, choose pears from the same group, although there is usually enough overlap between the flowering seasons to pair off trees from adjoining groups. 'Marguerite Marillat', for instance, flowers early and so would be a good companion for a pear such as 'Louise Bonne of Jersey', which comes into blossom at the same time. 'Conference' and 'Beurre Hardy' are equally good partners.

ROUTINE CARE

Mulch well in autumn or spring with a generous layer of farmyard manure or compost. Add 30g/sq m (1oz/sq yd) sulphate of potash. Digging around trees may damage the roots. Hoe off weeds or treat them with weedkiller. If trees are growing in grass, keep a circle at least 1.2m (4ft) wide of clear ground around them.

PRUNING

Pears need very little pruning in the early years and trees growing as standards can be left alone entirely. They are, by nature, more generous with fruiting

Pears in burgundy

For cooking, you need pears of firm texture and pleasing shape. For this purpose, use fruit with slight blemishes that may prevent them being stored successfully.

Serves 4

1kg (2lb) small pears	150ml ($1/4$ pint) water
250g (8oz) sugar	150ml ($1/4$ pint) red burgundy
ground cinnamon	

1. Peel the pears, leaving the stalks intact. Do not core them. Stand them upright, stalk end up, in a pan just large enough to hold them. Sprinkle the sugar and cinnamon over them and add the water. Simmer, covered, for 10–15 minutes.
2. Add the wine and simmer, uncovered for a further 10–15 minutes, until tender. Lift the pears carefully into a serving dish and allow to cool.
3. Bring the liquid to the boil and leave it to simmer, uncovered, for 5–7 minutes until it is reduced to a light syrup.
4. Pour the syrup over the pears and chill the whole dish. Serve with double cream.

Culinary notes

The true connoisseur of pears will eat them uncooked, dwelling, as the great fructivore Edward Bunyard did, on the texture and aroma of each different variety. 'As it is in my view the duty of an apple to be crisp and crunchable,' he wrote, 'a pear should have such a texture as leads to silent consumption.' A perfect 'Doyenné du Comice', he considered, should melt upon the palate 'with the facility of an ice'. A perfect 'Jargonelle' should have a slight musk flavour, delicately balanced.

spurs than apples. Trees growing as cordons or espaliers will need summer pruning. Cut back laterals (side branches) to three pairs of leaves, sub-laterals (the growth springing from the side branches) to one pair of leaves. Spread the work over the last six weeks of summer.

YIELD AND HARVESTING

Yield depends on the tree type and the variety of pear. Harvest pears before they are ripe, as soon as they will part from the tree. Summer pears such as 'Jargonelle' will be ready very quickly. Others such as 'Conference' need to be stored for up to a month before they can be eaten. Finish off the ripening process by bringing the pears, a few at a time, from their cool storage into a warm room.

PESTS AND DISEASES

Bullfinches can wreak havoc on the buds of pear blossom. For some reason, perhaps because the buds fit the cut of the bullfinch's beak, 'Conference', 'Williams' and 'Merton Pride' are particularly susceptible. 'Comice' and 'Beurre

Hardy' are usually left alone. Diseases are more likely to be due to poor growing conditions than anything else. Dwarfing rootstocks are demanding creatures and need clean ground, as well as regular food and water. Honey fungus is terminal but generally attacks only where a tree is old, sickly or suffering from some other major difficulty such as prolonged drought.

PLUMS/GREENGAGES & DAMSONS
Prunus domestica and P. institia

Feast or famine seems the rule with plums, the famines caused chiefly by badly timed frosts and insatiable bullfinches. The scale of the feasts will depend on the varieties you have chosen to plant. With 'Coe's Golden Drop', fifteen fruits on a tree is a cause for wonder and rejoicing. It is what is euphemistically described as a 'shy cropper', the meanest of all the plum family. But what a fruit! It has the melting sweet flavour of a perfect greengage, intensified threefold. It matures right at the end of the summer and is lemon shaped with a characteristic little bump at the stalk end. It has yellow skin and rich golden-yellow flesh. Once you have tasted it, you have an inkling what Paradise might be like.

Planted as orchard trees, or as fans against a sunny wall, the plum family are decorative in flower and fruit, though the blossom is not so heavy and eye-catching as that of an apple or pear. Choose half standards or standards for planting in grass. These will make long-lived garden features and you can mow under them without catching your hair in the branches.

RECOMMENDED CULTIVARS
- **Plums** (in order of ripening) 'Czar': heavy-cropping purple-black cooking plum. 'Early Laxton': small, golden, well-flavoured fruit on rather a weak tree. 'Ouillin's Gage': not a true gage but a dual-purpose plum, good eating when fully ripe and excellent for jam. 'Marjorie's Seedling': tall vigorous tree bearing large black cooking plums. 'Victoria': the most famous of all plums, oval, red, juicy when ripe, but useful for cooking when under-ripe. 'Jefferson': one of the best of the hardy dessert plums, oval, green and close to a greengage in flavour.
- **Greengages** 'Denniston's Superb' ('Imperial Gage'): hardy, self-fertile and reliable. 'Cambridge Gage': a vigorous tree bearing round green fruit of authentic gage flavour. 'Reine Claude de Bavais': large, reliable late gage, self-fertile and of good flavour.
- **Damsons** 'Farleigh Damson': small blue-black fruit of fine, rich flavour. 'Merryweather Damson': large, self-fertile spreading tree bearing big blue-black damsons.

Cultivation

As with apples and pears, plums are grafted on to different rootstocks which control their relative vigour. The most common is 'St Julien A'. Grown on this a 'Victoria' plum will spread at least 4.5m (15ft) after about ten years. Dwarfing rootstocks are less common with plums than with apples. Grafting is the horticultural equivalent of a piggyback: the graft borrows stronger legs than its own to do what it needs to do. But when you are planting, you need to be sure that the graft, which usually shows as a bump or a slight swelling on the trunk, is well clear of the soil. If you bury it, the top graft will try to grow its own roots and lose the benefit of the piggyback from its stronger companion.

Where there is room for only one tree it should be the self-fertile 'Victoria', which is not as fussy about its position as some other plums and crops well and regularly. In fact, it has a tendency to overcrop and, if you let it, will then want to rest the following year, like an enervated actor after a particularly stressful run of *Hamlet*.

SITE AND SOIL

Climate makes the biggest difference. Plums like hot summers, hard winters and a late, short spring. The Caucasus and the countries around the Caspian Sea are their home and they have not forgotten it. Situation is important too. The plum family needs shelter from the wind and as much protection as possible from late frosts. Late-flowering varieties such as the dual-purpose 'Ouillin's Gage' have a better chance of escaping frost than the early flowering 'Jefferson'. The most succulent fruit comes from fan-trained trees planted against south-facing walls.

Pickled damsons

All the plum family make superb conserves: pickled damsons, greengage jam, plum chutney. Add some sloe gin and you have the makings of a rich store cupboard.

Makes 10lb

4kg (8lb) damsons	1 tsp ground allspice
2kg (4lb) sugar	2cm (1in) root ginger, crushed
1.25 litre (2 pints) vinegar	2cm (1in) cinnamon stick, crushed
1 tsp cloves, crushed	Rind of half a lemon

1. Wash the damsons and take off their stalks. Dissolve the sugar in the vinegar in a preserving pan and add the crushed spices and lemon rind tied in a muslin bag. Simmer the fruit in the liquid until tender and then remove the bag of spices and drain off the liquid.
2. Pack the fruit neatly in jars. Return the liquid to the pan and boil it until it becomes slightly thick and syrupy. Pour it over the damsons and seal the jars securely.

Plums are too prolific in growth to make cordons or espaliers. Damsons, which in appearance are more like the wild plum, are generally hardier.

PLANTING

Plant in late autumn when the trees are dormant but while the ground is still warm enough to promote fresh root growth. If you are planting in grass, keep a circle at least 1.2m (4ft) in diameter clear round the base of the tree. Fans will need securing. If you buy them ready trained, they will probably already have six or eight long arms. Fix the corresponding number of bamboo canes to the wall or support so that they fan out to match the spread of the branches. Tie the branches to the canes and keep them tied in as they grow.

POLLINATION

Some plums, such as 'Victoria', are self-fertile and do not need pollinators to set a crop, but even self-fertile plums crop more liberally if they are cross-pollinated by a different variety. You have to work on setting up the right relationships. 'Jefferson' and 'Coe's Golden Drop' will not pollinate each other, nor will 'Cambridge Gage' help the common greengage. To pollinate each other, plums obviously need to be in flower at the same time and this is the most important thing to bear in mind when choosing varieties. Most good suppliers mark the season of flowering – early, mid-season or late – so that you can choose suitable companions. Flowering seasons overlap to some extent.

ROUTINE CARE

Firm down any trees that have been lifted by frost in the first winter after planting. Mulch trees heavily every year with bulky organic manure. If this is not available, dress established trees with sulphate of ammonia, using 60g/sq m (2oz/sq yd). Thin fruits if a tree overcrops, leaving no more than one fruit every 7–10cm (3–4in). The tree may shed some fruit itself, usually in early summer when the stones are beginning to harden.

PRUNING

Freestanding trees require very little pruning. Just take out dead wood and thin growth if it becomes overcrowded. Any cutting should be done in late spring or summer. This reduces the risk of spores of silver leaf getting into the system.

Fans require more attention to keep them in shape. Shoots sprouting from the main framework should be nipped out in two stages. In mid-summer, pinch back all side shoots to leave about six leaves. These will be the shoots that bear fruit in the subsequent summer. When they have fruited, cut back these side shoots by half, to about three leaves. Any shoots that are pointing directly forward or backwards into the wall should be rubbed out entirely.

YIELD AND HARVESTING

Fans are the most decorative way of growing plums and greengages, but the yields will not be so heavy. Expect about 14kg (30lb) of fruit from a ten-year-old tree. A freestanding plum of the same age should provide about 23kg (50lb) of fruit. The fruit should be left on the tree until fully ripe.

Plum chutney

Makes about 2.25kg (4¹/₂lb)
500g (1lb) apples, peeled, cored and chopped
500g (1lb) shallots, peeled and chopped
1kg (2lb) plums, quartered and stoned
500g (1lb) raisins
175g (6oz) brown sugar
1 tsp ground ginger
1 tsp allspice
¹/₄ tsp each of cayenne pepper, ground cloves, dry mustard and nutmeg
30g (1oz) salt
600ml (1 pint) vinegar

1. Put all the ingredients into a preserving pan. Bring slowly to the boil and simmer for 1–2 hours, or until the mixture has thickened and reduced.
2. Ladle the chutney into warm, sterilized jars. Cover with waxed discs while warm and secure with paper covers.

PESTS AND DISEASES
Silver leaf is the most serious problem and there is no cure. You can cut out infected branches and hope, but if more than a third of the tree is blighted, you will be lucky to see it recover.

PEACHES & NECTARINES
Prunus persica & *P.p.* var. *nectarina*

Most accounts of growing peaches and nectarines in cool climates concentrate on the disasters rather than the delights. By the time you have read through gloomy predictions of leaf curl, bacterial canker, red spider mite, scale insects, brown rot fungus, peach mildew and silver leaf, you may want to give up all ideas of growing your own and let the gardeners of California and Spain take the strain instead. Forget peach mildew: it may never happen. Remember instead Madame Recamier, siren, muse and toast of the salons of nineteenth-century Paris. When she and all those around her thought she was on her deathbed, when for days she had refused all offerings of food, however cunningly prepared, it was the smell and taste of a freshly picked peach that persuaded her that she would, after all, prefer to live.

For fresh, read FRESH. Over the years we have been bludgeoned into believing that 'fresh' can apply to any produce that has not actually been pickled or canned. But the day you pick your own fresh peach or nectarine from your own tree and carry it, pulsating with ripeness, inside for your breakfast, is the day you break faith with supermarket fruits in their cold plastic beds. These are bowdlerized wraiths compared with the real thing.

RECOMMENDED CULTIVARS
- **Nectarine** 'Lord Napier': (early) regular heavy crops of white-fleshed, aromatic fruit. 'Pineapple' (late): yellow-fleshed fruit with a distinct pineapple flavour.
- **Peach** 'Duke of York' (early): heavy crops of pale yellow juicy fruit. 'Early Rivers': (early) tender, well-flavoured flesh. 'Peregrine' (mid-season): one of the easiest for outdoor cultivation in cool areas, well flavoured and juicy. 'Rochester' (late): firm and juicy and late flowering, which is an advantage in coolish areas, but not so well flavoured as 'Peregrine', raised on a farm near Rochester, New York, in 1900.

Cultivation
Peaches and nectarines are likely to succeed out of doors only when they have a sunny spring to ensure pollination, a hot summer to ripen the fruit, a dry autumn so that new shoots can mature ready for the next year's crops and a short, cold resting season during the winter. They need just enough rain to keep them growing but not so much that they succumb endlessly to the debilitating leaf curl disease. Under glass, suitable conditions are, of course, easier to arrange.

SITE AND SOIL
Only in countries with a Californian climate will peaches and nectarines succeed as freestanding trees. Elsewhere, grow them as fans with the protection of a sunny, south-facing wall. In cold areas they must be planted under glass. There are advantages in both methods. Outside, trees do not suffer so severely from red spider mite or scale insects. Inside, they are more unlikely to get leaf curl.

PLANTING
This is best done in late autumn so that the tree can get its roots settled before it has to think about its upper storey. Plant trees outside about 30cm (12in) away from a protecting wall, slanting the trunk back towards the wall. This will put the tree's roots in a better position to find moisture and will also enable you to mulch right round the trunk each spring. In a greenhouse, peaches and nectarines can be grown in big pots, but they do much better if they are set in a narrow border against a wall, if there is one.

POLLINATION
Both peaches and nectarines are self-fertile, so you do not have to plant different varieties to ensure pollination. Where cultivars flower very early, there may be no insects on the wing to pollinate for you, in which case

---

Poached peaches in raspberry sauce

Only in glut seasons will you want to cook a peach or nectarine or do anything other than sink your teeth straight into its luscious melting flesh. This recipe combines peaches with a piquant raspberry sauce.

Serves 4

4 ripe peaches
125g (4oz) caster sugar
150ml (1/4 pint) water

250g (8oz) raspberries
2–3 tbs peach syrup (see below)

1. Skin the peaches by immersing them in boiling water for 1 minute. Drain, carefully peel off the skin and cut the fruit in half.
2. Combine the sugar and water in a saucepan over a low heat and stir continuously until the sugar has dissolved. Bring the syrup to the boil, add the peaches, and then simmer gently for about 5 minutes until the peaches are tender.
3. Spoon out the peaches into a serving dish and boil the syrup until it is reduced by half.
4. Purée the raspberries by rubbing them through a sieve with a wooden spoon, gradually adding the peach syrup to ease the process. You should be left with a fairly thin sauce. Spoon this over the peach halves and chill before serving.

---

you must do it yourself. Flick a camel-hair brush (or rabbit's tail or powder puff) from one flower to the next, shifting pollen from one set of stamens to another. You will have to do this several times as new batches of flowers open up. Unless doors are left open, trees grown under glass will always have to be hand-pollinated. Traditionally this job was done at noon and the peach house floor damped down immediately afterwards to help the fruit set.

ROUTINE CARE

Mulch around trees growing outside each spring with a thick layer of well-rotted manure. Refresh the soil around glasshouse peaches and nectarines in late winter, scooping off the top layer and replacing it with good garden soil mixed with 1kg (2lb) of bonemeal and 500g (1lb) of sulphate of potash. When the fruits are no more than the size of hazelnuts, start to thin them out, so that they are eventually spaced about 23cm (9in) apart on the branches.

PRUNING

Fruit of peaches and nectarines is borne on the shoots produced in the previous season. Make life easy for yourself by buying a tree ready trained as a fan. Rub out unwanted shoots (including those pointing either forward or back) in spring, leaving three growth buds on each lateral branch. In early summer prune back each of these three shoots to six leaves. When you have picked the fruit, cut out the growth that bore it and tie in a replacement shoot.

YIELD AND HARVESTING
Expect about 9kg (20lb) of peaches or nectarines from a mature trained fan. Freestanding trees, where they can be grown, will give much heavier crops. The fruit is ready to pick when the flesh round the stalk feels soft. Twist the fruit gently to detach it from the tree.

PESTS AND DISEASES
Pests are most troublesome where peaches and nectarines are grown under glass. Damping down regularly will deter red spider. Peach leaf curl is the most likely problem to affect trees growing outside. You can sometimes check it by spraying with a copper-based fungicide at leaf fall and again in early spring just after the tree has started into growth. Once the disease has struck, you can curb it by spraying at fortnightly intervals. As the fungal spores that cause leaf curl are carried by rain, the most effective method of combating leaf curl is to cover trees growing outside with a polythene shelter from mid-winter until mid-spring. Roll up the polythene in good weather at blossom time to allow pollinating insects to get at the flowers.

APRICOTS *Prunus armeniaca*

The perfect apricot is not easy to find. Too often you sink your teeth into the fruit to find nothing better than a mouthful of cotton wool. When they are good, they are very, very good but, like peaches, in cool climates they need the help of a warm wall if they are to ripen to perfection. Although they are not subject to leaf curl, apricot trees have a distressing habit of suddenly dying back. The strongest branches are usually the first to go. This problem has been known ever since apricots were first introduced into England in the reign of Henry VIII. The knowledgeable gardeners of Edwardian times suggested that apricots should be root pruned, to curb the speed at which new branches grow. 'Thrifty' growth, they felt, resulted in a sturdier tree. The famous old variety 'Moor Park', brought back to England in 1760 by Lord Anson, who named it after his Hertfordshire home, is more susceptible to this problem than modern cultivars.

RECOMMENDED CULTIVARS
'New Large Early' (early): larger and earlier than 'Moor Park' with better resistance to dieback; not exactly new since it has been grown since the 1870s. 'Tomcot' (early): a newish cultivar coming from a French breeding programme – big, orange fruits flushed with crimson. 'Flavorcot' ('Bayoto'): a late variety bearing juicy orange-red fruit. 'Moor Park' (late): a popular variety with superb flavour but prone to dieback.

Cultivation

The apricot, which was spread by silk merchants westward from China into Armenia, needs cold winters and early springs to perform well. Then it must have a long warm summer to ripen the fruit. It copes, just, with an English summer, but is more reliable outdoors in warmer climates.

SITE AND SOIL

Choose a sunny, warm wall against which to train a fan-shaped tree. The soil needs to be well drained, but not too well fed.

PLANTING

Plant in late autumn. The most popular rootstocks are St Julien A and Torinel, on which a full-grown fan is likely to spread 3.5m (12ft). If you are planting more than one tree, allow 4.5m (15ft) between them. Set the tree about 30cm (12in) away from the wall with the stem leaning back towards it. Secure the branches of the fan to bamboo canes or to wires stretched between vine eyes.

POLLINATION

Apricots are self-fertile, but blossom very early, often in late winter. Protect trees outside from frost with fine-meshed net. If no insects are about, hand-pollinate the flowers with a fine camel-hair brush.

ROUTINE CARE

Water copiously in dry summers to help the fruit swell. Keep the soil around

---

Quick apricot tarts

In cool climates, a gardener will be lucky ever to get a glut of home-grown apricots, but if there should ever be a few spare, try these quick apricot tarts.

Serves 6
a pack of puff pastry, either in a block or ready rolled
12 halved apricots (less or more depending on the number of tarts you want to make)
a little sugar

1. Make sure the oven is really hot (230°C/450°F/gas mark 8). Roll out the pastry until it is no thicker than a pound coin. Cut out circles for the tarts (a saucer makes a suitable template) and then, using a slightly smaller saucer, score the pastry round, leaving a rim round the edge of the circle.
2. Poach the apricots very gently in water and a little sugar until they are soft but not sloppy.
3. Put the pastry circles on a baking tray and prick the centre of each one with a fork. Cover each one with apricot halves – cut side down, leaving the pastry rim clear. This will rise separately and hold in the fruit. Bake for 10–15 minutes until the pastry is crisp.

---

the tree free of weeds but do not disturb the roots by cultivating deeply. Thin the fruit at intervals during mid- and late spring, so that they are spaced roughly every 10cm (4in) along the branches.

PRUNING
Aim to build up a series of fruiting spurs about 15cm (6in) apart all the way along the branches of the fan. Do this by pinching back the lateral growths in early summer, leaving about 7cm (3in) of each growth in place. Any growths springing from these laterals should be pinched back, leaving just one leaf. Keep tying in the new growth on the ends of the main branches of the tree to maintain the fan shape. Because fruit is borne on stems formed the previous season, on mature, freestanding trees cut back a proportion of old wood in early spring to encourage new growth each year.

YIELD AND HARVESTING
Expect about 9kg (20lb) of fruit from a well-grown fan, twice as much from a freestanding tree. Pick the fruit carefully – they bruise easily – when the stem parts easily from the branch. They will keep two weeks or more if stored in a cool place.

PESTS AND DISEASES
Dieback is the biggest problem and there is no cure. Choose resistant cultivars and do not feed trees too liberally. Rust may be a problem in late summer, showing as powdery orange pustules on the leaves. Spray with a fungicide if the attack is severe.

CHERRIES *Prunus avium* & *P. cerasus*

A cherry left to its own devices will quickly make a tall, wide-spreading tree, and is best in an orchard, where it can spread its wings up to 9m (27ft) or more. Allow grass and wildflowers to grow uncut underneath it for the kind of scene that drove the French Impressionists to their paintboxes. Cherries are extremely decorative when covered with blossom, and often perform well again in autumn, when the foliage may turn fiery shades of red and orange. Sweet cherries can be trained as decorative fans on a wall, but the wall will need to be big and you will have to fight to keep the cherry under control. The best cherry for a wall, particularly a north wall, is the acid-flavoured 'Morello' cherry, black fleshed and excellent for pies and tarts. You can also drown cherries in brandy. Fished out several months later, they make suitably drunken toppings for home-made ice cream.

RECOMMENDED CULTIVARS
• **Sweet cherries** 'Early Rivers': very early, juicy, shiny, black-fleshed fruit, grown since 1869. 'Merton Glory': early, sweet white-fleshed fruit, bred in

the 1930s. 'Celeste': large, dark red fruit and, grafted on Tabel rootstock, a compact tree suitable for a tub on a terrace. 'Lapins': a Canadian mid-season variety with big, black fruit on an upright tree. 'Bigarreau Napoleon': mid-season with firm, sweet white flesh. 'Sunburst': a mid- to late-season cherry on a spreading, self-fertile tree. 'Stella': a self-fertile sweet cherry with large, juicy, dark red fruit. 'Summer Sun': compact, self-fertile tree with dark red fruit, late maturing. 'Sweetheart': a very late Canadian variety with well-flavoured fruit.

- **Acid cherries** 'Morello': self-fertile, making a spreading tree wider than it is high, bearing dark red fruit.

Cultivation

Many cherries need to be cross-pollinated if they are to bear fruit. If there is not enough room for two cherry trees in your garden, plant 'Lapins', 'Stella', 'Summer Sun' or 'Sunburst', all of which are self-fertile. So is the acid cherry 'Morello'.

SITE AND SOIL

Cherries fruit best in places where the climate is dry and reasonably warm. It is not worth planting them in areas where late frosts may ruin the blossom. The soil should be rich but well drained.

PLANTING

Plant in late autumn, setting half standard or standard orchard trees 12m (40ft) apart and fan-trained trees 6m (20ft) apart.

POLLINATION

The self-fertile acid 'Morello' cherry will pollinate sweet cherries such as

---

Clafoutis with cherries

Serves 6

butter, for greasing	a little salt
50g (2oz) flour	250ml (1/2 pint) milk
3 eggs	450g (1lb) sweet cherries
100g (4oz) sugar	a little icing sugar
1 tbsp vanilla extract	

1. Butter an ovenproof dish and shake a dusting of flour around in it.
2. Whisk the eggs and add the sugar, vanilla extract and a pinch of salt. Sift in the flour and mix in the milk. Leave the batter to stand for an hour if you can.
3. Pour about half the batter into the floured dish, add the cherries (stone them if possible) and then cover with the rest of the batter.
4. Bake for about 40 minutes at 190°C/375°F/gas mark 5. Serve warm, with icing sugar sprinkled on it and with some good Jersey cream alongside.

'Bigarreau Napoleon' that flower at the same time. 'Stella' and 'Merton Glory' will both pollinate 'Early Rivers'. 'Stella' and 'Sunburst' will pollinate 'Merton Glory'.

ROUTINE CARE

Mulch sweet cherries with well-rotted manure in spring and fix bird scarers if bullfinches or other birds attack the flower buds. Keep fan-trained trees well watered during summer.

PRUNING

Sweet cherries growing as standards or half standards in an orchard do not need pruning. Simply cut out any dead wood and remove crossing branches. 'Morello' cherries fruit only on new wood, so you must prune to force the tree to produce plenty of the necessary new growth. When a wall-trained tree has fruited, cut out the long growths at its extremities so that it will make new shoots in the centre. Without this 'sides to middle' treatment, you will find the tree bears only at the tips of its branches. Tie in as many new shoots as you can fit in among the framework of the main branches.

YIELD AND HARVESTING

A fully mature freestanding cherry may provide 32kg (70lb) of fruit, while a fan-trained 'Morello' will yield about 9kg (20lb). Sweet cherries are ready to pick by mid summer, 'Morello' cherries are usually later. Both kinds freeze well.

PESTS AND DISEASES

Bacterial canker is the most troublesome disease and is most likely to occur when trees are growing too fast as a result of overfeeding. Spores enter the tree through wounds or cuts, so avoid damaging the bark and prune as late as possible in the summer. Blackfly cluster as thick as soot around new shoots in spring, distorting growth. Cut off the worst affected shoots and burn them.

CITRUS FRUIT *Citrus* spp.

Citrus trees, growing in fancy terracotta pots or big square wooden boxes with elaborate finials at the corners, can be used like statues to decorate a garden, however small. Standing in a row along a terrace, used as a centrepiece for a potager or set like guardsmen at the side of a series of steps leading from one level of the garden to another, they look grand and faintly unreal. The leaves are glossily evergreen and the fruit hangs on the branches like decorations on a Christmas tree. They are not hardy and wherever frost strikes they will need to be brought inside a conservatory for the winter. But here too they are immensely decorative and the flowers, which begin to open in late spring, will scent the air for weeks. The fruit takes a whole year to develop, so while the present season's flowers are opening, curling back their fleshy petals to reveal prominent stamens, the previous season's fruit is maturing on the tree.

Caramelized oranges

Many recipes involving citrus fruit include the peel in some way, for the zest of the skin gives an extra sharp kick to the taste of the dish. This simple orange salad is enhanced both in taste and appearance by a sprinkling of finely cut strips of caramelized peel.

Serves 6
6 large oranges
300ml (¹/₂ pint) of water
125g (4oz) sugar

1. Peel the skin of one orange as thinly as you can, leaving the pith behind. Cut the skin into very fine strips, each about 2cm (1in) long.
2. Put the peel in a small pan with the sugar and water. Bring to the boil and simmer gently for about half an hour until the liquid is reduced.
3. Peel all the oranges and cut them thinly into rounds, taking out any pips. Arrange the slices in a dish and pour the syrup with the strips of slightly caramelized peel over them. Chill before serving.

Culinary notes
* The arrival of bitter Seville oranges in the new year is the signal in Britain for a brief orgy of marmalade-making, for no other citrus gives a marmalade of such sharp, tangy quality. You can experiment, though, with mixes of other citrus fruit to make marmalades that, if not so sharp, are no less good to eat. Lime marmalade, wonderful to eat, is unfortunately the most difficult to make, as the skins are exceptionally tough and difficult to cut. Easier to prepare is a grapefruit marmalade. With each 1kg (2lb) of grapefruit, include 300g (10oz) of lemons, to provide the necessary pectin to set the conserve. A three-fruit marmalade using two grapefruit, four lemons and two sweet oranges also makes a very good breakfast treat.

RECOMMENDED CULTIVARS
- **Lime** *Citrus aurantifolia* 'Tahiti': compact and prolific, producing large, sweet seedless fruit.
- **Seville orange** *Citrus aurantium* 'Seville': bitter fruit on spiny tree with slender pointed leaves.
- **Lemon** *Citrus limon* 'Garey's Eureka': open, spreading habit, excellent juicy fruit.
- **Lemon/mandarin cross** *Citrus × meyeri* 'Meyer': small, bushy, slow growing, ideal in containers.
- **Calamondin** *Citrus mitis*: one of the best citrus trees for pots as it flowers and fruits while still small (also known as x *Citrofortunella microcarpa*).
- **Grapefruit** *Citrus × paradisi* 'Star Ruby': well branched but not too vigorous tree with glossy, ovate leaves.

- **Mandarin** *Citrus reticulata* 'Clementine': vigorous, large bushy tree with rounded fruit.
- **Sweet orange** *Citrus sinensis* 'Navelina': distinctive navel orange first introduced to the US in 1870, *C. sinensis* 'Washington': a navel type producing an early crop.
- **Kumquat** *Fortunella japonica* 'Nagami': makes an ornamental dwarf tree bearing oblong fruit.

Cultivation

Citrus are now synonymous with Florida, California, Israel and Spain but the fruit originated in China, where the ultra-refined Chinese did not eat it but held it in their hands to savour the aroma released by the gradually warming peel. Growing in containers will be the only option for many gardeners who do not share the balmy climate of the Mediterranean or the west coast of America. Fortunately, citrus trees – particularly the calamondin, kumquat and Meyer's lemon – adapt well to this form of culture.

SITE AND SOIL

All citrus need to be kept frost free during the winter, and fruiting is more likely to occur if the plants can be maintained at about 10°C/50°F during the winter season. Use an ericaceous compost (pH 6–6.5, slightly lower for lemons) and make sure that the container has adequate drainage. Coarse grit mixed with the compost will help in this respect.

PLANTING

Trees may start their lives in small containers but must be potted on where necessary into larger tubs. Winter is the best time to carry out this job. When the trees are in their final homes, scrape off the top 5cm (2in) of compost in mid-spring each year and replace with fresh ericaceous compost.

POLLINATION

Citrus trees are parthenocarpic – they set fruit even when the flowers do not contain viable pollen. So you do not need more than one to get a crop.

ROUTINE CARE

Watering and feeding are of prime importance in maintaining healthy container-grown plants. Feeding should continue throughout the year with a different solution used in summer and winter. In summer the trees need a high-nitrogen formula to maintain growth. Winter feed should contain the trace elements, particularly iron, magnesium, manganese and zinc, that are essential for healthy growth. Without these trace elements trees will have dull, yellowish foliage, growth will be stunted and fruit liable to drop in winter. Never allow the compost to dry out.

PRUNING

Citrus trees do not need regular pruning. Trim new growth in early spring if necessary to keep the plants balanced and shapely.

YIELD AND HARVESTING

Yield depends on the size and maturity of the tree. Expect twenty or thirty fruit from a well-grown specimen. Fruit can be harvested from late autumn through until early spring.

PESTS AND DISEASES

Like other conservatory plants, citrus trees may suffer from red spider mite, aphids, scale and mealy bug, especially when they are growing under cover. Sooty mould is then likely to develop on the sticky excretions produced by the aphids. You can wash over the trees regularly with slightly soapy water. Wipe away mealy bug and scale insects with cotton wool soaked in methylated spirit.

FIGS & MULBERRIES *Ficus carica & Morus nigra*

These trees are both great survivors, hanging on in old gardens long after the lawns and walls on which they were displayed have disappeared. Both give an air of distinction to a garden, for they are fruits with an ancient lineage, and make splendid specimen trees, though they will need protection from cold winds and are unlikely to succeed in the open in very cold areas. Figs can be grown very successfully in cool greenhouses, or splayed out as fans on a warm wall, but the mulberry, which makes a big, bushy round-headed tree, needs an expanse of lawn to set it off properly. Although both lose their leaves in winter, the trees, starkly stripped, still contribute to the garden scene. They have the attribute of all true aristocrats: good bones.

RECOMMENDED CULTIVARS

- **Fig** 'Brown Turkey': the hardiest type, producing chocolate-coloured fruit with deep red flesh. 'Brunswick': large fruit with red flesh and yellow-green skin. 'White Marseilles' ('White Genoa'): pale green fruit with opalescent flesh.
- **Mulberry** *Morus nigra* (black mulberry): slow growing at first, but at ten years old a fine tree bearing a useful crop of fruit. 'Chelsea': earlier into fruit than the equally good 'Wellington'.

Cultivation

Where space is limited, a fig can be grown in a large pot to stand in a sheltered corner, but a mulberry needs space. It will gradually develop into a tree at least 6m (20ft) high and 4.5m (15ft) wide. You sometimes see veteran trees leaning on their elbows in a relaxed way, which makes them spread even further. They grow old very gracefully.

SITE AND SOIL

Figs are forgiving trees, as you might guess from the fact that they grow so successfully trained on the façade of the National Gallery in London's

---

Fig tart

Serves 6

70g (3oz) butter	2 dessertspoons caster sugar
pinch of salt	1 tbsp sweet white wine
150g (6oz) plain flour	40g (2oz) toasted flaked almonds
4 eggs	7 fresh figs
275ml double cream (or crème fraiche)	

1. Make the pastry by rubbing the butter into the salt and flour until the mixture is like breadcrumbs. Beat up one of the eggs with a little iced water and use as much as you need of this to turn the pastry into a firm dough. If you have time, allow the pastry to rest in the fridge for an hour.
2. Roll out the pastry and line a tart tin (22cm/8in diameter) with it. Prick the bottom with a fork and cover the base with some beans to stop it rising. Bake the pastry case in a medium oven (180°C/350°F/gas mark 4) for 20–25 minutes. Remove the beans.
3. Mix the cream with the caster sugar, the wine and the remaining three eggs (beaten). Scatter the toasted almonds on the bottom of the tart.
4. Quarter the figs and set them on top of the almonds. Pour the cream mixture over the top. Cook for 15 minutes or so until the tart is just beginning to brown.

Trafalgar Square, where they are drenched by the fumes of a thousand buses. There, they were planted for their architectural foliage. If you want them to fruit, they must have sun and shelter, which may mean a south-facing wall or a cool greenhouse. A mulberry needs deep, well-drained rich soil that does not dry out in summer.

PLANTING

Both figs and mulberries are best planted in spring. Figs, which are inclined to make too much growth in the kind of climate prevailing in the southern part of the UK, fruit more freely if the roots are restricted. Dig a hole about 1m (3ft) deep and wide and line it with brick or concrete slabs. Plant the fig inside this box, mixing plenty of bonemeal with the earth that you replace.

ROUTINE CARE

Mulch trees thickly in late spring with well-rotted manure. Water mulberries if necessary in summer. Water figs in dry weather while the fruits are swelling, but do not overwater while they are ripening or they may split.

PRUNING

Mulberries bleed badly if cut, so should not be pruned on a regular basis. On mature trees it may be necessary in winter to cut out dead wood or branches that cross over each other. Remove frost-damaged shoots and overcrowded young growth from fig trees in mid-spring and tie in growth on fan-trained specimens. If necessary, you can thin out branches again in mid-summer. By taking out one of the oldest branches each year, you can persuade the tree to throw up more productive young growth from the base of the fan.

YIELD AND HARVEST
Yields depend on winter weather and the age of the tree. Figs are usually ready to pick by late summer or early autumn. Wait until the fruit droops on its stem, with the skin just beginning to split and a drop of nectar hanging from the eye. The easiest way to gather mulberries is to spread sheets out under the tree and shake the branches.

PESTS AND DISEASES
Neither tree is usually troubled by pests but grey mould may attack the young shoots of fig, causing them to die back. You can see the brownish-grey pustules on the dead wood. The same mould may attack fruit, causing it to rot.

MEDLARS & QUINCES
Mespilus germanica & Cydonia oblonga

Both medlars and quinces are as attractive in bloom as any purely ornamental tree and by planting one or the other you have the added advantage of an autumn crop. Both fruits make excellent jellies. The quince was a popular fruit before the upstart apple ever appeared in south-eastern Europe and it is still a favourite in Turkey, though elsewhere it is no longer widely grown as a commercial crop. Like figs and mulberries, quinces and medlars bring an air of ancient peace to a garden. The medlar, with its angular branches makes a tree rather wider than it is high, casting a dense shade. Where soil and weather conditions suit it, the leaves flame into an orange-yellow and red blaze before dropping in late autumn. Quince trees turn clear butter yellow.

RECOMMENDED CULTIVARS
- **Medlar** 'Dutch': very large fruit on a small weeping tree. 'Nottingham': prolific, often bearing fruit when only three years old.
- **Quince** 'Champion': large apple-shaped fruit. 'Lusitanica': vigorous but slow to crop, bearing big oblong fruit with exceptionally woolly skins. 'Meech's Prolific': slow growing but often bearing its pear-shaped fruit when only three years old. 'Vranja': large pear-shaped fruit.

Cultivation
Quinces usually make round-headed trees not more than 3.5m (12ft) tall, but where they are suited they can reach 6m (20ft). Allow them room for expansion. All cultivars are self-fertile and should start to crop by the time they are six years old. 'Meech's Prolific' is more precocious. The medlar is an anciently

cultivated tree, with fruit that looks lilke large, bronze rosehips. Watch for suckers on medlars, which are often grafted on to hawthorn rootstock.

SITE AND SOIL

Quinces like warmth, and a deep rich soil which is not too limey. They love moisture and you sometimes see old specimens planted by the side of ponds. A damp corner of the garden will suit it just as well. Medlars are hardier than quinces and will succeed in any ordinary well-drained garden soil.

PLANTING

Plant any time after leaf fall, digging a hole large enough to accommodate the roots easily, and stake the trees to provide support for their first year. Keep the ground round the trunks clear of grass or weeds.

ROUTINE CARE

Mulch around the trees in spring with well-rotted manure.

PRUNING

Thin out crowded branches of quince if necessary during winter. Treat medlars in the same way, removing branches that are weak or crossing over each other.

YIELD AND HARVESTING

Expect about 23kg (50lb) of quinces and perhaps 14kg (30lb) of medlars from a mature half-standard tree. Pick quinces in mid-autumn before the first frost. Store them in trays in a cool dark place where they will keep for up to a month. Keep them as far away as possible from other fruit, which will otherwise pick up the quince's strong aroma. Medlars are still very hard when you gather them from the tree in late autumn. In Tudor times the fruits were stored in damp bran or sawdust until they were 'bletted' – that is until the flesh had become soft, brown and faintly alcoholic. Then the pulp was sucked straight from the skin, like wine from a winebag.

PESTS AND DISEASES

Leaf spot is sometimes a problem on quinces. Spray with a fungicide as the leaf buds burst and again after the fruit has set. The medlar is usually free of any troubles.

NUTS

The most useful nuts for the gardener are cobnuts and filberts, both types of hazel. The trees are extremely decorative in winter, hung with long, soft catkins. Where squirrels allow, they produce heavy crops of nuts in the autumn. Left to themselves they make multi-stemmed thickets, which you can plunder for pea sticks, bean poles and twiggy stems to weave into decorative supportive lattices for your French beans. You can use them as part of an informal boundary hedge, or plant them as an understorey beneath taller trees such as oaks or beeches, the way they often grow in the wild.

Other nuts, such as walnut and almond, are better used as specimen trees. Almonds are breathtaking in spring, iced all over with pink blossom. Walnuts are grander, more restrained – and slow. You may have to wait twenty years for a crop, but you will meanwhile have the pleasure of anticipation. A fresh walnut, soft and creamy, bears no relation to the dry, slightly rancid, shop-bought nuts that masquerade under the name around Christmas.

RECOMMENDED CULTIVARS
- **Cobnut** (*Corylus avellana*) 'Cosford Cob': vigorous upright growth producing large, thin-shelled nuts. 'Pearson's Prolific': compact habit with abundant crops of small nuts.
- **Filbert** (*Corylus maxima*) 'Kentish Cob': prolific bearer of well-flavoured nuts. 'Purpurea': extremely decorative tree with purple foliage and dark catkins producing well-flavoured though small nuts.
- **Walnut** (*Juglans regia*) 'Broadview': a self-fertile type. 'Buccaneer': a self-fertile type.
- **Almond** (*Prunus dulcis*) 'Mandaline': self-fertile, bearing nuts of excellent quality. 'Ardechoise': a hardy French variety.

Cultivation
Country of origin is the best guide as to what these different nuts need in order to bear good crops. Cobnuts and filberts (hazelnuts) do well in the moist temperate climate of the UK but do not like summer heat. The cobnut is a rounded nut only partly covered by its husk. A filbert is longer and enclosed completely by the husk. Walnuts are also better in generally cool climates, but almonds, natives of North Africa, fruit most successfully in Mediterranean areas.

SITE AND SOIL
Because a walnut is so long lived you need to think very carefully about its planting position. It may inhabit it for 200 years, spreading eventually to make a tree 30m (100ft) high and at least 15m (50ft) wide. Hazels will

grow in full sun or partial shade, doing best in deep, damp limestone soils. Almonds are not as fussy about soil as they are about climate.

PLANTING

Mid-autumn is the best time to plant, so that roots can establish themselves while the soil is still reasonably warm. Spread the roots out well when planting so that they will eventually provide a well-balanced anchorage for the trees above. Choose only young walnut trees for planting, as they resent being moved when they are older.

POLLINATION

Hazels are wind pollinated, with male and female flowers borne on the same bushes, but for the best crops, plant several different kinds together. New cultivars of walnut are self-fertile. Almonds are not and cross-pollinating varieties must be planted to produce a crop.

ROUTINE CARE

Mulch thickly round trees to conserve moisture and keep down weeds. Water young trees in summer until they are properly established.

PRUNING

When hazels are well established (after 4–5 years) start to cut out some of the oldest stems at ground level to encourage the production of new shoots. Walnuts bleed horribly when cut and fortunately require no regular pruning. Occasionally it may be necessary to remove a crossing branch. Do this in mid-April or late summer. Do not let the tree develop a forked trunk. Almonds need no regular pruning, though you should cut out dead wood where it occurs.

YIELD AND HARVESTING

Yield varies enormously according to age and climatic conditions. Expect about 11kg (25lb) of nuts from a hazel, 9kg (20lb) from an established almond and 23kg (50lb) from a full-grown walnut. Hazelnuts fall to the ground when they are ripe, but almonds can be harvested from the tree when the shells split. Husks still cling round the shell of walnuts when they are ready to harvest in autumn and must be removed before you store the nuts. Use gloves. The juice stains skin a startling dark brown.

PESTS AND DISEASES

Squirrels are the chief pests, for they have an insatiable appetite for nuts and bury more in autumn than they can ever rediscover. Compared with their depredations, no other pest can be considered a problem. Honey fungus will usually attack only those trees that are already weakened by drought, starvation or old age. Frost may cause young shoots of walnut to die back.

Afghan compote

Nuts, which store beautifully in their shells, were once a highly valued winter food and are still associated with winter dishes. Ground almonds make traditional marchpane for a Christmas cake. Chestnuts combined with Brussels sprouts are served with the turkey. This compote of dried fruit and nuts is popular in Muslim countries. It is traditionally made with seven fruits and seven passages from the Koran are read out before it is eaten.

Serves 4–6

100g (4oz) small dried apricots
100g (4oz) dark seedless raisins
50g (2oz) sultanas
50g (2oz) pistachios (unsalted)

50g (2oz) almonds
50g (2oz) walnuts
6 cherries (fresh or preserved)

1. Wash the dried fruit, put it in a serving bowl and cover it with cold water. Set the bowl of fruit aside for a couple of days.
2. Put the pistachio nuts and almonds in a bowl and cover them with boiling water. Slip the skins off the nuts.
3. Add the walnuts with the skinned almonds and pistachio nuts to the soaked fruit in the bowl. Decorate with cherries. Put the bowl in the refrigerator for a day or two before serving with cream.

Culinary notes

Ground hazelnuts can be used very successfully to thicken soups and combine particularly well with delicately flavoured vegetables such as cauliflower or celery.

SOFT FRUIT & VINES

The most spectacular vines are not those with the best grapes, so you will have to decide which is more important: appearance or taste. All vines, though, have handsome foliage, which can be used to good effect on arbours and trellises, pergolas and porches. *Vitis vinifera* 'Purpurea' provides a fine contrast for a scrambler such as *Clematis flammula*, or you could combine its purple leaves with pale blue clematis and deep red climbing roses. Soft fruits such as redcurrants and gooseberries are no less decorative when carefully trained. Grow gooseberries as mop-headed standards to mark the corners of a herb garden. Train redcurrants on wires as U-shaped cordons to make an unusual airy screen. Large-fruited strawberries need fresh ground every few years. Remember that birds will be waiting for the fruit even more eagerly than you. Protect plants with nets or cloches.

Old-fashioned hand-lights, each one a miniature crystal palace, are decorative as well as practical. Plain glass cloches, jam jars or fine-meshed netting will do the same job less prettily. Alpine strawberries can wander at will over a semi-shaded bank in the garden. These alpine kinds are pretty enough to grow as ground cover, with woodruff and hostas. They will succeed in any moist, rich soil.

Autumn-fruiting raspberries such as 'Autumn Bliss' are not attacked by birds in the way that summer fruiting ones are. This is a great advantage, as it saves the trouble of netting the crop. Use them to make a hedge-like screen between one part of the garden and another. Blueberries will only be happy in acid soil, where they can be used to good effect as ground cover under other lime-hating plants such as rhododendron and azalea. The late summer crop of berries is followed by a brilliant blaze of orange from the leaves before they fall.

In warm climates, melons can be trained over an arbour. Elsewhere, they will need the protection of a greenhouse or cold frame, where ripening fruit can be protected by straw or an underlying sheet of black plastic. Musk melons are generally smaller than cantaloupes. A greenhouse also gives extra protection to dessert grapes. Traditionally, the vine would be planted outside, with the rods or stems trained up inside against the ribs of the roof. The handsome foliage makes a dappled pattern against the light and provides useful natural shading for crops growing underneath. For the best grapes, fruit must be thinned as it develops.

RASPBERRIES *Rubus idaeus*

Though not particularly ornamental in themselves, raspberries, trained tidily on wires, make useful summer screens in a garden or can be used to divide a fruit

Summer pudding

Summer pudding is one of the great classic dishes of summer and can be made with any mixture of summer berries. It should always contain a good proportion of raspberries.

Serves 4–6
butter, for greasing
6 slices proper white bread (stale is better than fresh)
1kg (2lb) mixed summer fruit (such as raspberries, strawberries, redcurrants, blackcurrants)
250g (8oz) sugar
double cream, to serve

1. Butter the inside of a 1.25 litre (2 pint) pudding basin. Cut the crusts off the bread and use the slices to line the bottom and sides of the basin.
2. Heat the prepared fruit gently with the sugar in a saucepan until the fruit is just soft. Do not overcook it. Pour the fruit mixture into the lined basin without dislodging the bread. The fruit should be close to the top of the basin, but not up to the rim.
3. Use the rest of the bread to make a lid on top of the fruit. Put a saucer on top of the basin, weight it down and leave it in the refrigerator overnight.
4. Turn the pudding out onto a plate and serve with plenty of thick double cream.

Culinary notes
* To make a delicious, sharp sauce, press fresh raspberries through a fine-meshed sieve. For a striking as well as healthy dessert, serve as an accompaniment to peaches, which are conveniently in season at the same time of year.

patch into different areas. Plant them from corner to corner in a square plot to make four triangular spaces for gooseberry bushes, currants and strawberries. This is a potentially more decorative way of using them than planting them in parallel rows, the more traditional way. Autumn-fruiting raspberries grow much more densely than summer-fruiting ones and make great thickets of canes. Apart from providing a delicious crop at an unexpected time of year, autumn raspberries have the added advantage of not attracting birds for a free meal. Do not plant other fruit too close to the rows for it is likely to be overwhelmed.

RECOMMENDED CULTIVARS
• **Summer fruiting** 'Glen Ample': large crops of delicious fruit. 'Glen Moy': a thornless cane bearing large firm fruit early in the season. 'Glen Prosen': thornless but needs good soil. 'Leo': useful late-cropping raspberry, but sparse in growth. 'Malling Admiral': vigorous and resistant to botrytis and some viruses.

• **Autumn fruiting** 'All Gold': sweet golden-yellow fruit. 'Autumn Bliss': high yielding, bright red fruit with firm texture. 'Polka': generally a couple of weeks earlier than 'Autumn Bliss'.

Cultivation

Think of Scotland before you plant raspberries. They like moisture and an acid soil. They also need support. You can fence them in between two sets of parallel wires, or tie them in separately in a single row on wires stretched between 1.8m (6ft) poles.

SITE AND SOIL

Raspberries like a deeply dug, light, moist soil and are often disappointing in heavy soils which may bake and crack in summer. This disturbs the fine surface roots that feed the canes. They grow best in slightly acid soils (pH6.5–6.7) and will succeed in light shade.

PLANTING

Plant canes in late November, setting them so that the fibrous mat of roots is no more than 7cm (3in) below the surface of the soil. They will not grow if they are planted too deeply. Set the canes 38–60cm (15–24in) apart, the more vigorous varieties at the wider spacing. If you are planting more than one row, allow at least 1.2–1.8m (4–6ft) between the rows. Cut down the canes to about 23cm (9in) after planting, to encourage new growth from the base. The most even growth comes in rows that run from north to south.

ROUTINE CARE

Mulch the rows in early spring with manure, compost or any other mulch that does not contain lime. Keep the ground weed free, but do not dig deeply around the raspberries, as this will disturb their shallow roots. Water well if necessary during the summer.

PRUNING

After summer cultivars have fruited, cut out the old canes close to the ground and thin out the new canes, leaving no more than five or six strong stems growing from each original plant. Tie in the new canes to their wires, if you are using this method of support. In late winter, cut off the top of each cane just above the top wire. Autumn-fruiting raspberries need slightly different treatment, as they carry fruit on canes formed earlier in the same season. Cut the old fruited canes to the ground in late winter and thin out the thicket of new growth gradually as it grows during the season.

YIELD AND HARVESTING

Summer-fruiting varieties may be early, mid- or late season, bearing crops from mid- to late summer. Autumn-fruiting raspberries can be gathered from early to mid-autumn. Expect about 5.5kg (12lb) of summer raspberries from a 3m (10ft) row and half that amount from the autumn types.

PESTS AND DISEASES

Raspberries sometimes show signs of chlorosis (yellowing of the leaves) if they are planted in limey soil. Spread green sulphur on the soil, use sequestrene or fertilize with sulphate of ammonia to correct this problem. Plant virus-resistant varieties where possible to minimize the possibility of virus disease, which is spread by the large raspberry aphid. Cane spot is a fungus that appears as small purplish spots on the canes in late spring or early summer. Cut out affected canes and spray fortnightly with a systemic fungicide from bud burst until the end of flowering.

LOGANBERRIES & TAYBERRIES
Rubus x *loganobaccus*

Promiscuity generally gets a bad press, but in the plant world at least there is a great deal to be said for it. The wantonness of the raspberry and blackberry families, for instance, has produced several excellent hybrid berries to swell the summer harvest. The first and most famous of these hybrids was the loganberry, bred more than a century ago by Judge Logan of California. He raised it by crossing a raspberry with a blackberry, and the same cross has since produced other hybrids such as the tayberry. The tayberry's parents were an American blackberry called 'Aurora' and an unnamed tetraploid raspberry known tersely as No. 626/67. They were brought together in 1962 by Dr David Jennings of the Scottish Crop Research Institute.

RECOMMENDED CULTIVARS
- **Loganberry** 'LY59': long fruit with a sharp taste. 'LY654': a thornless type which is easy to handle, though it is not as vigorous as 'LY59'.
- **Tayberry** 'Medana Tayberry': the best strain, resistant to virus. 'Buckingham' is also good. Tayberries are larger and sweeter than loganberries.

Cultivation

Both plants are very vigorous with long canes that need tying in to wires or against walls and fences. They do not like cold winters and, if frosted, the canes may die back quite severely, though the plant itself usually recovers.

SITE AND SOIL

All the hybrid berries like roughly the same treatment. They hate waterlogged soil and are unlikely to do well where there is only a thin skim of earth over chalk.

PLANTING

The best planting time is late autumn, but hybrid berries can be planted any time up until early spring. Set them quite shallowly in the soil to encourage plenty of suckers. Leave 3–3.5m (10–12ft) between plants.

TRAINING
If you are training hybrid berries on wires to make a screen, put in posts that stand at least 1.8m (6ft) high, at convenient intervals. Stretch the first wire between them just under 1m (3ft) from the ground with another three wires above it fixed at 30cm (12in) intervals. Tie the growths securely along the wires, keeping the new canes bunched up in a fountain in the middle and the older fruiting growths trained horizontally away from the centre. When you have finished picking the fruit, cut out the old canes, unbundle the new ones and tie them in where the old ones were.

ROUTINE CARE
A spring mulch of well-rotted manure or compost will conserve moisture and help to feed the plants. In really cold areas you may find it best to leave the bundle of new canes lying on the ground all winter and tie them up in spring. Research has shown that canes treated like this suffer less from die back and other effects of intense cold.

YIELD AND HARVESTING
In the first year after planting expect about 2.5kg (5lb) of fruit from each plant, increasing to about 6kg (14lb) when the plant is mature. The fruiting season stretches from mid- to late summer.

PESTS AND DISEASES
Maggots of raspberry beetle may tunnel into the fruit. To prevent this, spray the plants at petal fall with a contact insecticide.

BLACKBERRIES *Rubus fruticosus*

As blackberries are so prolific in the wild, gardeners may wonder whether they should devote space to them in the garden. But modern varieties bear bigger fruit than wild brambles and, carefully trained, the canes make useful, windproof screens around a growing area. The most vigorous types, such as 'Himalayan Giant', have spiny canes that may be 3m (10ft) long. This is the one to use where a prickly barrier may be an effective deterrent against marauding animals.

Other types such as 'Oregon Thornless' are easier to deal with, as the canes have no prickles. The leaves of this variety are deeply cut like parsley and extremely decorative. In some areas the foliage in autumn turns rich shades of orange and red. Blackberries grow and crop well in shade. Think perhaps of training one on a north wall.

RECOMMENDED CULTIVARS
'Bedford Giant': well-flavoured fruit of an outstanding size. 'Himalayan Giant': the largest and thorniest of the blackberries with fruit of a decidedly

Bramble jelly

Wild berries, such as blackberries, make excellent fruit jellies. Since the fruit is free you do not worry that the yield of jelly is less than that for jam. If you cannot find enough blackberries, use a mixture of blackberry and apple, which gives an equally good jelly, though with a less intense flavour.

Makes about 750g (1.5lb) for every 500g (1lb) sugar used
4kg (8lb) blackberries
juice of 3 large or 4 small lemons (or 2 tsp citric acid)
900ml (1 1/2 pints) water
sugar (see below)

1. Wash the fruit and put it in a preserving pan with the lemon juice (or citric acid). Add the water and simmer until tender. The fruit should be cooked slowly and gently until it has completely broken down.
2. Strain the resulting pulp through a scalded jelly bag. If you want a clear, sparkling jelly, do not squeeze the bag.
3. Measure the extract, bring it to the boil in the cleaned preserving pan and add the sugar, using 500g (1lb) of sugar for each 600ml (1 pint) of strained juice. Stir well.
4. Boil the mixture rapidly without stirring until the setting point has been reached. This should not take longer than 10 minutes. Skim any froth from the surface of the liquid and pour it into small jars as quickly as possible. Put wax circles on top of the jelly as soon as the jars are filled. Finish them off with lids or circles of cellophane kept in place with elastic bands.

Culinary notes
* Once you have grasped the principles of jelly-making, you can fill a store cupboard with a range of delicious conserves. To get a well-set jelly, you need pectin (the natural setting agent present in fruit), acid and sugar available in the right proportions. Fruits such as cherries, pears and strawberries are low in pectin and do not make successful jellies. But try apple and sloe, apple and mulberry, apple and damson, apple and blueberry, or redcurrant with raspberry.

acid flavour. 'Loch Ness': one of the most widely grown, with thornless canes and handsome, glossy fruit. 'Oregon Thornless': one of the most decorative of the blackberries, excellent foliage, thornless with mild-flavoured fruit.

Cultivation
Even the less vigorous varieties need plenty of space, so bear this in mind before planting. Train blackberries on a fence or on a series of parallel wires stretched between posts. You can also grow blackberries in a hedge, as they grow in the wild. If you are planting a new hedge, let the trees become

established before you put in the blackberries; otherwise they will be smothered in the blackberries' prickly embrace.

SITE AND SOIL
Blackberries grow best in soil that retains moisture and is not too limey. You can improve the soil texture by digging in plenty of muck or compost before you plant. As they do not flower until early summer, they can be grown in frost pockets and seem to do equally well in sun or shade, provided the ground is not dry.

PLANTING
Plant in late autumn or at any time up until early spring. Cut the canes down to about 23cm (9in) immediately after planting. If you are growing two or more plants, set them at least 3.5m (12ft) apart. If you are using a vigorous type such as 'Himalayan Giant', increase the spacing to 4.5m (15ft). Train the new canes against a wall or fence, or along parallel sets of wire. If planted in a hedge, blackberries need no formal training.

ROUTINE CARE
Water if necessary in dry spells during summer. Mulch each spring with manure or compost.

PRUNING
As with raspberries and loganberries, the fruited canes should be cut out each year after the crop has been gathered. With a late-fruiting variety such as 'Himalayan Giant' this may not be until mid-autumn. Tie in the new canes to replace the old. With 'Himalayan Giant', which does not produce canes quite as freely as other varieties, a proportion of the old wood may be left in each season.

YIELD AND HARVESTING
Expect about 5–9kg (10–20lb) of fruit from each plant, depending on variety. Blackberries crop in late summer and early autumn. 'Himalayan Giant', the latest to crop, bear fruit until mid-autumn.

PESTS AND DISEASES
Grey mould may attack the fruit, especially in wet summers. Pick off the worst affected fruit. Spraying will need to continue every two weeks through the summer.

BLUEBERRIES *Vaccinium* spp

Blueberries will only succeed in the kind of moist, peaty soil in which rhododendrons and azaleas flourish. The best way to use them in the garden is as an understorey among other lime-hating shrubs planted in an informal border or a woodland setting. The modern cultivated blueberry is a mixture of several wild American species including *Vaccinium corymbosum*, the swamp or highbush blueberry, which is a shrubby, woody plant common in the eastern United States. White flowers, tinged with pink, appear in little tassels during late spring and early summer. The blue-black fruits, covered in a greyish-silvery bloom, are ready in late summer and early autumn.

RECOMMENDED CULTIVARS

'Berkeley': large, prolific pale blue berries on a vigorous spreading bush. 'Bluecrop': firm, good-quality berries among leaves that colour well in autumn. 'Duke': flowers late but crops early, a good choice for cold areas. 'Herbert': said by connoisseurs to have the best-flavoured fruit. 'Spartan': hardy, early to mid-season cultivar with large fruit. 'Sunshine Blue': a self-fertile type with pretty pink flowers.

Cultivation

It is not worth bothering with these fruit unless you can supply the very specific growing conditions they need. They will not survive in ordinary loams and certainly not in limey or heavy clay soil.

SITE AND SOIL

Blueberries should be planted in damp, peaty soil with a pH lower than 5.5. The position should be relatively open, but they will grow in sun or partial shade.

PLANTING

Plant between mid-autumn and early spring, using two- or three-year-old plants and setting them 1.5m (5ft) apart.

POLLINATION

To ensure good pollination, two different cultivars should be planted together.

ROUTINE CARE

The plants should be netted against birds as the fruit begins to ripen. Feed them with bonemeal in spring and mulch with an acid compost. Water regularly in dry summers.

PRUNING

Start pruning the plants in winter by cutting out dead, or damaged branches together with a proportion of old wood. In spring shear over the tops of the bushes to keep them compact.

YIELD AND HARVESTING

Expect about 3kg (6lb) of fruit from a fully established mature bush. You will need to pick over the bushes several times, as the berries ripen over a relatively long period during late summer and early autumn.

PESTS AND DISEASES

Blueberries do not generally get attacked by pests or diseases.

STRAWBERRIES *Fragaria* x *ananassa*

Nothing speaks of summer so eloquently as a dish of strawberries, eaten warm and richly glowing, straight from the garden. Recent breeding has concentrated on producing fruits that travel well. Gardeners can happily ignore that criterion and choose cultivars only on the basis of their taste. The strawberry is the only fruit that, like the Pompidou Centre in Paris, carries its vital working parts on the outside. The seeds, dotted in the flesh, are the true fruits of the plant. The berry is just the carrier, but for epicureans it is the only bit that matters.

Wild strawberries are found in both the Old and the New World, and a fusion of the two types produced the forerunners of most modern cultivars. It started in 1702 when a French naval officer, M. Frezier, brought back from Chile the pine strawberry, so called because it tasted of pineapples. The French crossed this fruit with a wild Virginian strawberry that had originally been introduced into Europe by the royal English gardener John Tradescant.

The Revolution brought French strawberry breeding to an abrupt halt and the work was taken up by an English market gardener, Michael Keens, who caused a sensation when he showed his plump, sweet, ruby-coloured 'Keens Seedling' at the Royal Horticultural Society's show in 1821.

When choosing cultivars for your fruit patch, get both early and late fruiting types. And do not forget the alpine strawberry, which with its pretty leaves and flowers makes an excellent edging for potager or path. The fruits are small but there are plenty of them and they do not seem to be attacked by birds.

RECOMMENDED CULTIVARS
'Aromel' (perpetual): fruits medium to large with excellent flavour. 'Baron Solemacher' (alpine): a useful habit as it grows in neat clumps without runners. 'Cambridge Favourite': a reliable, heavy cropper with moderately flavoured fruits. 'Hapil': heavy yields of sweet mid-season fruit. 'Honeoye': an early variety that crops heavily. 'Mae': the best early strawberry, to pick in early June. 'Marshmello': vigorous and sweet, ready in late June. 'Pegasus': a good mid-season type with excellent resistance to disease. 'Perfection': fine-flavoured berries, abundantly produced in late June. 'Royal Sovereign': superb flavour, though yields are lower than those of more recent cultivars. 'Symphony': glossy red late-season fruit.

Cultivation
The strawberry season is short, although the plants tie up the ground for twelve months of the year. In a small garden you may feel that pick-your-own is a better solution, but commercial growers may not put taste at the top of their list. They will be looking for robust plants that crop heavily. And bear in mind, even if you do grow your own, that children, birds and slugs will always find ripe berries before you do.

SITE AND SOIL
To grow good crops you must have ground that is in good heart: deep, porous, well fed and well drained. Prepare the beds in summer, digging in

Strawberry shortcake

Serves 6

250g (8oz) flour	a little milk
2 tsp baking powder	500g (1lb) strawberries
¹/2 tsp salt	a little caster sugar
1 tbs sugar	300ml (¹/2 pint) cream
125g (4oz) butter	

1. Sift the flour, baking powder and salt into a bowl and sprinkle in the sugar. Add the butter, cut into little pieces and rub it in with your fingers until the mixture is like breadcrumbs. Add just enough milk to bind the mixture, working it in with a knife.
2. Turn the mixture on to a floured surface, divide it in half and, with the palm of your hand, press out each half into a rough circle, about 15cm (6in) across. Butter two 23cm (9in) flan tins and put a circle of dough in each. Press out the dough until each circle reaches the edge of its tin.
3. Bake at 230°C/450°F/gas mark 8 for 15 minutes or until the shortcake starts to colour slightly. Remove from the oven and allow to cool.
4. Halve the strawberries, keeping some of the best whole to decorate the top of the shortcake. Sprinkle caster sugar over them.
5. Whip the cream and spread half of it over one of the circles of shortcake. Cover the cream with the halved strawberries and sandwich them with the second round of shortcake. Spread the rest of the cream on top and decorate with the whole strawberries.

Culinary notes
* The advantage of growing your own strawberries is that you can pick them when they are properly ripened. A squeeze of lemon juice on a bowl of fresh fruit intensifies the flavour.

plenty of muck. Old gardening books recommend trenching 1m (3ft) deep. That is pure sadism.

PLANTING
You must buy stock that is certified virus free as early as possible in summer and practice a three-year rotation of the strawberry patch. This is difficult to arrange in a very small garden. Plant rooted runners in late summer so that the plants can settle before winter weather sets in. Strawberries should be set 45cm (18in) apart in rows 1m (3ft) apart. Alpine strawberries can be planted at 30cm (12in) intervals.

ROUTINE CARE
A dressing of sulphate of potash in late January or early February will help develop flavour. Spread straw around plants as the berries form, to keep them

clean and well aired. Plastic is sometimes used but seems to encourage grey mould (*Botrytis*). Nip off runners as they form, unless you need to raise a fresh crop of plants. After cropping, chop off all the old leaves about 10cm (4in) above the crown of the plant and dress the ground lightly with a general fertilizer. Discard old plants after three years and plant a new bed with runners rooted from your old plants.

YIELD AND HARVESTING

Some cultivars yield much more heavily than others, but flavour tends to decrease as productivity rises. Expect about 250g (8oz) of fruit from each plant. Alpine strawberries will crop intermittently from mid-summer to autumn. 'Perpetual' strawberries are not in fact perpetual but carry a second, lighter crop of autumn fruit after the main summer crop. The summer-fruiting strawberry can be early or late, depending on the cultivar.

PESTS AND DISEASES

You will need to net crops to keep the fruit safe from birds. If you use cloches to hasten on the crop, they will provide the necessary protection. Slugs can also be a problem. Grey mould (*Botrytis*) is the most distressing disease, as it rots the berries, covering them with a fluffy, brownish-grey fungus. It is worst in wet summers. Water plants in the morning rather than the evening so that the flowers and fruit dry off quickly.

BLACK, RED & WHITE CURRANTS
Ribes nigrum & R. rubrum

For the gardener, there are three different kinds of currant: black, red and white. For the botanist, there are only two, for the white currant is nothing more than a variant of the red one, *Ribes rubrum*. For translucent, luminous beauty, nothing can match the redcurrant, which you often see glowing in the still-life paintings of Dutch artists. Though they are most often grown as ordinary bushes, red and white currants can be trained into extremely decorative cordons to make screens round a vegetable patch. Blackcurrant bushes are living medicine chests. Half a dozen of these tiny fruit have more vitamin C in them than the biggest lemon. Choose compact varieties such as 'Ben Sarek' if you are gardening in a small space.

RECOMMENDED CULTIVARS

- **Blackcurrant** 'Ben Connan': reliable crops of large fruit. 'Ben Lomond': a medium-sized bush carrying heavy crops of large fruit. 'Ben Sarek': the most compact in terms of bush size, but bearing heavy crops of large fruit.
- **Redcurrant** 'Jonkheer van Tets': large fruit on an early cropping, upright bush. 'Red Lake': one of the most popular varieties bearing very large fruit

on an upright bush. 'Rovada': heavy yields between mid-July and mid-August. 'Stanza': small, dark fruit on an upright bush.
- **White currant** 'Blanka': sweet, ivory-coloured fruit. 'White Grape': best for flavour, the large fruit growing on an upright bush.

Cultivation

Currants grown in bush form need no support, but if you decide to grow redcurrants as one-, two- or three-stem cordons, they will need to be either trained against a wall or fence, or tied in to parallel wires stretched at intervals between posts. Provide a bamboo stake to support the main stem. The eventual height of bushes depends on the cultivar, but is usually about 1.2–1.5m (4–5ft). Blackcurrants tend to make large, spreading bushes, red and white currants more upright shapes. As cordons, red and whitecurrants will reach 1.5–1.8m (5–6ft).

SITE AND SOIL

All currants do best in open situations, but all will tolerate some shade. Blackcurrants are greedier feeders than red and white currants. Dig in plenty of compost or farmyard manure before planting.

PLANTING

Bushes are best planted in late autumn, but can be put in any time until early spring. Plant blackcurrants deeply – more deeply than they were growing in their containers – to ensure a good supply of fresh growth springing from the base. Leave 1.5–1.8m (5–6ft) between bushes. Cut down all branches of blackcurrant to within 7–10cm (3–4in) of the ground immediately after planting.

ROUTINE CARE

Mulch all bushes in spring with well-rotted manure or compost and dress red and white currants with sulphate of potash, about 30g (1oz) for each bush. Do not dig deeply around the bushes, as you will disturb the roots, but keep them well weeded. Protect the fruit from birds.

PRUNING

Blackcurrants are treated differently from red and white currants as blackcurrants fruit on young, one-year old wood and the other two fruit on spurs made on old wood. When blackcurrants have fruited, cut out at least a third of the old dark wood, leaving as much of the new light brown growth as possible. It is on these new, pale stems that the following season's fruit will be produced. As red and white currants bear on old wood, pruning is less drastic. After fruiting, or during the following autumn and winter, shorten branches by about a third to keep the bushes shapely and compact. On red and white currants grown as cordons, cut the lateral branches back to within 3cm (1 1/2in) of the main stem.

YIELD AND HARVESTING

Currants are ready to pick in mid- and late summer. Expect about 5kg (10lb) of fruit from each bush when they are fully established.

PESTS AND DISEASES

Aphids may infect currants, causing blisters on the leaves and other distorted growth. Spray if necessary with a systemic insecticide. If blackcurrant bushes lose vigour and crop poorly, they may be suffering from reversion disease spread by blackcurrant gall mites. There is no cure. Bushes should be dug up and destroyed.

GOOSEBERRIES *Ribes uva-crispa*

'The freedom of the bush should be given to all visitors,' wrote the Edwardian epicure and fruit grower Edward Bunyard. He was thinking of the gooseberry in its dessert state, pale yellow, squidgy, sweet, highly scented – an almost forgotten delight, for gooseberries are most often gathered hard and green to be cooked in pies and tarts. They also make a good sauce for mackerel, which comes in at the same time.

Gooseberries can be bought or trained as very pretty little standard trees, grown up on 90cm (36in) stems with a round head of foliage on top, like a piece of topiary. They need strong stakes, however, as the stems are rather spindly in relation to the topknot.

RECOMMENDED CULTIVARS

'Careless': one of the most popular types bearing large, pale green fruit on a spreading bush. 'Hinnomaki Gul': produces succulent yellow dessert gooseberries in July. 'Invicta': makes a vigorous, spreading bush immune to mildew. 'Leveller': ripens into an excellent dessert gooseberry, extra large, oval, greenish yellow. 'Pax': gives red dessert gooseberries if left until July. 'Whinham's Industry': an upright bush succeeding well in shade and bearing medium-sized dark red fruits which are equally good cooked or used as dessert.

Cultivation

Gooseberries grow wild in most northern, temperate zones and seem to flourish in cool, moist, high places. They can be used as bushes, cordons or standards. Eventual height varies with the cultivar. Bushes generally grow to about 1.2–1.5m (4–5ft) and cordons to 1.5–1.8m (5–6ft).

SITE AND SOIL

The soil should be well drained but moisture retentive. On shallow, dry soil, the fruit will not swell properly. Gooseberries thrive in sun or partial shade.

PLANTING

Plant in late autumn or at any time until early spring. Bushes are best grown on a short stem to prevent suckering at ground level. Set the bushes about 1.5m (5ft) apart. Do not plant too deeply. Cordons can be set just 30cm (12in) apart.

Gooseberry wine

Gooseberries, along with white currants, make a very good clear, white wine, refreshing to drink chilled on a summer evening. To make home made wine, you need large sterilized containers which can be corked with an air lock. In this way, gases can escape while the fruit pulp is fermenting.

Makes 4.5 litres (1 gallon)

1kg (2lb) gooseberries
3 Campden tablets
3.5 litres (6 pints) water
15g (1/2oz) pectin enzyme

1.1kg (2¼lb) sugar
1 level tsp yeast nutrient
1 heaped tsp wine yeast

1. Crush the uncooked fruit in a clean plastic bucket. Dissolve the Campden tablets in the water and add to the gooseberries. Add the pectin enzyme and stir.
2. Cover the bucket securely with a lid or a film of polythene and leave the mixture to steep for 48 hours in a warm place. Strain the mixture through a jelly bag or similar into a fresh plastic bucket. Squeeze out all the liquid.
3. Dissolve the sugar in 600ml (1 pint) of boiling water, cool and add this syrup together with the nutrients to the liquid. Make up the volume to 4.5 litres (1 gallon) with more water if necessary.
4. Pour the liquid into its fermenting container (4.5 litres/1 gallon) and add the yeast. Keep under an air lock at a temperature of about 15°C/60°F until the mixture has stopped fermenting. This may take 12 weeks.
5. Siphon off the mixture through a filter into a fresh container, taking care not to siphon off any sediment from the bottom of the original container. Add another Campden tablet and fit a new air lock. When the wine is completely clear (a matter of weeks rather than days), bottle it and store it in a cool place.

ROUTINE CARE

Mulch with well-rotted compost or manure in early spring. Water newly planted bushes if necessary in summer. Feed each winter with sulphate of potash, using 30g (1oz) for each bush. Keep the bushes well weeded and remove any suckers that sprout round the base.

PRUNING

Gooseberries will bear fruit even if they are not regularly pruned, but it is easier to pick the fruit if you remove some of the growth each year to keep the centre of the bush open and to shorten long branches, which may be weighed down to the ground with fruit. On cordons, shorten the side growths to three buds, and cut the branches of standards back by at least a third to maintain a well-shaped head.

YIELD AND HARVESTING

For cooking, green fruit can be thinned out in late spring and early summer. Dessert fruit should be left to ripen on the bush until mid- or late summer. Expect 3–5kg (6–10lb) of fruit from a bush, 1–1.5kg (2–3lb) from a cordon.

PESTS AND DISEASES

American gooseberry mildew is the most debilitating disease, starting as a white powder on new foliage. Keep bushes open so that air can flow through them. Spray if necessary with a systemic fungicide or plant a resistant variety such as 'Invicta'. Birds may attack flower buds. Net bushes if this is a problem.

GRAPES *Vitis vinifera*

Grapes make up the biggest single fruit crop in the world. Given the amount of liquid that finds its way down the throats of wine buffs each year, this is perhaps not surprising. Gardeners will probably not be growing grapes primarily for their alcoholic potential. Vines are blessed with an elegant, venerable habit of growth and excellent, shading foliage. Trained over a seat or an arbour, a vine gives just the right air of productive ease in a garden. Combined with clematis, they are ideal plants to decorate a pergola. In hot countries they can be trained to make a shaded lattice roof over a terrace where you can sit in dappled light under the shifting leaves. In conservatories, a vine carefully tied in to wires strung underneath the glass of the roof will provide useful summer shading for the plants inside. Choosing the right variety is important. Some are more tolerant of cold conditions than others. One of the most widely grown grapes in the US is 'Concord'; the vines most commonly used in Europe are derived from a different species.

RECOMMENDED CULTIVARS

- **Outdoor (white)** 'Madeleine Silvaner': not high yielding but does well in cool conditions. 'Muller Thurgau': one of the best for making wine, dessert quality only fair. 'Perlette': almost seedless grapes, larger than 'Phoenix'. 'Phoenix': Muscat-flavoured almost seedless grapes. 'Siegerrebe': dual-purpose grape producing sweet Muscat-like fruit.
- **Outdoor (black)** 'Alphonse Lavallée': known in France since the 1850s. 'Brant': one of the best, crops prolifically and foliage turns beautiful colours in autumn. 'Dornfelder': reliable outdoor crops.
- **Indoor (white)** 'Buckland Sweetwater': not vigorous, so suitable for a smallish greenhouse. 'Foster's Seedling': heavy crops of well-flavoured fruit. 'Muscat of Alexandria': an old variety unparalleled for taste, but needs heat.
- **Indoor (black)** 'Schiava Grossa' ('Black Hamburg'): one of the best of the dessert grapes, setting freely and ripening well.

Cultivation

The correct pruning and training are vital whether you are growing grapes inside or out. In cool, wet areas, vines make far too much growth, which must be restricted if the plants are to be persuaded to fruit. Purely ornamental vines such as *Vitis coignetiae* do not need this kind of treatment.

SITE AND SOIL

Although they are hardy, vines will ripen their crop most successfully in areas where the summers are long and warm. In the UK grapes will rarely succeed outside north of a line drawn from Gloucester to the Wash. Give them a sheltered sunny wall and fertile, well-drained soil.

PLANTING

Greenhouse and conservatory beds should be made up with a rich mixture of loam mixed with farmyard manure. Alternatively, vines can be planted outside with the main stem fed through to the inside of the house, so that subsequent growth is sheltered by the glass. Outside, plant vines between mid-autumn and late winter, setting them 1.2–1.5m (4–5ft) apart.

ROUTINE CARE

Keep the atmosphere in greenhouses humid by damping down the floor at regular intervals. Ventilate the greenhouse well as soon as the vines begin to flower. Pollinate the vines by hand with a soft brush. Thin the bunches of grapes, leaving one for every 30cm (12in) of stem. As the grapes begin to swell, cut out the smallest and most overcrowded fruits in the centre of the bunch. Give a liquid feed every ten days until the grapes have fully ripened. As they are ripening, ventilate the greenhouse well and keep it less moist. Rest the vines in winter by reducing the temperature, untying the rods (branches) from their wires and laying the vines down on the ground. In this way, the rising sap in spring will run right to the end of the growths. If the vines are not dropped, there is a tendency for the lower buds only to break into growth. Tie the rods back into place in early spring. Varieties such as 'Muscat of Alexandria' may need extra heat in spring and do best if growing temperatures can be maintained between 10–13°C (50–55°F). Mulch outdoor vines annually in early spring with well-rotted manure or compost.

PRUNING AND TRAINING

When grown under glass, vines should be trained on wires set about 30cm (12in) apart and at least 15cm (6in) away from the glass itself. The leading shoot should be trained vertically, the laterals horizontally along the wires. When the vines have flowered, prune the laterals back, leaving just two leaves beyond the clusters of fruit. Any subsequent shoots breaking from the laterals should be pinched out, leaving one or two leaves at most. After fruiting, in the autumn, cut the leading stem back to well-ripened wood and cut the laterals back to two buds.

Crème brûlée with grapes

Grapes add texture to the smooth bland creamy base of this pudding with its caramelized coating. Large grapes should be halved and their seeds taken out. Smaller seedless grapes can be washed and used as they are.

500g (1lb) grapes
4 egg yolks

600ml (1 pint) cream
90g (3oz) brown sugar

1. Take the seeds out of the grapes if necessary and arrange the grapes in a thick layer on the bottom of a fireproof dish.
2. Beat the egg yolks in the top of a double saucepan. Heat the cream gently, pour it on top of the egg yolks and mix well.
3. Stir the mixture over hot water in the double saucepan until it begins to thicken. Do not let it boil. When the mixture has thickened, pour it over the grapes and leave overnight.
4. Next day, cover the cream with an even layer of the brown sugar. Put the dish under a very hot grill until the sugar has caramelized. Remove the dish, allow it cool and chill before serving.

Culinary notes
* Home-grown black grapes have a beautiful bloom on the skin that is very easily rubbed off and spoiled. Handle bunches with care and bring them to the table displayed on a few of their own handsome leaves.
* Grapes also look beautiful divided into small bunches and piled in a glass bowl, together with sparkling ice cubes and a scatter of small flowers such as borage.

Train vines outside on walls by allowing, at most, three or four main stems to develop from a single rootstock. After the first season's growth, cut back the growth by two thirds and repeat this in early autumn each year until all the available space is filled. On young plants, tie in the laterals and grow them on to about 60cm (24in) before pinching them out. On mature plants, the laterals should be stopped just beyond the clusters of flowers, leaving no more than two leaves. Sub-laterals (shoots springing from the side shoots) should be stopped at one leaf.

YIELD AND HARVESTING
A mature vine will give about 7kg (15lb) of fruit. Cut the bunches with a T-shaped piece of stem attached. If you want to keep them for any time, put one end of the T-stem in a jar of water.

PESTS AND DISEASES
Powdery mildew is the most serious disease of vines, whether they are grown under cover or outside. Leaves and new shoots become coated with floury

fungus. The disease is most likely to strike where vines are underwatered. Spraying with a systemic fungicide will control powdery mildew and also grey mould, which is worst on outdoor vines in wet seasons. Red spider mite may infect vines growing in hot, dry greenhouses. Regular damping down helps to keep this pest at bay.

MELONS *Cucumis melo*

Only in countries with a Mediterranean climate can melons be grown in open ground, trailing perhaps between tall sheaves of sweetcorn, or sitting proudly like kings on little heaped thrones of muck and compost. In warm areas, you may be able to train melons over trellis or an arch, but you will have to support the fruit in a net sling as it gets heavier. In growth they look like squashes, but you need to thin the fruit so that no more than four melons develop on each plant. In cool climates, melons will only ripen if they are grown with some protection: a cold frame, a cloche or a cool greenhouse. The most successful type in cool areas is the cantaloupe, small round fruit with heavily netted skin. 'Ogen' is typical of this group.

RECOMMENDED CULTIVARS
- **Cantaloupe** 'Minnesota Midget': small, sweet, fast-ripening fruit. 'Ogen': small, round yellow fruit with green ribs. 'Sweetheart': one of the best in cool conditions.
- **Musk** 'Durandal': small fruits with netted skin. 'Earlidawn': sweet, orange flesh.

Cultivation
To produce the best fruit, melons need a long, warm growing season, and if nature does not provide this naturally you will have to give her a helping hand. Fruits will also ripen more quickly if you train melon vines over some hard surface, such as concrete or paving stones that stores and reflects heat.

SITE AND SOIL
The site will depend on the prevailing climate. In the coldest areas, only a greenhouse will provide the necessary summer warmth. Melons grow well in grow bags, or can be planted in greenhouse borders, well enriched with muck. The soil in a cold frame needs to be similarly enhanced.

SOWING
Sow seeds in succession from early to late spring, setting each seed on edge 1cm (1/2in) deep in a 7cm (3in) pot of compost. Water the pots, cover them with cling film and keep them at a temperature of about 18°C/65°F until the seeds have germinated. The seedlings will be ready to plant out when they have four proper leaves.

TRANSPLANTING

Seedlings can be transplanted into their final quarters from late spring onwards. In a cold frame or in open ground, melons grow best planted on a slight mound with a wall of compost built up round the edge of the mound to retain water. Set the plants at least 1m (3ft) apart.

ROUTINE CARE

The flowers that will eventually become fruit form on the sub-laterals, so you need to pinch out growing tips to force the plant to concentrate on its fruit. The main stem will produce side stems (laterals), which you should stop when they have made five leaves. From these laterals will come sub-laterals, which you should pinch out at three leaves. Keep the soil permanently moist but the air around the plants as well ventilated as possible.

Pollinate the flowers by stripping the petals from a male flower and pushing it into a female flower. The females are the ones with slight swellings just underneath the flower heads. One male flower will pollinate at least four females. Pollination is best done at midday. Thin the fruit if necessary to leave no more than one melon on each lateral. Put a tile underneath each fruit as it develops to keep it off the earth.

YIELD AND HARVESTING

Expect four fruit from each plant. Do not pick melons until they are absolutely ripe. This is one of the advantages of a home-grown melon. You can leave it to ripen fully on the vine. The all-enveloping smell will be enough to tell you when to pounce.

PESTS AND DISEASES

Being cucurbits, like cucumbers, melons may suffer from cucumber mosaic virus, which makes the leaves crumple up and flecks the surface with bright yellow spots. There is no cure.

KIWI FRUIT & PASSION FRUIT
Actinidia deliciosa & *Passiflora edulis*

Both these fruits grow on extensive, twining vines that in the right conditions can be rampageous. The kiwi, or Chinese gooseberry, has big round leaves that are covered with a gingery fuzz when they are young. The fruit has a brown, furry coat and, where it gets sufficient heat and a long growing season, will ripen outside to be harvested in autumn. But the vine is not fully hardy and in order to ripen fruit needs an eight-month growing season.

The passion fruit is a cousin of the garden climber *Passiflora caerulea*, the common passion flower, and in mid-summer has showy white flowers with purple centres, set off against handsome, three-lobed leaves. Its home is in the South American tropics and it is not frost hardy. It is only likely to fruit where the winter temperature rarely falls below 8–10°C/45–50°F. Grown outside, growth is likely to be cut down each year by frost, as sometimes happens with *P. caerulea*. Then the plant, having to start growing from the base again, cannot set flowers soon enough for the fruit to ripen before the first frost.

RECOMMENDED CULTIVARS
- **Passion fruit** 'Crackerjack': a reliable selection.
- **Kiwi** 'Hayward': the most reliable female available. 'Jenny': self-pollinating. 'Tomuri': a good male.

Cultivation

Give these plants the hottest spots you can find in the garden, trained on a sunny wall, or else grow them in a greenhouse or conservatory. In order to get kiwis other than 'Jenny' to fruit, you will need two vines: a male and a female.

SITE AND SOIL
Both these vines do best in rich, well-drained ground.

PLANTING
Set out plants in late spring when all danger of frost has passed. They will both need to be trained and securely tied in to supports. These should be strong for a kiwi vine, which can be up to 9m (27ft) long, and heavy with it. Plant male and female plants next to each other, but leave 4m (14ft) between each pair.

POLLINATION
'Jenny' is self-pollinating but all-female kiwi plants will only set fruit when there is a male plant growing close by. The passion fruit is self-fertile.

ROUTINE CARE
Both plants are greedy for food and water. Mulch liberally in spring with manure or compost and water regularly through the growing season.

PRUNING
Growth is rampant in the right conditions and may need curbing to persuade the plants to concentrate on the job in hand. For the gardener, this means the production of fruit rather than foliage. Kiwis fruit on the first three to six buds of the current year's growth. Treat them like vines, summer pruning new growth to a point just beyond the setting fruit. Winter pruning can be more drastic and entail, if necessary, the removal of whole stems. Prune passion fruit in early spring, thinning out overgrown plants and pinching back the lateral shoots to about 15cm (6in).

YIELD AND HARVESTING
Expect about 9kg (20lb) of fruit from both kiwi and passion fruit vines, when they are well established. This may take up to seven years. Pick fruit when it gives slightly under thumb pressure, like a peach.

PESTS AND DISEASES
These crops are generally trouble free.

3

PLANNING &
CULTIVATION
TECHNIQUES

In this final section are some ground rules you may find useful. Humus and hardening off, intercropping and insects, pricking out and pollination, they are all here, explained in a way that makes them simple to follow. Garden rules, however, exist only to be broken. Your own ability to tune in to the ebb and flow of the seasons and your plants' reactions to those changes will, in the end, be much more useful than any other source of knowledge. Learn, too, to be sanguine. Even if you follow all the rules you may still have disasters. Do not worry. There is always another spring.

SIZING UP THE OPTIONS

The options available to new kitchen gardeners will depend entirely on the space available. You can grow some excellent vegetables on a balcony or a roof garden, but you would not expect to build an asparagus bed there. If all you have is a kitchen windowsill, then you may become the world's expert on basil or rocket, but you are unlikely to be able to pull a decent carrot. Finding the right place for the right plant is the secret of success in gardening and this is as true for fruit and vegetables as it is for flowers. Some vegetables will grow in partial shade. Some demand sun. Some want lashings of food and drink. Others will spin a crop out of little more than thin air. Think of these things when you are planning what to grow.

The alternatives

Once you grasp hold of the notion that vegetables do not necessarily have to be grown in purdah, separate from the rest of the plants in the garden, all kinds of possibilities for using them arise. Instead of planting a rose on a sheltered wall of your house, you may put a pear there instead and train its malleable branches into a fan. Instead of raising a dividing screen of larchlap fencing, you may think of planting a loganberry or a tayberry and training it on parallel wires to make an extremely productive partition. Use structures such as tunnels to give you more growing space and plant vines and kiwi fruit among the mid-summer roses. You might think of bringing an artichoke into the back of the flower border to give height and architectural substance to flowers that are lacking in both. You might edge a path with crinkly-leaved parsley, perhaps planting it alternately with groups of chubby violas. One of the best foreground groups in Christopher Lloyd's Long Border at Great Dixter was once a bright patch of parsley mixed with the rich-blue pimpernel flowers of *Anagallis monellii*.

You might experiment with using lettuces as foliage plants among bright marigolds and zinnias. Lettuce has come on a long way since 'Webbs Wonderful'. Now they are frilled and flounced and may be red or bronze or one of forty shades of green. You may decide for once to do without the Surfinia petunias in the hanging basket and fill it instead with tumbling bush tomatoes. All these things are possible, and look beautiful as well as providing you with food. There is no pleasure to equal that of picking your own supper, on a summer evening. The pleasure is more muted when are trying to hack a parsnip out of frozen ground in winter, but even that may have a masochistic charm. Divert yourself by thinking of the mouthwatering parsnip purée that will be the reward for your labours.

Fruitful features

When you are sizing up the options, think hardest about the features that will be the most permanent. These are likely to be fruit trees. Could you fit an apple on to the lawn? The answer is probably yes, but your life will be made easier if you choose a half standard with at least 1.2m (4ft) of clear stem before the branches start to arch out. This will grow into a fine tree, will be easy to mow under, suitable to sling a hammock from and infinitely more beautiful to look at than a squat bush reined in by a dwarfing rootstock.

Could you make better use of paths in the garden by turning one or more of them into a curving tunnel dripping with grapes from a vine (if you are a romantic) or runner beans and purple-podded climbing French beans (if you take a more pragmatic view)? Again, the answer is probably yes. Tunnels for the vine can be permanent structures – hoops of iron joined by cross pieces – or temporary. For the runner beans you could make a simple tunnel from hazel poles bent and lashed together over the path and joined at the sides with horizontal poles. This would suit a cottage garden, where you might have borders of courgettes and alliums bobbing around busily under the beans.

Then cast your eye on your beds and borders. Occasional drama is what you want in a border to wake up the sleepy hordes of geraniums and well-bred campanulas. Vegetables can provide that drama as easily as flowers. The best borders, as gardeners are told a thousand times, are those that include plenty of good foliage. Only the slightest shift in focus is needed before you reach for a scarlet-stemmed chard instead of a bergenia, plant a globe artichoke rather than an acanthus or fill a gap with the supremely decorative endive 'Variegata di Castelfranco' rather than a hosta. What could be a more fitting companion for a rich-red verbena than the elegant drooping flags of a leek, especially the French blue-leaved type 'Bleu de Solaise'?

Think about bringing in flowers to mix with the vegetables too. Allow nasturtiums to sprawl among the sweetcorn. Use pot marigolds to paint lines of orange between green strips of spinach and carrot. Scatter seed of the California poppy, eschscholzia, to spring up in beds of cut-and-come-again salad crops such as mizuna or saladini.

Pick of the plants

Deciding what to grow has to come after sizing up the options. You might not have enough space to do all that you want to do. You might not have enough sunny sites to be able to grow your chosen crops. Taste matters too. However longingly you may dream up visions of purple *Verbena bonariensis* waving above the blue-green flags of a leek bed, it will be a waste of space to grow leeks if you have a family that is resolutely anti-leek. With some vegetables, such as tomatoes, there is no such thing as too much. Tomatoes are decorative, they can be trained to grow in vertical space rather than horizontal – which is always at a greater premium – and they make eye-catching centrepieces for the formal beds of a potager. They also crop well on a balcony, where you could make a miniature potager with a grow bag planted with tomatoes trained on canes, surrounded by well-watered pots of salad vegetables: cut-and-come-again lettuces, endive, rocket, mustard and cress.

If the way things look is more important to you than the process of producing food, you may be tempted to choose vegetables entirely on the grounds of their appearance. This is the mistake that supermarkets make and it would be a waste of your time to grow things that did not taste gorgeous too. If you choose carefully, you can have the best of both worlds: bounty and beauty combined in yellow courgettes and tiger-striped tomatoes, red-stemmed chard and purple-podded beans. Let rich, rampant profusion be the order of the day. Whichever option you choose, be generous.

SORTING OUT THE SPACE

The size of a garden need not limit your ambition. Indeed, the smaller the garden, the greater the need for a grand statement, and the greater the need for the gardener to feel that every square centimetre of the place is earning its keep in the best possible way. There are several ways you can bring this about. One is to consider the way the garden is laid out. You need bold, simple lines, with paths wider than you ever thought necessary and beds bigger than you ever thought possible. Introducing key plants, or highlighting existing ones, is another way to pull together a scheme that somehow always seems to have something missing. There is no strict formula to sorting out the space in a garden: each gardener finds his or her own solution. We may start working from the same set of principles but should finish with completely different results, which reflect what we want from our own patches.

Internal divisions

Imagine an average back garden where there is a small paved area with a central lawn beyond and narrow flower beds running up either side. At the end may be a shed, a tree or a play area with a climbing frame. How would it be if for a start you did away with the lawn and divided up the space in a more engaging way? If you have children, this may not be an option, although you could perhaps enlarge the area around the climbing frame and create extra playing space there. For the moment, forget children and concentrate on the space – the former lawn space – and its potential.

If you are sitting on the paved area immediately outside the house, or looking out from the windows, you will want something there to catch the

PLAN 1: DIAGONAL

A rectangular garden is divided by two wide paths running from corner to corner. These create four large triangular beds with plenty of space for an eyecatching display of plants.

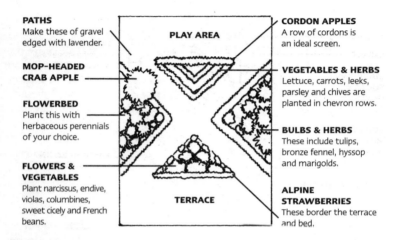

PATHS
Make these of gravel edged with lavender.

MOP-HEADED CRAB APPLE

FLOWERBED
Plant this with herbaceous perennials of your choice.

FLOWERS & VEGETABLES
Plant narcissus, endive, violas, columbines, sweet cicely and French beans.

CORDON APPLES
A row of cordons is an ideal screen.

VEGETABLES & HERBS
Lettuce, carrots, leeks, parsley and chives are planted in chevron rows.

BULBS & HERBS
These include tulips, bronze fennel, hyssop and marigolds.

ALPINE STRAWBERRIES
These border the terrace and bed.

PLAN 2: RECTANGULAR

Here, the garden has a paved area at the centre with two broad borders on either side. These are planted with trained fruit, plus flowers and vegetables to suit personal taste.

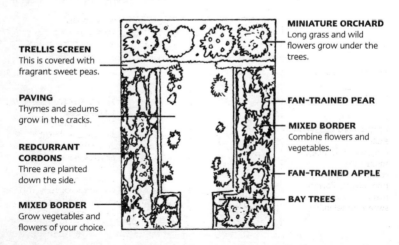

TRELLIS SCREEN
This is covered with fragrant sweet peas.

PAVING
Thymes and sedums grow in the cracks.

REDCURRANT CORDONS
Three are planted down the side.

MIXED BORDER
Grow vegetables and flowers of your choice.

MINIATURE ORCHARD
Long grass and wild flowers grow under the trees.

FAN-TRAINED PEAR

MIXED BORDER
Combine flowers and vegetables.

FAN-TRAINED APPLE

BAY TREES

PLAN 3: WINDING PATH

A path of flagstones surrounded by blue lobelia meanders through the garden, dividing it into two large planting areas filled with fruit, vegetables and flowers.

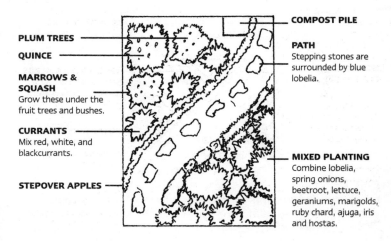

PLUM TREES

QUINCE

MARROWS & SQUASH
Grow these under the fruit trees and bushes.

CURRANTS
Mix red, white, and blackcurrants.

STEPOVER APPLES

COMPOST PILE

PATH
Stepping stones are surrounded by blue lobelia.

MIXED PLANTING
Combine lobelia, spring onions, beetroot, lettuce, geraniums, marigolds, ruby chard, ajuga, iris and hostas.

PLAN 4: SYMMETRICAL

This very symmetrical design has raised beds around its sides, two patches of grass, and three wigwams of climbing plants that act as a focal point as well as a screen.

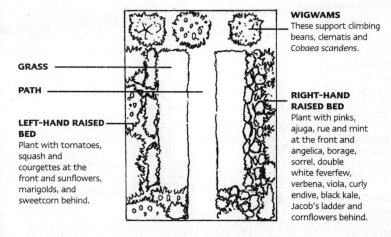

GRASS

PATH

LEFT-HAND RAISED BED
Plant with tomatoes, squash and courgettes at the front and sunflowers, marigolds, and sweetcorn behind.

WIGWAMS
These support climbing beans, clematis and *Cobaea scandens*.

RIGHT-HAND RAISED BED
Plant with pinks, ajuga, rue and mint at the front and angelica, borage, sorrel, double white feverfew, verbena, viola, curly endive, black kale, Jacob's ladder and cornflowers behind.

eye. The garden itself should appear as luxuriant as possible. We are not talking about fearful gardening here. Faced with a plot of ground to divide up, many gardeners turn first to the edges and work their way round the boundaries digging borders which are usually too narrow to be useful and leave a void at the centre. Perhaps this is a remnant of some atavistic urge to mark territory. If instead you think out from the centre of the space towards the boundaries, quite different patterns will emerge.

DIAGONAL PLAN

If the squarish space in front of you were divided with a giant X to mark the lines of two new diagonal paths, as in Plan 1, several advantages immediately become clear. Space is apportioned in a clean, simple way, creating the maximum area for growing flowers, fruit and vegetables in the four triangles formed by the X. It becomes possible to create an eye-catching display alongside the paved area outside the house, where you most need something to admire. And the crossing of the paths in the middle creates a pivot for the design. The two diagonal paths need to be wide. This is possible since there is untrammelled planting space in between. Be generous.

The style of planting in the four triangles can be formal or not, depending on your taste. Each of the four pieces of ground should have one big outstanding specimen: a giant fennel, perhaps, or a neat mop-headed crab apple with different kinds of mint tumbling around in the shade underneath it. Depending on the size of the garden, the far side of the X-shape may mark the back boundary. Or there may be a necessary but messy drifting off into the shed/climbing frame scene. Cut this off by a bold semi-screen, which will hold in the top end of the X and create a separate area beyond. You do not want anything solid, as otherwise your eye will bounce off it like a rubber ball and come back to you too quickly, giving the impression there is nothing to look at in between. Nor do you want anything fussy, for nothing should detract, either from the importance of your central assemblage or from the stars of the four planted beds. This is where fruit trees planted in rows of slanting single-stem cordons or splayed out in fans are ideal. Nothing makes a more effective screen in this kind of situation.

RECTANGULAR PLAN

You might like the idea of a rectangular paved area in the middle of the plot, as in Plan 2, with wide borders of mixed vegetables and flowers on either side, and a miniature orchard at the end. A trelliswork screen covered with sweet peas divides the orchard from the rest of the garden, and cracks between the paving stones are planted with mats of thyme and fleshy leaved sedums.

WINDING PATH PLAN

This divides the garden with a path that curves up through the centre, as in Plan 3. A thick planting of lobelia makes the flagstones look like stepping stones in a river of blue. Stepover apples (like long, low, one-tier espaliers) have been planted along its edge. Other fruit trees and bushes include plums, a quince and a mixture of currants. Vegetables share the bed with flowers, while marrows and squash have room to roam under the fruit trees.

SYMMETRICAL PLAN

A fourth option, shown in Plan 4, has rectangles of grass either side of a central path, with plants contained in raised beds built round the sides. The path could be made of bricks or stone, to suit the surroundings. Bush tomatoes tumble over the edges of one raised bed, with tall stands of sunflowers and sweetcorn behind. The other raised bed combines vegetables, herbs and flowers. Three wigwams at the end add height, and are used to support runner beans, clematis and the cup-and-saucer vine, *Cobaea scandens*.

Getting started

New gardeners are usually told that they must draw out a plan on paper before they start flailing around outside with spades and wheelbarrows. Because this is the way professional garden designers work, it is assumed that this is also the best way forward for amateurs. The problem with paper designs is that they tend to get overcomplicated. The obvious is avoided at all costs. Another difficulty with paper is that it cannot contain the information you need to make the right decisions and which you get as you prowl over your patch. You take in the slight rises and falls in the ground and the consequences that these will have on your design. You are aware of things beyond your boundary that you would rather not see and which a well-placed plum tree may be able to conceal. You sense where the sun falls and which patches are permanently in shade. You become aware of the wind and the problems that this might cause with a too hastily erected wigwam of peas. Above all, working on the ground you develop a proper sense of proportion. Think simple is the best advice. And think big, however small your plot.

CHOOSING PATHS

Paths define the main lines of the design in a garden. They do not all need to be of equal importance. The main thoroughfares may be wide and hard-surfaced, but there may be an interconnecting web of narrow paths between beds that are no more than beaten earth. You need to get these lines of communication sorted out before you proceed with the rest of the plan for your garden. You need also to think of the kind of surfaces you want to use on your paths. The most sympathetic coverings in terms of looks and texture will probably also be the ones that need most care and maintenance. If you don't like weeds but have an equal antipathy to weedkiller, then you had better start learning to love concrete.

Simple surfaces

The way you treat the paths in your garden will be dictated by cost as well as taste. The simplest and cheapest method is to leave the paths as beaten earth, but your design will become more muted as a result, for you will have lost contrasts of colour and texture between paths and vegetable beds; they will also be muddy after rain. The big advantage of trodden earth paths is that they cost nothing. And they are easily re-routed if you feel like a change in layout.

Another cheap treatment is to cover the paths with chipped or ground bark, though not if you already use a good deal of the stuff as a mulch on your borders. Used on both, your garden will begin to look like a demonstration plot for the Forestry Commission's waste products. Lay the bark over black polythene if you want to cut down on weeding, but not if you like the idea of the bark itself slowly transmuting to soil. Ground, composted bark disappears faster, but gives a smooth, sleek finish. Chipped bark is coarse and rustic in effect. Both are dark treacle-coloured. Straw is even more rustic and, in country areas at least, easy to get hold of. It quickly sops up dampness in the soil and treads down to make friendly paths in vegetable gardens, especially those made in the cottage style. Both bark and straw will need to be regularly topped up.

Gravel and hoggin

Gravel, if you have not used it elsewhere, makes a good path, although it sticks to the bottom of your shoes and then magically unsticks as soon as you walk into the house. The noise that it makes when you walk on it is very satisfying, so crunchy and distinctive that police forces now recommend gravel as a useful deterrent to burglars. Plants will seed themselves into it; bulbs (and weeds) will grow through it. This may be the effect you want. If you like the idea of gravel, but want to retain it as a formal, clean, unplanted area, lay a plastic membrane down on the earth and put the gravel on top of that. Different gravels give different colours and textures. Stick to one kind and make sure it tones in with the colour and texture of the brick or stone around you. For a serene, calming finish, rake the gravel in parallel lines with a wide-tined rake. Gravel can be used in combination with other materials – perhaps a few good York paving stones set at regular intervals down the length of the path. Sea shingle, its sharp edges rubbed smooth by the waves, gives a softer look than the more usual hard-edged gravel.

Hoggin is the term for a mixture of sand, gravel and pebbles often used in kitchen gardens to provide a firm surface for heavily used work routes. It must be properly rolled, so that the constituents bind together to make a hard, durable crust. The best hoggin paths are made with a 'batter', a slightly humped profile, so that water is shed from the centre of the path to run along gutters on either side.

Edgings

If you use bark or gravel, both of which kick about easily, you will probably need an edging to the beds, to prevent the one straying into the other. Lengths of board, about 7cm (3in) deep, are simple to fix with a few wooden pegs bashed into the ground to keep them where you want them. Avoid rolls of corrugated plastic edging. It draws attention to itself without having the looks to warrant it.

If you use more permanent forms of paving for the paths, you can dispense with fixed edgings, relying on borders of parsley, alpine strawberries and the like to keep the earth vaguely in place. There will always be some sweeping up to do. Birds do not understand the pleasures of clean paths. Blackbirds in particular have beaks that excavate as efficiently as JCBs. In an ornamental kitchen garden, the paths will always tend to be on a lower level than the beds. The mulching that should be an annual routine in all gardens gradually builds up the level of the soil in the beds, which is then more likely to topple on to the paths. In this respect, plants make better nets for catching the earth than narrow planks of wood.

Permanent paths

Old bricks make good paths. DIY experts will suck their teeth knowingly if you use indoor bricks outside. Yes, they do flake in bad frosts, but they do not disintegrate entirely and the texture and colour of ordinary bricks is infinitely more pleasant than the unvarying liverish look of what is called engineering brick. Stableyard bricks are equally good, shallower and cross-hatched on the top with a regular diamond pattern.

To do the job properly, you need to excavate the soil along the route of the path to a level of about 18cm (7in) plus the thickness of the brick. Lay down hardcore 15cm (6in) deep along the path and top it off with a layer of cement, about 2cm (1in) thick. Lay the bricks on the cement, leaving narrow gaps between them. Fill the gaps with more cement, mixed very dry. Press the mixture down between the bricks with a trowel or a stick, then run the top of a stick down along the joints to take away any surplus cement. Wipe the bricks clean before any spare cement on them sets hard and is impossible to remove. Cobbles are also best laid on hardcore and cement.

Some of the best paths, such as those at Sissinghurst, the famous National Trust garden in Kent, are made from a random selection of bricks, cobbles and rubble. Some patterning of the materials – using bricks always in threes, incorporating regular roundels made from bits of blue and white china, making parallel lines of cobbles down the sides – gives a better effect than total anarchy. The advantage of this sort of path is that it gives a home to all kinds of bits and pieces that you don't want to throw away, but which don't, on their own, have much purpose. Gertrude Jekyll used to sink families of clay flower pots, one inside the other, to fill the open centres of the millstones that were such a feature of paths in Edwardian gardens designed in the Arts and Crafts style.

Asphalt is perhaps the most unpleasant surface to look at in a garden. Concrete runs it a close second but has been in the past a favourite way of surfacing a path. Laid on an uneven surface, it cracks and splits and becomes as lethal as it is unsightly. If you have got a path like that in your garden, abandon all thoughts of repairing it. Invite round a couple of aggrieved friends and get them to work out their spleen by smashing up the old concrete, which you can then cart off to the tip.

PAVING PATTERNS
Bricks, being relatively small paving units and very regular in shape, can be laid in a wide variety of patterns. Stretcher bond may mirror the pattern of a house wall. Herringbone is much more decorative, but leaves you with the interesting problem of what to do with the leftover triangles which the design will produce at the edges of the path. Basketweave is equally comfortable and less problematic to lay. When you are working with large, irregular slabs of stone, patterning is not so easy. Artificial stone does not have quite the same appeal, but it is cheap and comes in even shapes.

SCREENS AND STRUCTURES

The need for a focal point in a planting scheme dawns on you gradually. If you want your garden to be comfortable and unselfconscious, you tend not to use words like focal point. But in certain places, the eye needs something to fix on to bring the area into focus. A good focal point should seem inevitable: otherwise you get the uncomfortable feeling of being manipulated. A degree of manipulation in a garden is interesting, but if it is well done you should not be aware of it. A focal point needs to show that it is important, without divorcing itself from the rest of the garden. A bench or a seat might do the trick, particularly if you signal its importance by giving it pots as outriders, or by surrounding it with a bower or an arbour, swathed in vines and honeysuckle. Use hazel or willow hurdles if you want to screen one part of the garden from another, and tailor-made wigwams to bring height and importance to a low planting of vegetables and herbs. Such a structure is itself appealing, but it is practical too and can support useful crops of climbing beans and peas.

Using screens

Hazel and willow are the materials traditionally used to make structures such as wigwams and hurdles for the garden. Both are pliable, easy to get hold of in country areas and grow quickly from clumps that are regularly 'stooled' (cut down in rotation) to provide a non-stop, renewable supply of stems.

Boundaries made from willow or hazel hurdles will not be long lasting and they are best used for internal divisions in a garden. They blend sympathetically with plants around them and can be used, like wigwams, to support climbers or trained fruit. You might think of stretching willow hurdles end to end to divide a fruit plot from a flower plot. Use them to support a loganberry, whose stems can stretch out along the structure. The loose, woven pattern of these supports means that you will easily find spots to tie the stems in place. Plant golden hops to scramble over a woven hazel hurdle. Hops die down in winter and allow you to get in and repair the hurdles where necessary.

Criss-cross open lattice made from lengths of softwood also makes a decorative structure in the garden and would be suitable for a light boundary fence. A screen such as this would be strong enough to support the weight of a colonizing pumpkin, or you could use it to provide the background for a row of slanting cordon apples.

Wigwams to scarecrows

You can buy plant supports such as wigwams ready made from metal or wood, but, with a little practice, you can also make your own. A professional basket-maker usually works sitting down and would start a wigwam with a bunch of hazel sticks clasped between his knees. As he progresses, working further and further down the spiral of the wigwam, the whole structure is pushed under and through his knees. You might find it easier to stick the uprights in the ground, using a dustbin lid or the wheel of a bicycle to mark out the size and shape of the base. Hazel, sweet chestnut or willow can be used for the uprights, and willow, old man's beard or clematis stems for the woven spiral that holds the whole thing in place. Freshly cut stems do not need to be soaked, but you would need to soften up material that has been cut and stored by soaking it in water for a few hours. You can make the thin wands of willow that you use for the weaving even more supple by swinging them round against your finger and thumb, rather like a cowboy in a Western about to lasso a steer.

In a big wigwam there may be eighteen uprights, which makes a very stable structure. You could use fewer, but there should not be too much space between the uprights if the wigwam is to make a bold feature in your planting. Structures such as this do not last for ever. Eventually the bottoms of the uprights will begin to rot and, as the wood ages, it will become more brittle and more likely to snap under the weight of the growth it is supporting. If you have the necessary space, bring wooden structures such as this under cover in the winter after you have gathered in all your crops.

Once you have grasped the potential of materials such as willow and hazel, all kinds of possibilities open up. You may even feel you could tackle something as complex as a woven basketwork seat. You may start dreaming about a futuristic scarecrow, with a body made from bowed lengths of hazel and strong chestnut crosspieces for its arms. Dream on. Then get weaving.

UNDERSTANDING THE SOIL

Vegetable heaven is a soil that is well drained, fertile, open and neither too acid nor too alkaline. If you have an old garden, somebody else might have already converted the underlying sand or clay into a workable tilth. If not, grit your teeth and prepare to mulch, mulch, mulch. Soil is a mixture of bits of rock, water and organic matter such as rotted leaves. Sandy soils (ideal for carrots, which swell easily in this open, free-draining medium) are made from relatively large bits of rock, clay soils (good for brassicas, which prefer a solid soil) from small particles. One is called light, the other heavy. Adding bulky manures to soil is the only way to improve soil structure. The extra organic matter (humus) closes up the big spaces in sandy soils, making them capable of holding more water. In clay soils, humus adds extra air spaces between the too closely packed particles and so improves drainage.

Types of soil

What you grow and how you grow it is to some extent determined by type of soil. The five main kinds each display characteristics that make them reasonably easy to recognize.

CHALK A pale, shallow, stony topsoil indicates chalk. It is free draining and moderately fertile.

CLAY Clay is heavy, slow draining and often quite sticky. It can be hard to work but is full of nutrients.

PEAT Rich in organic matter, peat looks very dark and crumbly. It retains moisture well and makes an acid soil.

SANDY SOIL Light, gritty and free draining, sandy soil is easy to work, but it needs lots of humus to make it fertile.

SILT Silt is fertile and retains moisture well but is easily compacted. It has rather a silky feel if you squeeze it.

How soil works

Before plants can take up food, they need roots that can find it. Plant roots need passages along which they can run and from which they can then absorb the nutrients necessary for healthy growth. Humus helps to create these vital passages. No amount of chemical fertilizer will change the structure of your soil.

In town gardens it may be difficult to acquire bulky manure – the best source of humus – but make a resolution to haul in a sack of some nourishing mulch once a week until the whole plot has been covered. It will pay enormous dividends in improved growth. If you have space, you can make your own compost (see page 219) and add that to the soil. Home-made compost should have the colour and texture of rich fruit cake.

The minerals that plants need for healthy growth are generally lumped together under the heading 'trace elements' and include boron, copper, iron, manganese and zinc. In fertile soils they are present naturally, but lack of them shows up in plant deficiency diseases. Organic animal manures are rich in trace elements and if you use these regularly, you are unlikely to have problems. Magnesium deficiency (which makes leaves turn brown and wither) is more prevalent on acid soils than on alkaline ones. Chlorosis is more likely on limey soils: leaves that should be a bright, pulsating green turn a pallid, sickly yellow. It is caused by the fact that the plant cannot absorb the minerals it needs from the soil because they are locked up by too much lime. Correct the imbalance by watering with a solution of chelated iron (sequestrene).

Acid or alkaline?

Acid and alkaline are terms that apply to the pH (the potential of hydrogen) in the soil. The scale runs from 1 to 14, with neutral around 7. Most vegetables and fruit do best in this middle range. Asparagus is not happy on very acid soils, whereas blueberries demand it. Raspberries always look happier in slightly acid soils than they do in heavy, clay ground. Generally, though, good fertility and drainage have a greater effect on growth than the precise nature of the pH level.

There are simple kits available with which you can gauge the pH level of your soil, but remember to take readings from more than one part of your garden.

You can tinker with acid soils by adding extra lime if you want to make them more amenable to the growing of vegetables. It is far more difficult to convert an alkaline soil to a comfortable home for lime-hating plants.

Cultivation methods

Prepare beds for planting during autumn, winter and early spring, working only when the soil is dry enough not to stick on the bottom of your boots. Only masochists make digging loom large in the gardening calendar.

On heavy ground, you dig to expose clods of earth so that they can get broken up by frost. You dig to get air into compacted soil, to bury weeds or other organic material and to give robins a decent breakfast. Digging no longer has the heroic status it once had, along with bastard trenching and double digging, which was twice as back breaking. On light soils, forking over will often be enough. Mushroom compost or any other weed-free compost that you can spread thickly on top of the ground will eventually be pulled down into the earth by worms. That is a lot less trouble than doing it yourself.

If you are making a new bed, it may not be necessary to dig the earth at all. If you garden on light, sandy soil, weedkill it thoroughly, mulch it heavily and plant direct into the ground. Heavy ground, or places which have been used as throughways, need more attention.

Digging improves drainage and introduces air into earth that has been hard packed by feet. Heavy clay soils should be dug at the beginning of winter, light soils as late as possible in spring. Light soils do not need to be broken down by frost. The main problem here is hanging on to water and nutrients. By leaving the soil firm over winter, you will be helping it to hold as much water as possible.

The no-dig method

If you have a light, well-drained, fertile soil, the sort of soil that everyone dreams of, then you may well be able to run a fruit and vegetable garden without ever having to dig at all. Some light forking and hoeing to get rid of weeds will be all that is necessary. To maintain fertility you will have to mulch heavily. The no-dig method works well in areas of the garden where you have permanent crops such as fruit bushes or asparagus. You can use it successfully on ground where you grow transplanted crops such as tomatoes, courgettes and leeks, and also for potatoes. It is more difficult, however, to produce the fine tilth needed for seedbeds without doing any digging. A mulch in these circumstances is a hindrance rather than a help.

MULCHING, FEEDING AND WATERING

If you take care of the mulching, the feeding and watering will mostly take care of themselves. A mulch works like a biodegradable blanket: by putting a layer of compost, grass cuttings, rotted leaves or farmyard manure on top of the soil you can control weeds, retain moisture, improve soil structure, add nutrients (slowly) and keep plants and crops clean. Thick and regular mulches will make watering and feeding far less imperative. Mulches of materials that have once been plants themselves add a complex cocktail of nutrients to the soil. They also improve its condition, as earthworms gradually pull the mulch underground and aerate the soil. Without these air pockets roots cannot penetrate the soil. By mulching, you feed the soil, not the plants. Soil that is in good heart is the key to successful gardening.

Mulching

Spread mulches thickly over the soil to keep down annual weeds – no mulch will stop the growth of perennials such as bindweed. If they are to conserve moisture, do not apply mulches when the ground is dry. The following materials are ideal.

LEAFMOULD Making leafmould is a useful way of exploiting nature's own mulch. It improves soil texture and also, over time, releases valuable nutrients. Autumn leaves are far too valuable to be wasted on a bonfire. The easiest method is to pile up leaves inside a cage made from chicken wire, where they will gradually rot down. You will need a space about 1.2m (4ft) square. If you do not have room for this, pack leaves into dustbin liners instead. The best leaves to use are those of beech and oak. Leaves with thick midribs, such as ash and horse chestnut, take much longer to rot down.

MANURE A valuable source of organic matter, manure is best used when well rotted. In towns, pigeon lofts used to be a good source. Droppings are high in nitrogen and dry and light to handle.

GRASS CUTTINGS Lawn mowings are frowned on by some, but if you do not use herbicides on the lawn, you need have no worries about its safety as a mulch. They are excellent around soft fruit bushes, for instance, where they retain moisture in the soil and help keep down weeds.

GARDEN COMPOST If you have room to make a compost heap in the garden, you need never be short of humus. Any organic material – vegetable peelings, weeds, grass mowings, leaves, dead birds – can be added. Hair is excellent, full of minerals that plants need, though only in minute quantities. Gradually the whole lot rots down to something that looks very much like earth, your precious humus. Nettles are useful on compost heaps as they speed up the rate of decomposition. Covering the heap with old carpet also hurries things along but does not look very appealing. The hotter you can make your compost, the better. Heat destroys weed seeds, which are the only disadvantage of home-made compost.

MUSHROOM COMPOST Where it is available, this makes one of the best mulches. It is easy to use and sterile, but it is slightly limed, so you should not use it round blueberries.

GRAVEL You can also use inert materials such as gravel for mulching, but of course a material such as this will do nothing to feed the soil. Gravel does, however, provide extremely efficient drainage around the necks of plants prone to rot in too damp soil and can be used to great effect around herbs such as thyme, rosemary and marjoram.

Feeding

Fertilizers are compounds that you use to replace nutrients taken from the soil. They can be natural or manufactured and a fierce debate rages as to the benefits of one against the other. Organic fertilizers supply nutrients of plant or animal origin; extract of seaweed, hoof and horn, and bonemeal are typical. These are broken down by bacteria in the soil and then drawn in by the plants' roots. Inorganic fertilizers are either manufactured or of mineral origin, such as ground chalk or ammonium sulphate. Organic fertilizers are cheaper but tend to work more slowly than inorganic ones.

Using high-octane inorganic fertilizers is like using hard drugs. Instant benefit is cancelled out by long-term problems. Only plants growing in unnatural circumstances (usually confined spaces such as pots, hanging baskets and the like) are likely to need manufactured fertilizers. Leaving aside the larger argument against nitrates, leaching, pollution and the rest, think of what they do to your soil. Manufactured fertilizers work fast; that is one of the reasons they are popular. But they feed the plant rather than the soil. This upsets the delicate balance of the soil's own life, which includes important micro-organisms invisible to our eyes. Soil can die, although we cannot see the process. Manufactured fertilizers do not supply as clever a balance of nutrients as a plant can find for itself, if the soil is in good heart. Nitrates promote rapid growth, but plants fed in this way grow artificially fast, which may have a detrimental effect on taste. They often have too high a water content and, being sappy, are more open to attack by pest and disease. Which leads you to reach for a different bottle . . . Neither organic nor inorganic fertilizers are enough on their own. You need to add organic matter to the soil to enhance fertility and structure. Back to the mulch.

Watering

Watering gardens is a luxury, not a prerogative. Plants growing in restricted spaces such as pots, hanging baskets and grow bags need frequent drinks. The rest of the garden should not, if you use plenty of organic manures to enhance the water-retaining capacity of the soil. Watering unnecessarily may increase the growth of a plant, without increasing the quality of the bit you are going to eat. The crops that respond best to watering are leafy ones such as lettuce, cabbage and spinach. Crops that bear seeds and fruits such as beans, peas and tomatoes are best watered while the plants are in flower and the fruits swelling. Transplants of brassicas, celery and leeks need frequent watering until they are established. Overwatering of root crops such as parsnip or carrot after a prolonged dry spell tends to make the roots split. Once again, mulching is the long-term solution.

CROP ROTATION

The first thing that novice vegetable gardeners need to know about crop rotation is that their vegetables will not necessarily crumple up and weep if they are not moved to new homes each year. For many years crop rotation, along with double digging and bastard trenching, was one of the great shibboleths of vegetable growing. Yet the best gardeners are not those that rely on rules for success but those who use their eyes, take the trouble to learn the little vagaries of their own plot, work with the weather and have respect for their soil. Success in gardening comes from finding the right balance between what you want the plants to do and what they want you to do. Plants are successful because each has adapted over millions of years to make the most of a particular set of conditions. Learn to recognize each plant's needs. Crop rotation should reflect those needs, not become an end in itself.

The reason why
The most persuasive argument for the practice of some form of crop rotation has to do with the soil. Each different type of vegetable crop – brassicas, onions, legumes, potatoes – needs a slightly different cocktail of nutrients and trace elements from the soil. If you always grow your cauliflowers in the same place, it is likely that the soil there will eventually become drained of the ingredients that the cauliflowers most want. By moving them on to a different plot, you give the first plot a chance to recover and replenish itself from the liberal supplies of compost that you will, of course, be giving it.

The case for avoiding disease by rotating crops is less clear cut. If your brassicas have the misfortune to be struck by clubroot, they will of course do better if you plant them the following season in fresh ground. But the spores of clubroot, which causes swollen and distorted roots in all members of the cabbage family, can live for more than twenty years in the soil. Even if you practise a five-year rotation, those spores will still be lurking hungrily when the brassicas eventually return to their original plot. The spores of the fungus that causes white rot in onions is equally long lived. Also, in a small garden, it is unlikely that any of your plots will be distant enough from each other to prevent pests and diseases languidly drifting over the unmarked boundary lines into the neighbouring patch and re-infecting the crop. Your best defence against disease, in plants as with people, is to take every possible step to prevent it breaking out in the first place. And to be sanguine in those seasons when aphids outnumber predators and the noise of flea beetles jumping off cabbage leaves is louder than the crunch of your foot on the snails that are eating the lettuces.

The main groups

Traditional crop rotations revolve around three main groups of vegetables. First are the legumes (peas and beans), which are usually thrown together with a ragbag of other vegetables including sweetcorn, courgettes and tomatoes that do not fit tidily into any other compartment. Legumes are followed by the brassicas, which include swedes, turnips, kohl rabi and radishes as well as more obviously cabbage-like vegetables such as cauliflowers, Brussels sprouts and broccoli. Finally there are the roots and tubers: beetroots, carrots, Jerusalem artichokes, parsnips and potatoes. In a three-bed rotation, onions will be included with the legumes. In a four-bed rotation, onions will be hived off to make a separate group, with leeks, garlic and shallots. Lettuces and other salad crops can be fitted in wherever there is room.

As a group, the brassicas are the crops that are greediest for lime and muck, so they usually fit in at the beginning of a rotation, when if necessary you can lime a bed specially for them. By the following season, the muck will be well broken down and so you can follow with root crops. Root crops such as carrots should not be planted in freshly manured ground as it causes the roots to fork. In the third year, you follow the root crops with peas and beans, which have the useful trick of producing nitrogen-rich nodules on their roots. These will be much appreciated by the brassicas when they come round on the carousel again to the plot where they first started.

An inflexible attitude to crop rotation is not likely to help your vegetables as much as a common-sense appraisal of their needs. If you have one sheltered, sunny, south-facing plot, it would be a waste to use it for peas or cabbages, neither of which need that kind of protection. Tomatoes and sweetcorn, on the other hand, will be unlikely to crop successfully without it. If one part of your ground is markedly lighter and more free draining than another, then carrots will do better there than in the stiff ground that seems to suit members of the cabbage family. In thinking about rotations, you also have to be realistic about what you are most likely to eat and have the skill to grow. If you do not like cabbages and are unsuccessful in raising cauliflowers (not the easiest of crops to grow well), it will be a waste of valuable space to include them in a rotation.

The weather has an effect on crop rotation, as it does on all other aspects of gardening. Periods of very heavy rain may result in nitrogen leaching out of the soil and no amount of crop switching can remedy this. Nitrogen deficiency is the commonest of all mineral deficiencies. Leaves become pale in colour, growth is restricted and pink or purple patches may appear on the foliage of brassicas, which are particularly hungry for nitrogen.

HOW A 3-BED PLAN WORKS

Most gardeners will only need to use a simple 3-year, 3-bed rotation. The easiest way is to list the vegetables you want to grow and split them into the 3 main groups (in rotation terms, beds really means groups, not actual growing beds). Draw a rough plan of the garden and mark which crops can grow where, using a different colour for each group. The following year, move on the crops accordingly. Fit fast-growing vegetables (catch crops) into any convenient gaps.

YEAR 1 **YEAR 2** **YEAR 3**

PEAS	BRUSSELS SPROUTS	BEETS
BEANS	CABBAGES	CARROTS
CELERY	CAULIFLOWERS	CHICORY
ONIONS	BROCCOLI	JERUSALEM ARTICHOKES
LEEKS	KOHL RABI	PARSNIPS
LETTUCE	RUTABAGAS	POTATOES
SPINACH	TURNIPS	
SWEETCORN	RADISHES	
TOMATOES		
COURGETTES		

4-BED PLAN

In a 4-bed rotation, onions can be hived off into a separate group, along with leeks, garlic and shallots. Lettuce and other fast-growing salad leaves can be fitted in as catch crops wherever there is a spare patch of ground.

YEAR 1 **YEAR 2** **YEAR 3** **YEAR 4**

SCARLET RUNNER BEANS	BRUSSELS SPROUTS	ONIONS	PEPPERS
SNAP BEANS	CABBAGES	SHALLOTS	TOMATOES
PEAS	CAULIFLOWERS	LEEKS	CELERY
BROAD BEANS	BROCCOLI	GARLIC	CELERIAC
SWEETCORN	ORIENTAL VEGETABLES	COURGETTES	BEETS
	RUTABAGAS	LETTUCE	CARROTS
	TRUNIPS		PARSNIPS
	RADISHES		POTATOES

5-BED PLAN

A 5-bed rotation is for control freaks, whose chief joy is to lie awake at night dreaming up ever more complex ways of utilizing space, time and labour in the microcosm of the garden. But as gardeners, we take our pleasure and delight where we like. If you feel the best route to happiness lies in a 5-bed rotation system, follow the chart below. The onion family have a section all to themselves, as do potatoes and other root vegetables.

YEAR 1	YEAR 2	YEAR 3	YEAR 4	YEAR 5

BROAD BEANS	CAULIFLOWERS	COURGETTES	ONIONS	POTATOES
SCARLET RUNNER BEANS	BROCCOLI	SWEETCORN	GARLIC	PARSNIPS
PEAS	CABBAGES	TOMATOES	LEEKS	CARROTS
SNAP BEANS	TURNIPS	CELERY	LETTUCE	BEETS
	RADISHES	CELERIAC	SHALLOTS	RUTABAGAS
	BRUSSELS SPROUTS			JERUSALEM ARTICHOKES
	ORIENTAL BRASSICAS			

GROWING METHODS

The way that you grow is necessarily influenced by the kind of soil that you have. If you garden on heavy ground, the idea of making raised, deep beds may be more compelling than if you have light, free-draining sandy soil. If you live in a frost hollow where winter comes early and spring late, you'll have more reason to try out a floating polypropylene mulch to extend the growing season. Some growing techniques relate to particular crops. If you want fat white buds of chicory, you have to learn how to force them.

Deep beds

The deep bed system is not as luxuriously sybaritic as it sounds It is a way of growing plants, usually vegetables, in a series of beds no more than 1.5m (5ft) wide that are divided by narrow paths about 30cm (12in) wide. This sort of layout means you can do all the planting, weeding and general cultivation from the paths, without ever treading on the beds. This stops the soil becoming compacted, and helps drainage and soil structure. To make the beds, it is essential to dig the ground thoroughly and clear it of all perennial weeds. After that, heavy mulches of bulky organic matter must be applied regularly, making the beds higher than the paths. That is why they are called deep beds. What you lose on the pathways, you gain by more intensive cropping in the beds. Plant in short rows running across the beds with plants equidistant from one another. Because you are planting closely, you must feed the soil well. The best way is with a bulky organic mulch. The initial labour of making the beds is daunting, but once made you have only to maintain the layout and the system makes rotation of crops a very simple proposition.

Floating mulches

Plastic films have been used for many years by professional growers, either to protect crops or accelerate their rate of growth. Various types of film – clear, fleecy, perforated or plain – are now available to the amateur grower. They do not guard against frost, but you can use them to warm up the soil or to give extra protection to early crops. Brassicas, lettuce, early potatoes, radish and onions may all benefit from being covered with a plastic film for the first four or five weeks of the growing period. The film must be well anchored around the edges, either by being buried in the soil, or by being weighted down with stones or lengths of timber. If the edges are well sealed, plastic films can provide useful protection against pests such as cabbage root fly, carrot fly, flea beetle, cabbage white butterfly as well as predatory birds or rabbits. Soft fleecy films may be left in place over crops such as lettuce for the whole of its growing period. The term 'floating mulch' is confusing, as these films do not do what mulches do (keep down weeds, retain moisture, feed soil) but help to raise the soil temperature and guard against weather and pests.

Intercropping

On good, fertile soil you will be able to increase yields from the garden by intercropping, which is a way of squeezing more produce from less ground. It will only work if the crops are well fed and watered. You need, too, to find complementary crops, perhaps one that is faster than the other, or ones that grow in different directions. Radish is a classic example of a good intercropper. It grows fast and you can sow it between rows of carrots or parsnips, which take much longer to mature. You will have cleared away and eaten the radish before the parsnip needs the growing space for itself. Sweetcorn mostly needs vertical space and you set out the plants quite far apart. But you can use the space under them by intercropping with sprawling bush tomatoes or trailing marrows. Use small upright cos lettuce such as 'Tom Thumb' between rows of garlic, or ribbons of quick-growing saladini between newly planted out brassicas, which will take a long time to fill their allotted space.

Earthing up

It is more difficult to intercrop in the early stages between rows of vegetables such as potatoes because as they grow, they will need to be earthed up. You do this with potatoes to prevent any possibility of the tubers developing poisonous green patches, which they will do if they are exposed to the light. Start earthing up when the plants are about 30cm (12in) high, drawing up the soil around the stems on either side of the row. You can bury the lower leaves, but leave the tops uncovered. You can also earth up mature plants of Brussels sprouts to give the stems extra stability in exposed areas. Celery is earthed up in order to blanch the stems.

Forcing and blanching

These both have similar aims, which involve keeping light from the stems or leaves of vegetables to make them more tender (blanching) or to hurry them into growth (forcing). Vegetables to be blanched can be earthed up, wrapped in collars of thick paper or covered by a pot. Celery is usually given a paper collar and also earthed up. The hearts of endives can be blanched with a saucer upturned over the centre of the plant. Crops such as rhubarb can be forced by covering plants with tall terracotta pots shaped like chimneys, which make extremely attractive features in a kitchen garden. Stretching to reach the light at the top of the pot, the stems of rhubarb grow much longer than they would otherwise do. Belgian chicory needs both forcing and blanching. Outside, if the soil is not too heavy or cold, cut any leaves to 2cm (1in) above the neck of the plant and cover the stumps with at least 15cm (6in) of soil. Then fix cloches over the top.

The process is faster inside, when you can use plants that have been lifted, trimmed and stored in boxes of sand. Shorten the roots to 15cm (6in) and then set 3–6 plants upright in a 23cm (9in) pot of compost, leaving the tops exposed. Invert a similar-sized pot over the top to keep out light and store at 10–18°C/50–65°F while the blanched chicons develop. This will take about three weeks in the warmth of an airing cupboard, longer in a cooler cellar.

SOWING INSIDE

To the uninitiated, seed sowing is the impenetrable rite of passage that separates the novice from the seasoned gardener. It is not usually half as difficult, however, as experts try to make it and you do not need batteries of equipment. When you are sowing indoors, propagator heat will make seeds germinate more quickly and plants grow faster than they would otherwise do, but at some stage they must learn to do without it and take on the weather as it really is. The tougher plants have been raised, the better they will cope. The more sparsely you sow, the stronger plants will be for later transplanting. Greenhouses provide ideal conditions for sowing seed, but there is much that you can raise on a kitchen windowsill if it is light and warm.

Sowing in a container

Save your seed trays for pricking out and make your initial sowing in a clean plastic pot about 12cm (5in) across. Fill it with compost and firm it down gently. Scatter the seed as thinly and evenly as you can over the surface of the compost. Each gardener devises his or her own favourite way of doing this. Some like to tip it into the palm of one hand, and then take pinches of seed between the thumb and the forefinger of the other hand and sprinkle it thinly over the compost; others are confident enough to scatter seed directly from the packet with a series of gentle taps. Cover the seed with a thin layer of compost or vermiculite, which many gardeners find easier to use as a seed covering. Vermiculite is a lightweight mineral rather like mica, which retains moisture but also drains quickly. Perlite, made from expanded granules of volcanic minerals, has the same qualities, though the size of the granules makes it less suitable as a seed covering. You do not have to worry about the exact depth of a covering of vermiculite, as you do if you are using compost. Water the pot thoroughly before sealing it up in a cocoon of cling film, which will prevent the compost drying out. If you have a propagator, you can stand the pots in that.

Once the seeds have germinated, take the cover off the pot, keep the compost damp but not saturated and turn the pots round regularly, as the seedlings always tip themselves towards the light. Damping off may be a problem with seedlings raised indoors. Seedlings suddenly collapse at the point where stem meets soil and whole pots of seeds may be affected. Overwatering is the most common cause, but it may also arise from using old compost in dirty pots.

Large seeds, such as those of cucumber and melon, can be sown in single 7cm (3in) pots, setting one or two seeds on edge in each pot. If you sow two, you will need to remove the weaker of the two seedlings when they have germinated. Seeds sown in this way can stay in their pots until they are transplanted outside.

Pricking out

Seedlings grown *en masse* in a 12cm (5in) pot need to be pricked out – that is moved on to fresh quarters sooner rather than later. Growing close together, as they do in the initial seed pot, seedlings quickly get leggy, with too much stem to top, and then keel over at the slightest disturbance. One evening when you feel in need of some calming, therapeutic activity, fill some full-sized seed trays with compost, gently firm down the surface and, with your forefinger, poke a grid of holes in the compost, six along the long side, four along the short. With a lolly stick or teaspoon, gently ease up a few seedlings at a time from the pot. Pick each one up by a leaf and drop it into one of the holes you have made in the compost. Set the seedlings deep, so that the first pair of leaves sits on the surface of the compost. Firm the compost round them gently with your fingers. When the whole tray is planted, water it thoroughly with a fine-nozzled can.

Seedlings of tomatoes that have spent the first part of their lives in a 12cm (5in) pot should be pricked out into 7cm (3in) pots, one plant in each pot. Fill the small pots with compost, make a hole in the centre with your forefinger and drop in the seedling, setting it deeper than it was originally growing.

Gently firm the compost around the stem.

Plants that resent having their roots disturbed, such as Chinese cabbage, can be pricked out into modules, which are specially modified planting trays, divided into separate small compartments, which can be anything from 1cm (^{1}/2in) to 5cm (2in) across. You can improvise your own modules by using cardboard egg boxes. Sow in the lid and prick out seedlings into each of the six compartments. The advantage of modules is that roots have less competition for nutrients and are less disturbed when they are transplanted. You can also sow two or three seeds direct into modules and thin them after they have germinated.

Hardening off

The compost in the modules or the tray in which you have pricked out plants should contain enough food for the seedlings to live on until they can be planted out, usually in late spring. Watering is an important job, as is hardening off the plants, getting them acclimatized to the real world. Do this gently, putting the trays out on warmish days and bringing them in at nights until the plants seem sturdy enough to be planted out. You can help to harden off plants inside by brushing them over the top with the edge of a piece of card. Do this for about a minute each day, brushing in different directions. This flexing of the stems strengthens them, simulating the effect of wind out of doors. But even if you brush your plants, you will still have to acclimatize them gradually to lower temperatures outside. If you intend to grow plants such as melons, cucumbers, tomatoes and aubergines in a greenhouse, rather than outside in the garden, then you will not need to harden them off. They will be living their entire lives in luxurious warmth and shelter.

Transplanting

Planting out vegetables such as courgettes, cucumbers or tomatoes that you have been growing under cover in pots is not usually as detrimental to the plant as transplanting it from a drill or a seedbed. You can ease the rootball out of the pot without disturbing the roots and if you water them in well, these plants will not usually be too badly checked. In general, the earlier seedlings can be transplanted to their permanent quarters the better. Move lettuces when they have about four leaves, cabbages and other brassicas when they are about 10cm (4in) tall.

SOWING OUTSIDE

Vegetables are more often grown from seed sown direct in the ground outside than by any other means. Seed of frost-tender vegetables such as courgettes and tomatoes is sown inside in order to get as long a growing season as possible for the crops, but many vegetables, such as brassicas, carrots, and beetroot, do not need this treatment. Some vegetables are sown in short rows in seedbeds and transplanted later to their final growing positions. Brassicas and leeks are often treated in this way, though in very exposed situations, but both could if necessary be raised under cover and grown in pots and trays for planting out later. Other vegetables, such as parsnips, peas and radishes, are sown in the positions they will occupy for the whole of their growing lives. Remember this when preparing the site for sowing. Do not expect seedlings to hoist great clods of soil on their backs in their struggle to reach the light.

Sowing
PREPARING THE GROUND
If you are sowing outside, good preparation of the seedbed is the single most important factor in getting seeds to germinate. Some soils are easier to work than others. On sandy soils, you may only have to clear the soil of weeds and rake it, in order to create the fine, crumbly tilth that a seed likes to lie in. On clay you will hope that frost has helped during winter to break down obdurate clods of earth. Banging with the back of a rake also helps. The smaller the seed you are sowing, the finer the tilth should be.
SOWING IN A DRILL
This is the most usual way to grow vegetables from seed. Stretch out a line (usually stout twine attached to a short stake or peg either end) to make a straight row and take out a drill. The depth of the drill should depend on the size of the seed: shallow for small seed, deeper for big seed. Scatter small seed as thinly as possible along the drill, to avoid as far as possible the need for thinning. Seed such as beetroot or parsnip can be sown 'at stations' – that is, in little groups of two or three, spaced at intervals. Leave only the strongest seedling to grow on at each station. Cover the seed carefully with soil. If the ground is very dry, water the drill before sowing; otherwise water afterwards with a fine-nozzled can.
SOWING IN A WIDE DRILL
Use wide flat-bottomed drills for vegetables such as peas and cut-and-come-again crops like oriental saladini that are best grown in broad rows. The drill should be roughly 23cm (9in) wide. You can make it either with a hoe or with a spade. Space peas evenly along the drill, but broadcast seeds of cut-and-come-again crops as thinly as you can. Cover the drill with the earth you have removed and smooth it over carefully.
BROADCASTING
To broadcast seed is to scatter it over a relatively wide area, rather than confining it to a single drill. It is a technique that is most useful where you have a series of raised beds, each bearing a different crop, or where you

are filling part of a formally patterned potager, where you need blocks of crops, rather than rows. It is also the method to use when growing saladini – a mixture of salad leaves such as looseleaf lettuce and rocket – or oriental brassicas. Grow the plants as a cut-and-come-again crop, picking the leaves while they are still quite small.

Thinning

Seeds that are sown direct, such as carrots and beetroot, may need to be thinned to allow each plant a chance to develop its full potential. If you practise the art of sowing thinly in the first place, you can escape this wasteful task. Pests and diseases will do their own grim thinning, so carry out yours in stages, nipping off tiny seedlings rather than uprooting them and disturbing the roots of their neighbours. It is particularly important to avoid thinning carrots, because the smell of the bruised seedlings will act like a magnet for the carrot fly and the tiny holes you make by pulling up transplants will give it ready-made points of entry.

Transplanting

Vegetables such as leeks, Brussels sprouts and other brassicas are often grown in nursery seedbeds. These are small patches of ground where you can rake the soil to a mouthwatering tilth and use this to sow seeds in short drills. At some stage the plants will need to be moved to their final growing positions. Try to do this when the soil is damp and the weather overcast, so that the uprooted plants will not have to struggle too much to find their feet. Trowel up the plants with as much soil as possible around the roots and replant them in a hole that takes the root ball comfortably. Replant brassicas so that their lowest leaves are level with the soil. Leeks should be dropped into holes made with a dibber, so that they are set much deeper than they were growing in the nursery bed. Wash earth over their roots by watering them in liberally. They will need no other attention. Thinnings of crops such as lettuce may be transplanted with success, if the soil is moist and the temperature moderate, but you cannot transplant taprooted vegetables such as parsnip or carrot successfully.

PROPAGATION

Propagation can easily become an obsession. There is no more wildly parental feeling than watching your first successful cutting turn into a grown-up bush. In the kitchen garden, cuttings will mostly be of soft fruit: the currant family, gooseberries. When you become really ambitious, you may turn your hand to figs, which strike very easily from hardwood cuttings taken from the parent tree in mid- or late autumn. Fruits such as blackberry and loganberry require even less effort, for wherever the growing tip of a stem touches the ground, it will root and produce a fresh plant. But since they take up so much space – a loganberry can cover 4.8m (16ft) of wall without even trying – you may find that you are dissuading rather than persuading your specimen to reproduce itself. Vegetables in the kitchen garden are mostly grown each year from seed. Rhubarb and globe artichoke are perennials, and both produce offsets around the edge of the growing clump. A sharp spade is what you need here, to separate the siblings from their parent.

Dividing

RHUBARB Dividing is one of the easiest ways of increasing your stock of plants and, in the kitchen garden, rhubarb is a prime candidate for this particular type of propagation. Wait until the leaves die back in autumn before taking the spade to it. Then scrape the earth gently away to expose the buds. Drive a spade down between them, making sure that each section has a healthy bud. Replant the sections in their new quarters, spacing them about 1m (3ft) apart. Set them so that the bud just shows above the soil. On light soils, you should plant more deeply.

GLOBE ARTICHOKES You need to replace these on a regular basis, as old plants become woody and unproductive. As artichokes start into growth in spring, they produce a circlet of offsets around the woody crown. Each offset is made up of a plume of young leaves, all sprouting from the same point. Drive a sharp spade down alongside the clump to detach the offset, which may or may not have embryo roots (if not, it will quickly grow some). Plant the offset in fresh ground, burying it only just sufficiently to keep it standing upright. Water it frequently. The outer leaves will die back, but the plant will renew itself very quickly. Leave about 1m (3ft) between newly planted offsets.

Taking cuttings
SOFT FRUIT BUSHES

In order to propagate fruit such as currants or gooseberries, you need a spare plot of well-prepared ground where you can line out the cuttings. They will be there for a year, so think hard before you tie up ground for this length of time. There are only so many gooseberries that you can eat in a season. Propagate red and white currants and gooseberries by taking hardwood cuttings (30–37cm/12–15in long) in mid-autumn from vigorous, clean, well-ripened stems. Strip off all but the top four or five buds and bury the cuttings 15cm (6in) deep in your prepared nursery bed. Grow the cuttings on in this bed for a year before transplanting the new bushes to their permanent quarters in the following autumn. Don't forget that these bushes are most easily managed if they are grown on a short stem. Do not allow branches on the new bush to break from ground level.

Blackcurrants should be dealt with in a slightly different way. Take hardwood cuttings 20–25cm (8–10in) long in autumn and leave all the buds intact on the cutting. Bury it so that only two buds show above ground level. Whereas with gooseberries and red or white currants you want only one stem or leg to support the branches, a blackcurrant should constantly renew itself from below ground level. If you are lucky, each buried bud on the cutting will start into growth, so that when you dig it up in the following autumn, it will already have three or four decent-sized stems.

FIGS These take longer to find their feet. For your cuttings, choose 30cm (12in) sections of hardwood (that is well-ripened wood, not taken from the growing tip of a branch) and bury them up to half their length in well-drained soil in a sheltered, sunny spot. After two years, transplant the new young tree to its final growing position. Figs can also be layered. For this, you need a pliable one-year-old shoot growing near the ground. Strip off the leaves that are growing below the tip and bend the shoot down into a little depression that you have scraped in the earth below it. Cover the branch with soil and put a stone on top of it to keep it in place. After a year, you can cut the layer from the parent plant. Leave it in place for a further year so that it develops a strong root system.

BLUEBERRIES These are propagated from softwood cuttings, taken in early summer from healthy bushes. Choose growths 10–20cm (4–8in) long and strip off all but the top three leaves. Set each cutting in a 7cm (3in) pot of sandy, ericaceous compost, water the pot and cover it with a polythene bag. Cuttings can also be rooted in a propagator with the temperature set at about 18°C (65°F). Rooting will take between three and six weeks. When the cuttings are beginning to grow away, harden them off and pot them on into larger pots of lime-free compost before planting them out in autumn.

Layering

CANE FRUIT Blackberries, loganberries and other hybrid berries such as boysenberry and tayberry are propagated by tip layering, which is best done from early to late summer. Poke the growing tip of a cane into the ground, burying it about 10–12cm (4–5in) deep with the tip pointing downwards. In a few weeks a new growing tip will emerge and in the autumn you can sever the tip layer from the mother plant and put it in its new position.

STRAWBERRIES These increase by means of runners. All through summer, mature plants will send out long exploratory green stems which, when they have found a piece of bare ground away from the parent plant, will produce a small strawberry plant. This quickly sends down its own roots and starts to grow away. If you have just planted out a new strawberry bed, you will spend the first three years nipping off all these runners, as you want your plants to concentrate on producing fruit and you do not want your neat lines of plants to become a thick, matted mess. But strawberry plants lose vigour after three or four years. When you sense this is happening, you should leave enough runners in place to create an entirely new strawberry bed, planted in fresh, well-fed ground. The lazy (but effective) way is to wait for the runners to root themselves where they will. Or you can sink 7cm (3in) pots of compost into the ground, so that the rim of the pot is at the same level as the earth around it. Then peg down runners into each pot. Whichever method you choose, in early autumn you need to cut the baby plantlets from their runners and plant them out in their new bed. Old plants should be destroyed.

HERBS Some of the most useful herbs such as parsley, coriander and chervil are raised each year from seed, but shrubby herbs such as sage, rosemary and thyme can be propagated easily by mound layering. In spring pile free-draining soil over the base of the plant, leaving just the growing tops exposed. If your soil is thick and sticky, mix it in a bucket with sand or compost before mounding it up around the plant. Replenish the mound with fresh earth through summer if necessary. This technique stimulates roots to grow on the branches that are covered with soil. In late summer or autumn, you can carefully scrape away the earth, cut rooted sections of branch from the parent plant and set them out in their new homes. Cotton lavender (santolina), hyssop, lavender, southern wood, winter savory and wormwood can also be propagated by mound layering.

CHOOSING FRUIT TREES

Much pleasure in a decorative kitchen garden can come from trained fruit trees, perhaps curving to make a tunnel of blossom over a path, or splayed out on walls to make geometric espaliers and fans. Use parallel sets of cordons to screen off one part of the garden from another, or set low hedges of stepover apples around your salad plot. These low apple hurdles look equally good stretched out in front of a flower border. Fans of peaches and apricots are practical as well as beautiful, for spreadeagled on a sunny wall the blossom is protected from frost and the fruit has the best possible chance of ripening. The simplest route to success is to buy fruit trees ready trained in the shape you want.

Tree styles
CORDONS These are the answer where quantity rather than quality of fruit is the goal. A cordon is a single-stemmed tree which is usually planted at an angle of 45 degrees to reduce vigour and produce as much fruiting wood

as possible within easy reach. Cordons need to be tied in to parallel wires stretched between posts. They are normally grown on dwarfing rootstocks and several different cultivars of apples and pears can be grown together to make a fruitful screen. Double cordons are grown upright, the two arms making a goblet shape. For cordons use rootstocks M9, M26, MM106 (apples) and Quince A or Quince C for pears.

BUSH TREES Bushes start fruiting when they are very young, are easy to pick and spray but are difficult to mow under. They will never have the satisfying shape of a full-blown tree. Use rootstocks M27, M9, M26, MM106 (apples) and Quince A or Quince C for pears.

HALF STANDARDS AND STANDARDS These are the apple trees of picture books. Half standards have a clear stem of at least 1.2m (4ft) while full standards go up to 1.8m (6ft) before the branches break from the trunk. Their height makes spraying and picking slightly more difficult to manage, but they are infinitely more pleasing to look at than a dwarfed bush. When you plant a half standard, you dream of picnicking in its shade, of slinging a hammock from its branches. There is no such romance with a bush. For half standards use rootstocks MM106 or MM111 (apples) and Quince A for pears. For standards use MM111 or M25 (apples) and pear seedling for pears.

FANS These are more often used for cherries, plums, peaches and pears than they are for apples. The name explains the shape, which looks particularly good against a stone or brick wall. The branches are best trained on rigid canes of bamboo and, as with all trained forms of fruit tree, summer pruning is essential. Use rootstocks M26 or MM106 for apples, and Quince A or Quince C for pears.

ESPALIERS An espalier is trained to make several flat tiers of branches, like a wedding cake. It may have two, three or four sets of parallel branches, depending on the space available. Naturally, they take up more space than cordons, but can be used in the same way, to make a geometric screen. The branches need to be tied in regularly as they grow and careful pruning is imperative if the espalier is to keep its formal two-dimensional shape. If the main trunk is trained on a curved hoop over a path, espaliers can be used to make beautiful fruit tunnels. Use rootstocks M26 or MM106 for apples and Quince A or Quince C for pears.

STEPOVER A stepover tree is a miniature espalier, with only one set of arms, growing out about 30cm (12in) above the ground. Use rootstocks M27 or M9 for apples. Pears are generally too vigorous to make manageable stepovers.

The style of tree you choose should be considered hand in hand with site, cultivar and rootstock. Some of the most aristocratic and fussy dessert pears such as 'Marie Louise', 'Winter Nelis' and 'Glou Morceau' are best grown as fans or espaliers against a wall where they can develop full flavour. An apple tree such as 'Bramley's Seedling', however, would not be a good cultivar to choose for a trained tree: it is too vigorous and would be difficult to control by pruning. If you have poor soil, then you are unlikely to succeed with dwarfing rootstocks. They are demanding things and need weed-free ground as well as careful feeding and watering.

Rootstocks

A rootstock lends its roots to another plant, which if grown on its own roots would behave differently. While roses are often grafted on to briar rootstocks to make them more vigorous, fruit trees are sometimes put on dwarfing rootstocks, which make them less vigorous. Good grafts are imperceptible. Bad ones are like a crooked elbow. Sometimes the rootstock makes a bid to take over the graft. In roses, this is called suckering, but it happens with fruit trees too. The suckers should be cut or pulled out as soon as you see them.

Good nurserymen will offer fruit grafted on to more than one type of rootstock, so you can choose the right one for your particular needs. You might want to grow the early dessert apple 'Discovery'. This is of only medium vigour, so you would not generally want it on the extremely dwarfing M27 stock. For a cordon in a restricted situation on good soil, you might choose M9 as the rootstock. On poor soil, you would be better off with MM106. This would also be the best choice for growing 'Discovery' as an espalier or fan, but if you wanted to grow it as a specimen half standard in the lawn, then you need to look for a tree grafted on MM111 stock.

Types of rootstock

Fruit trees are usually grafted on to a range of rootstocks that control the rate at which the trees grow, as well as the eventual size they will reach. As a rule, dwarfing rootstocks bring a tree into production earlier, but are more demanding in terms of growing conditions.

APPLES

M27 Extremely dwarfing, producing trees that are unlikely to exceed 1.8m (6ft) in height or spread. They crop very early in life (2–3 years old), need little pruning and can, with care, be grown in tubs. As their root systems are sparse, they only succeed in very fertile soil and must be kept staked throughout their lives. Trees grown on this rootstock are usually more expensive than those on MM106 or M9.

M9 Very dwarfing, producing trees from 2–2.5m (7–8ft) in height and spread and cropping while still young (3–4 years). Though slightly more tolerant than M27, this rootstock still needs good soil to succeed and trees must be permanently staked.

MM106 For the average garden, this produces a tree of an ideal size, from 3.5–4.8m (12–16ft) in height and spread, cropping when 4–5 years old. Roots become well anchored, so the tree does not have to be permanently staked and will grow vigorously even on poor, sandy soils.

MM111 A vigorous rootstock which produces trees from 4.5–5.5m (15–18ft) in height and width. It is generally used for standards and half standards, but trees do not start fruiting for 6–7 years.

M25 This is the rootstock to use for posterity. Ideal for orchard and specimen trees, it is forgiving of poor growing conditions, but produces big trees from 4.8–5.5m (16–18ft) at maturity.

PEARS

Quince C Trees on Quince C start fruiting earlier and make smaller trees, generally about 3m (10ft) high and wide, than those on Quince A, but the rootstock is only suitable for very fertile soils, or where you are growing cordons in a confined space.

Quince A This semi-vigorous rootstock is a good all-round performer, producing trees from 3.5-4.5m (12–15ft) high and wide. It is said to be more frost resistant than Quince C.

Pear seedling rootstock Plant pears for your heirs, gardeners used to say. Pears on pear roots, not necessarily their own, grow slowly to produce some of the most beautiful trees you could desire. Only suitable for standards or half standards.

PLUMS

Pixy This produces trees 3–4.5m (10–15ft) high and wide, from a half to two-thirds the size of trees on St Julien A. Only suitable for very fertile soil and attentive gardeners. Trees must be permanently staked.

Ferlenain Like Pixy, semi-dwarfing and used for pyramids and fans, gives bigger fruit than Pixy but prone to suckering.

St Julien A Widely available and compatible with all cultivars. Semi-vigorous rootstock producing trees up to 6m (20ft) high and wide.

Brompton Too vigorous for small gardens, but good for standards in an orchard setting, where it may eventually produce trees 7.5m (25ft) high and wide.

PEACHES AND NECTARINES

St Julien A A semi-vigorous rootstock, capable of producing a fan 3.5–4.5m (12–15ft) wide.

Brompton A more vigorous rootstock, producing fans 4.5–6m (15–20ft) wide.

APRICOT

St Julien A Apricots are generally grafted on to this plum rootstock, which produces a fan about 4.5m (15ft) wide or a bush of about the same size.

Torinel Another popular semi-vigorous rootstock.

CHERRY

Gisela 5 Perhaps the best choice for bushes, half standards and fans.

Tabel This is a semi-dwarfing rootstock, producing trees 3–3.75m (10–12ft) high and wide. It is a good choice for fan-trained trees.

Colt This is an old and reliable rootstock for standard trees from 4.5–6mm (15–20ft) high and wide.

PLANTING AND POLLINATION

Take time to plant a fruit tree. It deserves your full attention, for it has the potential to be one of the longest-serving features in your new kitchen garden. That potential is unlikely to be realized if you cram it into a measly little hole with its roots coiled around as dizzily as vipers in a basket. Excavate generously, remain oblivious to the siren calls of the mobile phone, the coffee pot or any other distraction, and do not leave the tree's roots drying in the wind while you dig. Give some thought, too, to your tree's sex life. Some fruit trees are self-fertile, which relieves you of any further worry on this score. Others need to have suitable pollinating partners not more than a bee's hop away.

Planting

If your fruit tree comes in a container, do not plant the pot as well as the contents. There is a certain logic in doing so (plant easier to move if you have made a mistake, roots not disturbed, job quicker and simpler to carry out) but it does nothing for the long-term future of the plant in question. Roots must run. Autumn is the best time to plant as fruit trees are dormant then and can settle themselves in, getting their roots firmly plugged in to supplies before they have to fuss about flowering.

Make a hole bigger than the one you first thought of and have a bucket of compost mixed with bonemeal standing by. Ease the tree out of its container and settle it so that the stem sits in relation to the ground at the same level as it was sitting in the pot. Put in a short stake to stand about 50cm (20in) above the ground for half standard and standard trees. You should also stake bushes on very dwarfing rootstock. Always plant with the join of the graft above the level of the soil; otherwise the plant that is grafted may try to make its own roots and the benefit of the rootstock will be lost. Spread the tree's roots out comfortably, so that the main ones go off in different directions. Work the compost in the bucket around the plant's roots, firming it as you go. Fill in with the soil that you took out of the hole. Water the plant thoroughly – a drench, not a sprinkle. If it is very dry, mulch round the base of the tree after watering.

Pollination

Many fruit trees need to be cross-pollinated if they are to produce fruit. The job is usually done by insects, who transfer pollen from the anther of a flower on one tree to the stigma of a flower on another. Some fruit trees such as the 'Morello' cherry are self-fertile, in which case you can expect fruit even if it is the only tree in the garden. Some trees, such as the 'Conference' pear, are technically self-fertile, though this will set fruit more readily if it is also cross-pollinated by another type of pear. Where trees need to be cross-pollinated, the pollinator obviously needs to be out in bloom at the same time as the tree it is pollinating.

Most specialist nurseries number the fruit trees in their catalogues to indicate the different flowering seasons. The apple 'James Grieve', for instance, might be paired with 'Egremont Russet', the 'Beurre Hardy' pear with 'Doyenne du Comice'. Whereas most fruit trees are diploids, with two basic sets of chromosomes, a few are triploids with three and this makes them sterile. These need to be pollinated by two different cultivars. 'Ribston Pippin', 'Bramley's Seedling' and 'Jupiter' are triploid apples, 'Jargonelle' a triploid pear.

The other vital factor in pollination is a good supply of insects. Commercial growers hire hives of bees to move into their fruit orchards. Others release specially bred bumblebees to work in their glasshouses. Bees have suffered appallingly from the thoughtless use of insecticides. Think before you spray.

Both peaches and nectarines are self-fertile, so you do not have to plant different cultivars to ensure pollination. But they flower very early in the year, when there may be few insects on the wing. To ensure a good set of fruit, you can help with the process of pollination by flicking a camel-hair brush (or a rabbit's tail or powder puff) from one flower to the next, shifting pollen from one set of stamens to another. You will have to do this several times as new batches of flowers open up. Unless doors are left open, trees grown under glass will always have to be hand-pollinated. Traditionally, this job was done at noon and the greenhouse floor damped down immediately afterwards to help fruit set.

Pollination groups
APPLES
Crops will be much improved if trees are cross-pollinated – that is if the blossom on a tree is fertilized with pollen brought from a tree of a different kind. It need not be in your own garden. Varieties described as triploids are not good pollinators. If you plant these, you need *two* other pollinators to get them to set fruit. To pollinate each other, trees must be in blossom at the same time. Check flowering times in a catalogue and choose trees from the same, or bordering, flowering groups.

- **Early flowering** 'Baker's Delicious', 'Beauty of Bath', 'Christmas Pearmain', 'Crispin', 'Discovery', 'Egremont Russet', 'George Cave', 'George Neal', 'Idared', 'Lord Lambourne', 'Red Melba', 'Rev W. Wilks', 'Ribston Pippin', 'St Edmund's Pippin', 'Sunset'.
- **Mid-season flowering** 'Arthur Turner', 'Ashmead's Kernel', 'Blenheim Orange', 'Bramley Seedling', 'Charles Ross', 'Chivers Delight', 'Cox's Orange Pippin', 'Crown Gold', 'Early Victoria', 'Elstar', 'Fiesta', 'Greensleeves', 'Grenadier', 'Howgate Wonder', 'James Grieve', 'Jester', 'Jonagold', 'Jonagored', 'Jupiter', 'Katya', 'Kidd's Orange Red', 'Laxton's Epicure', 'Laxton's Fortune', 'Malling Kent', 'Merton Knave', 'Queen Cox', 'Rosemary Russet', 'Rubinette', 'Sanspareil', 'Sturmer Pippin', 'Tydeman's Early Worcester', 'Tydeman's Late Orange', 'Wagener', 'Worcester Pearmain'.
- **Late flowering** 'American Mother', 'Annie Elizabeth', 'Crawley Beauty', 'Edward VII', 'Ellison's Orange', 'Gala', 'Golden Delicious', 'Golden Noble', 'Harvey', 'Lane's Prince Albert', 'Laxton's Superb', 'Lord Derby', 'Monarch', 'Newton Wonder', 'Orleans Reinette', 'Pixie', 'Suntan', 'Winston'.
- **Triploids** 'Belle de Boskoop', 'Blenheim', 'Bramley's Seedling', 'Crispin', 'Gascoyne's Scarlet', 'Gravenstein', 'Jonagold', 'Jupiter', 'King of Tomkins Country', 'Reinette du Canada', 'Ribston Pippin', 'Suntan' 'Warner's King'.

PEARS

These should be treated as for apples. Triploid pears will need two pollinators. Despite overlapping pollination times, some pears are not compatible. 'Fondante d'Automne', 'Louise Bonne', 'Seckle' and 'Williams', for instance, will not pollinate each other. 'Conference' is self-fertile, but will set a better crop if another pollinator is at hand.

- **Early flowering** 'Louise Bonne of Jersey', 'Marguerite Marillat', 'Ovid'.
- **Mid-season flowering** 'Beth', 'Beurre d'Amanlis', 'Concorde', 'Conference', 'Dr Jules Guyot', 'Durondeau', 'Fertility Improved', 'Fondante d'Automne', 'Glow Red Williams', 'Josephine de Malines', 'Merton Pride', 'Nouveau Poitou', 'Packham's Triumph', 'William's Bon Chretien'.
- **Late flowering** 'Beurre Hardy', 'Bristol Cross', 'Catillac', 'Doyenne du Comice', 'Glou Morceau', 'Gorham', 'Onward', 'Winter Nelis'.
- **Triploid** 'Beurre Alexander Lucas', 'Beurre Bedford', 'Beurre d'Amanlis', 'Beurre Diel', 'Bristol Cross', 'Catillac', 'Jargonelle', 'Merton Pride' and 'Pitmaston'.

PLUMS/DAMSONS/GREENGAGES

Some of the plum family such as 'Belle de Louvain', 'Czar', 'Denniston's Superb', 'Early Transparent Gage', 'Marjorie's Seeedling', 'Merryweather', 'Ontario', 'Opal', 'Ouillin's Gage', 'Reine Claude de Bavay', 'Victoria' and 'Warwickshire Drooper' are self-fertile, but as with the 'Conference' pear, crops are much improved if you provide a suitable pollinator. As with apples and pears, flowering time is the key to choosing suitable pollinators.

Some plums are incompatible. 'Jefferson' and 'Coe's Golden Drop' will not pollinate each other and 'Cambridge Gage' will not pollinate the common greengage.

- **Early flowering** 'Coe's Golden Drop', 'Denniston's Superb', 'Farleigh Damson', 'Jefferson', 'Ontario', 'Reine Claude de Bavay', 'Warwickshire Drooper'.
- **Mid-season flowering** 'Anna Spath', 'Czar', 'Early Laxton', 'Goldfinch', 'Kirke's Blue', 'Merryweather', 'Opal', 'Reeves Seedling', 'Rivers Early Prolific', 'Victoria'.
- **Late flowering** 'Belle de Louvain', 'Cambridge Gage', 'Count Althann's Gage', 'Early Transparent Gage', 'Marjorie's Seedling', 'Old Greengage', 'Ouillin's Gage'

PEACHES/NECTARINES

Both peaches and nectarines are self-fertile, but may need hand-pollinating if there are no insects on the wing to do the job.

APRICOTS/CHERRIES

Apricots are self-fertile but blossom very early, often in late winter. Protect trees outside from frost with fine-meshed net. If no insects are about, hand-pollinate the flowers with a fine camel-hair brush as for peaches (above).

The acid cherry 'Morello' is self fertile and will pollinate sweet cherries such as 'Napoleon Bigarreau' that flower at the same time. With the exception of 'Stella', sweet cherries are not self-fertile. 'Governor Wood' and 'Merton Bigarreau' will pollinate each other. 'Governor Wood' and 'Roundel' will also pollinate each other. 'Merton Heart' will pollinate 'Early Rivers'.

MELONS/KIWI/PASSION FRUIT

Pollinate the flowers by stripping the petals from a male flower and pushing it into a female flower. The females are the ones with slight swellings just underneath the flower heads. One male flower will pollinate at least four females. Pollination is best done at midday.

Female kiwi plants will only set fruit when there is a male plant growing close by. The passion fruit is self-fertile.

PRUNING & TRAINING TREE FRUIT

Plants do not die if they are not pruned. There is no ghostly pruner in the wild, flitting about with secateurs to get wild blackberries into shape or to trim up the hawthorn. Gardeners prune fruit trees to enhance fruiting, to keep on top of a tree that is growing in a particular way, as with a cordon or fan, or because they are tidy minded. Accept that the diagram in your manual will never look like the tree that confronts you in the garden. Once you understand the principles, the practice becomes easier to carry out.

Principles of pruning

You cannot rely on pruning alone to contain the size of a tree. If an apple has been grafted on to M25 rootstock, it will always have the will to do what destiny dictates: grow into a big, beautiful prize fighter of a tree. Heavy pruning will lead only to renewed efforts on the part of the tree to fulfil the imperative of its genes. If you want a small tree, choose a cultivar that is inherently only moderately vigorous and check the rootstock on which it has been grafted. If you buy a tree trained as a cordon, espalier or fan, the appropriate rootstock is likely to have been already chosen for you.

Most apples and pears produce their fruit buds on new shoots, which develop from short, woody clusters known as spurs. These are called spur-bearing trees. A few cultivars, such as the apples 'Bramley's Seedling' and 'George Cave' and the pears 'Jargonelle' and 'Josephine de Malines', are tip bearers, producing their flower buds on the ends of two-year-old shoots. If you are constantly cutting these back, there is little chance of getting any fruit. Tip-bearing cultivars should not be the ones you choose to grow as cordons or espaliers.

Before you home in, brandishing a pruning saw, remind yourself why you want to prune. It may be to maintain the tree in a particular form, to increase vigour, to encourage more fruit buds to form, to improve the quality or the quantity of the fruit, to thin out overcrowded branches (which will in turn help prevent diseases) or to cut out diseased or dead wood. Just as you need to balance suitable rootstocks with particular styles of tree, so you should regulate your pruning to the vigour of the cultivar. Winter pruning stimulates a tree to produce more growth, so the harder a tree is pruned, the more growth it produces. This may be at the expense of more useful fruit buds. The more vigorous a tree is, the more lightly it should be pruned. Conversely, if a tree has weak, droopy branches, it can be pruned hard.

APPLES AND PEARS

Trees growing as bushes, half standards and standards will need only winter pruning, if you prune them at all. They will grow and fruit quite happily, though not at maximum potential, if you leave them entirely alone. If you want to prune, do it on the replacement principle. Encourage new growth by cutting back some of the old growth at the ends of the branches, making the cut where there is a new shoot waiting to take over.

On trees growing as cordons, espaliers and fans, summer pruning is more important than winter pruning, as it is by this means that you control the amount of growth that the tree produces and keep it in the particular shape you want. To summer prune an apple or a pear which is growing as a cordon or an espalier, cut back the new leafy shoots that have been produced during spring and early summer. If the shoot is springing directly from one of the main arms of the tree, cut it back to the third leaf above the basal cluster of leaves. Leave the cluster itself intact. If the shoot is springing from a knobbly spur formed by previous pruning, cut it back to just one leaf above the cluster. The time to do this is in mid- to late summer, when the greenish stems of the shoots have started to turn brown. In winter, you may have to shorten any other long shoots that have grown since the summer pruning.

A fan is slightly less rigid in its underlying structure than a cordon or espalier. You can continue to tie in side shoots springing from the main branches, until all the space between is filled. After that, you must summer prune side shoots, cutting them back to one leaf above the basal cluster. If one of the main stems starts to outgrow its space, cut it back to a strong replacement shoot, which you can tie in in its place.

PLUM, GREENGAGES AND DAMSONS Freestanding trees require very little pruning. Simply take out dead wood and thin growth if it becomes overcrowded. Any cutting should be done in late spring or summer. This reduces the risk of spores of silverleaf getting into the system.

Fans require more attention to keep them in shape. Shoots sprouting from the main framework should be nipped out in two stages. In mid-summer, pinch back all side shoots to leave about six leaves. These will be the shoots that bear fruit in the subsequent summer. When they have fruited, cut back these side shoots by half, to about three leaves. Any shoots that are pointing directly forwards or backwards into the wall should be rubbed out entirely.

PEACHES AND NECTARINES These can most conveniently be grown as fans. Make life easy for yourself by buying one ready trained. Their fruit is borne on the shoots produced in the previous season. Rub out any shoots that you do not want (including those pointing either forward or back) in spring, leaving three growth buds on each lateral branch. In early summer, prune back each of these three shoots to six leaves. When you have picked the fruit, cut out the shoot that bore it and tie in a replacement shoot. On freestanding trees, trim out crowded or crossing branches in summer. In mid-spring prune back any shoots killed by winter frost.

APRICOTS Fan apricots are treated in a similar way to peaches. Aim to build up a series of fruiting spurs about 15cm (6in) apart all the way along the branches of the fan. Do this by pinching back the lateral growths in early summer, leaving about 7cm (3in) of each growth in place. Any growths springing from these laterals should be pinched back, leaving just one leaf. Keep tying in the new growth on the ends of the main branches of the tree to maintain the fan shape. No regular pruning is needed for established bushes.

CHERRIES Sweet cherries growing as standards or half standards in an orchard do not need pruning. Simply cut out any dead wood and remove crossing branches. 'Morello' cherries only fruit on new wood, so you must prune to force the tree to produce plenty of the necessary growth. When a wall-trained tree has fruited, cut out the long growths at its extremities so that it will make new shoots in the centre. Without this 'sides to middle' treatment, you will find the tree bears only at the tips of its branches. Tie in as many new shoots as you can fit in among the framework of the main branches.

CITRUS FRUIT Citrus trees do not need regular pruning. Trim new growth in early spring if necessary to keep the plants balanced and shapely.

PRUNING & TRAINING SOFT FRUIT & VINES

With soft fruit, as with tree fruit, you can choose to grow bushes in a decorative manner, perhaps using a standard, mop-headed gooseberry on a 1.2m (4ft) stem to rise among your annual flowers. Redcurrants respond well to being trained too. You can turn them into double cordons, which grow in the shape of a wine glass, the two stems trained out and up from a single clear trunk. Of this group, vines need the most careful pruning. In good soil, they tend to grow too much leaf and you must prune to remind it to flower and fruit. Where you are growing a vine to cover an arbour you need not be too particular about the pruning. Greenhouse vines are more demanding.

Cane fruit

RASPBERRIES These need pruning every year, but this is a simple process. After summer cultivars have fruited, cut out the old canes close to the ground and thin out the new canes, leaving no more than five or six strong stems growing from each original clump. Tie in the new canes to supporting wires, if you are using this method. In late winter, cut off the top of each cane just above the top wire. Autumn-fruiting raspberries need slightly different treatment as they carry fruit on canes formed earlier in the same season. Cut the old fruited canes to the ground in late winter and thin out the thicket of new growth gradually as it grows during the season.

HYBRID BERRIES If you are training hybrid berries such as loganberries or tayberries on wires to make a screen, fix the first wire about 1m (3ft) from the ground, with another three wires above it, fixed at 1m (3ft) intervals. Tie the growths securely along the wires, keeping the new canes bunched up in a fountain in the middle and the older, fruiting growths trained horizontally away from the centre. When you have finished picking the fruit, cut out the old canes, unbundle the new ones and tie them in where the old ones were.

BLACKBERRIES These are treated in the same way as hybrid berries. Cut out the fruited canes each year after the crop has been gathered. With a late-fruiting cultivar such as 'Himalaya Giant', this may not be until mid-autumn.

Tie in the new canes to replace the old. With 'Himalaya Giant', which does not produce canes quite as freely as other varieties, a proportion of the old wood may be left in place each season.

Soft fruit bushes

BLUEBERRIES Bushes can be trimmed, rather than severely pruned. Start in winter by cutting out dead or damaged branches together with a proportion of old wood. In spring, shear over the tops of the bushes to keep them compact.

CURRANTS Although red and white currants are pruned in the same way, you need to treat blackcurrants differently. While red and white currants fruit on spurs made on old wood, blackcurrants fruit on young, one-year-old wood. When they have finished fruiting, cut out at least a third of the old, dark wood, leaving as much of the new, light brown growth as possible. It is on these new, pale stems that the following season's fruit will be produced. As red and white currants bear on old wood, pruning can be less drastic. After fruiting, or during the following autumn and winter, shorten branches by about a third to keep the bushes shapely and compact. On red and white currants grown as cordons, cut the lateral branches back to within 3cm (1.5in) of the main stem.

Redcurrants are especially good trained as goblet-shaped double cordons. Allow a rooted cutting of redcurrant to grow up as a single stem, without any side branches. It needs to be planted against the parallel wires that will support it. When it is well established, and is about 75cm (30in) high, cut the stem back to about 25cm (10in) from the ground, leaving a strong bud on either side, below the cut. These two buds will break into side shoots, which you should train on canes set at an angle of 45 degrees. When the tips of these shoots are at least 45cm (18in) apart, lower the training canes to an angle of 30 degrees and attach more canes vertically to the wires. Continue to train the two side shoots in the new vertical position. Prune them as you would a single cordon.

GOOSEBERRIES These will bear fruit even if they are not regularly pruned, but it is easier to pick the fruit if you remove some of the growth each year to keep the centre of the bush open and to shorten long branches, which may be weighed down to the ground with fruit. On cordons, shorten the side growths to three buds, and cut the branches of standards back by at least a third to maintain a well-shaped head.

Grapevines

CORDONS When grown under glass, vines should be trained on wires set about 30cm (12in) apart and at least 15cm (6in) away from the glass itself. The leading shoot should be trained vertically, the laterals horizontally along the wires. When the vines have flowered, prune the laterals back, leaving just two leaves beyond the clusters of fruit. Any subsequent shoots breaking from the laterals should be pinched out, leaving one or two leaves at most. After fruiting, in autumn, cut the leading shoots back to well-ripened wood and cut the laterals back to two buds.

WALL-TRAINED VINES Train vines outside on walls by allowing, at most, three or four main stems to develop from a single rootstock. After the first season's growth, cut back the branches by two-thirds and repeat this in early autumn each year until all the available space is filled. On young plants, tie in the laterals and grow them on to about 60cm (24in) before pinching them out. On mature plants, the laterals should be stopped just beyond the clusters of flowers, leaving no more than two leaves. Sub-laterals (shoots springing from the side shoots) should be stopped at one leaf.

THE GUYOT SYSTEM Vines growing outside can also be trained according to the Guyot system, named after the person who invented it. For this you need parallel sets of wires spaced 30cm (12in) apart stretched between posts, or fastened to a wall. After planting the vines in the dormant season in late autumn, cut hard back the growth made on the vine the previous season, leaving just one or two buds. During the first summer, train a single shoot vertically up the wires, tying it in at regular intervals. Prune away any other shoots that develop.

In autumn or early winter, cut back this shoot, leaving about 75cm (30in) of growth. Undo the ties and retie this stem horizontally along the bottom wire. The following season, several shoots will break from this stem. Train them vertically up the wires. When the grapes have been gathered, cut out all except two shoots nearest the original rootstock. Shorten these down to about 75cm (30in) and tie them along the bottom wire. As before, train the new summer shoots vertically to the wires, then repeat the process of cutting out most of the growth and selecting new shoots to tie in on the lowest wire every autumn or early winter.

GROWING IN GREENHOUSES

The chief benefits of a greenhouse are the extra warmth and shelter it will give plants, although it can also be decorative in its own right. Under glass, you can extend the growing season of all plants and grow fruit and vegetables that may not survive outside in the garden. Unfortunately, greenhouses provide ideal living conditions for pests as well as plants. Be prepared for armies of whitefly and red spider. The options available will depend on the type of structure that you have. Old-fashioned kitchen gardens will have lean-to greenhouses built against a south-facing wall, where apricots, peaches and nectarines can be trained in fans. Protected from frost, the trees blossom fearlessly and the fruit ripens more easily than it would outside. Vines, too, benefit from the shelter of a greenhouse. The rootstock is best planted outside, with the trunk leading through an opening in the side of the greenhouse. Branches, or rods, can then be trained up the ribs of the greenhouse roof, where in high summer the foliage will provide welcome shade for the crops underneath.

Choosing a greenhouse

Freestanding aluminium greenhouses glassed to the ground are one of the most popular options for amateur gardeners. Although maintenance is minimal and the design allows maximum light to reach the plants, a greenhouse such as this is cold and condensation may be a greater problem than in a similar house made of wood. But wood, even cedar, needs looking after. The cheapest option is some kind of polytunnel, made from plastic sheeting stretched over big metal hoops. Unfortunately polytunnels add nothing in terms of decorative value to the garden. Even polythene sheeting that has been treated against ultraviolet light rarely lasts for more than a few years and is easily punctured; it is also liable to tear in high winds.

Whatever type of greenhouse you choose, make sure that it can be well ventilated. With a simple polytunnel, you might do this by arranging doors at either end of the structure, but not if they face into the prevailing wind. In a greenhouse, you will need roof ventilators, equal in area to at least 20 per cent of the floor space. If you are away from home a good deal, you may find it wise to invest in automatic ventilators. These are designed round a cylinder of sensitive wax that expands or contracts according to the temperature. The cylinder moves a piston rod attached to the ventilator. All automatic ventilators should be marked with the weight they can lift. Check that you have got one that is man enough for the job.

The manner and amount of heating in a greenhouse will depend on your purse. In any case, arrange the space so that you can partition off at least part of it to keep frost free in winter. Electricity is reckoned an expensive option, though installing it is relatively cheap. Remember that keeping a greenhouse at a winter temperature of 10°C/50°F costs twice as much as keeping it at 8°C/45°F. Paraffin heaters are cheap, but not so precise as electric ones. Insulation is the best way to save on heating costs. Use heavy-duty bubble polythene fixed with clips to the inside of the greenhouse frame. In very cold areas, leave this insulation in place on the north side to provide extra protection and warmth through the summer.

Greenhouse crops

Even in an unheated greenhouse you can extend the growing season of basic crops such as carrots, lettuces, French beans and potatoes. Tender vegetables such as aubergines, cucumbers, peppers and tomatoes can be grown outside, but you will not be able to set out plants until late spring or early summer when all danger of frost is past. In the shelter of a greenhouse, tomatoes can be planted earlier and so will start cropping sooner. Frost-tender herbs such as basil also benefit from the extra warmth and protection of a greenhouse and grow extremely well in polytunnels. Some vegetables such as endive, chard and certain oriental vegetables may be reasonably hardy, but will be more succulent if they are grown under cover during the winter months.

Your greenhouse or polytunnel can also function as a nursery in which to bring on seedlings of lettuce, courgettes or sweetcorn that you intend to plant out later on in the garden. You can raise seedlings such as this on a window ledge indoors, but the light levels are unlikely to be as good as those available in a greenhouse and the temperature may be too warm. Both of these could induce the seedlings to become leggy and weak.

Grow tomatoes in a greenhouse as cordons rather than bushes, setting a short, strong cane, about 60cm (24in) high, by the side of each plant. Tie a double string between the cane and the roof of the greenhouse. Tie the plants to the canes and, as they grow, twist the string around the stems to support them. Stop each leading shoot by pinching it out in late summer, or when six trusses of fruit have formed, if that is sooner.

Damping down is one of the simplest ways of keeping pests at bay in a greenhouse. Some of the most troublesome, such as red spider, thrive in hot dry conditions. If you hose down the floor of a greenhouse every day during hot weather, you will keep the air inside moistly humid, which is what makes plants purr and pests cough. When the weather itself is moistly humid, though, you need to keep air moving through the greenhouse to prevent plants rotting off.

Planning the space

You can use the space inside a greenhouse more economically if you grow crops in earth borders either side of a central pathway. Where greenhouses are set on a solid base in a back yard, all crops will have to be grown in grow bags or other containers. In the main, borders are easier to manage in terms of watering and feeding, but there is one important disadvantage of this kind of layout: if you grow the same crops (such as tomatoes) year after year in the same soil, it is likely to suffer from a build-up of salts, causing 'soil sickness'. This will mean that crops will not continue to thrive in that position unless the soil is sterilized or replaced. If you have three greenhouse borders, one at either side of a central path and one at the end, you can practise a simple crop rotation and grow tomatoes and cucumbers in a different border each year.

COLD FRAMES, CLOCHES & LIGHTS

If your garden is too small for a greenhouse, you can still arrange useful protection for fruit and vegetables by investing in a cold frame or some cloches. A cold frame is a kind of doll's greenhouse, unheated as the name suggests and built low, with a sloping glass roof which you slide on and off depending on the weather. Old-fashioned cloches were always made of glass, which allows the maximum amount of light through on to the crops underneath. Modern cloches may be made from Perspex or different types of plastic, either transparent or translucent, ridged or smooth. Victorian lantern lights, or modern replicas, are attractive and easy to move round the garden, but expensive to buy. Considerably cheaper are jam jars or plastic bottles with their bottoms chopped off that can be used to cover seeds or newly emerging plants.

Cold frames
The warmest type of cold frame has brick rather than glass walls. Use it to harden off plants that you have raised from seed, before planting them out in the vegetable garden. Set the young plants as close as possible to the top of the frame by raising the seed trays on piles of bricks or some similar support. If you do not have a greenhouse, use the cold frame to grow crops such as peppers, aubergines and melons that will only thrive in cool areas with the kind of added protection that a cold frame can provide. Position your frame so that it faces south and is in full sun. Protect it if you can from winds, especially those from the north and east. Do not leave the frame closed on hot, sunny days, as the temperature will rise dramatically and plants inside will suffer. In the tricky days of late spring, when sudden frosts can wreak havoc on plants, give extra protection to a cold frame by covering the top with sacking, newspapers, old carpet or any other material that will provide extra insulation. Fork over the soil inside the frame to a depth of at least 15cm (6in) before direct sowing any vegetables such as carrot, lettuce or radish. Remember that 'soil sickness' can as easily build up in a permanent cold frame as it can in a greenhouse border. Vary the crops that you grow in a cold frame and keep the soil in good heart by mulching areas that are free of crops in the late autumn and winter.

Low polytunnels
The cheapest way of protecting vegetables is to grow them under a continuous plastic cloche, in effect a mini polytunnel, made by stretching polythene sheeting over hoops of sturdy, galvanized wire. These types of cloches are usually available as kits and give you a protected growing area as long as you choose, but usually no more than 30–45cm (12–18in) high. It

is wasteful of polythene to make runs less than 1.8m (6ft) long. Secure the plastic at either end of the tunnel by bunching it up together and tying it to a stake driven into the ground. Long low tunnel cloches of this kind are ideal for protecting strawberries and carrots. The strawberries ripen more quickly with some protection and the tunnel keeps them safe from birds. Carrots do not need extra heat to grow well, but a covering of some kind prevents them being attacked by carrot fly, whose grubs tunnel into the roots.

Cloches

Plastic does not hold on to heat as well as glass and temperatures under a glass cloche will usually be two or three degrees higher than those under a plastic one. Glass cloches do not deteriorate with age as plastic does, but they are more fragile – and heavier to move about. Sometimes, though, weight is an advantage. Wind can get under a light plastic cloche and whirl it away in a fashion that obliterates not only the cloche but also the crop underneath.

The simplest style of cloche is tent shaped and you can easily make such cloches yourself, either from two sheets of glass held together with a specially designed clip, or from polythene stretched over batons, held together with a bulldog clip. For bulkier crops, barn cloches are a better shape. These have tent-shaped roofs supported on two slightly slanting side pieces. Either type can be placed end to end to protect a row. Leave a little space between each one for ventilation. You do not have to move the cloches to water the crops underneath. Water over the tops of them so that the water drips down and soaks in either side of the row. The roots of the vegetables or fruit underneath will reach out to find it.

Use your cloches to warm up and dry out the soil before planting and to protect emerging crops of seedlings. With such protection, you should get crops ready to harvest two or three weeks sooner than if you had grown them without shelter. Warming the soil is as valuable as any other benefit of a cloche, for seeds sulk and may rot in cold, wet ground. Cloches are particularly valuable during the last month of winter and the first one of spring, when the ground is often cold and temperatures fluctuate in a way that is not favourable to young seedlings. Beetroot, carrots, lettuce and peas will all benefit from the protection of a cloche. Later on in the season, you can use cloches to help along tender vegetables such as French beans, sweetcorn, outdoor cucumbers and tomatoes. Cucumber, sweetcorn and courgette plants can be grown in the early stages under mini cloches, made by cutting the bottoms off clear plastic drinks bottles. In early autumn, you can use cloches to extend the growing season and give protection to carrots and lettuce sown in late summer. You can also use them to hasten the ripening of the last crops of bush tomatoes or to protect onions that you are drying off for storage.

Use cloches in cold areas to warm up the soil before transplanting brassicas such as cauliflowers. Leave the cloches in place for as long as possible, before the cauliflower outgrows the space. You can also use them to good effect with peas. If you have made a very late sowing, say in early or mid-summer, you may find, in cold areas, that the only way to bring the crop to fruition is to cover it with cloches. This of course would only be possible with a dwarf cultivar. But you could also use cloches to protect peas sown in early or late winter to crop in mid- or late spring. Unprotected, you lose most of your winter peas to birds looking for a quick breakfast.

Lights, bottles and jars
Old lantern lights make attractive covers for plants or patches of seedlings and are easy to remove during the day and replace at night. But for the cheapest covers of all, use upturned jam jars or cut the bottoms off clear plastic drink bottles. Put these over seeds of plants such as cucumbers, sweetcorn and courgettes while they are germinating. Keep them over the seedlings until the nights have warmed up.

HARVESTING & STORING

Vegetables and fruit gathered fresh from the garden and eaten as soon as possible nearly always taste better than produce that has been stored, however carefully. The exceptions, of course, are apples and pears, some varieties of which need to be stored, either to finish ripening (as with pears) or for full flavour to develop (as with late-season apples such as 'Orleans Reinette'). But generally, there is no good reason to starve yourself of fresh crops during the summer and autumn in order to fill a storehouse with fruit and vegetables which may then rot quietly through winter and early spring. By trial and error you will sort out those crops that you are most likely to use and which will store most successfully; your choice will also depend on the amount of storage space you have available.

The freezer has revolutionized the whole business of keeping fruit and vegetables. Few people now preserve peas by drying them, but once dried peas were a winter staple. And in the days before freezers, if you had a glut of tomatoes you bottled them in preserving jars. You can still do this, but it is actually much easier to freeze them. Frozen whole, with their skins on, they maintain an excellent flavour. When you need some for cooking, you just put them under the tap and the skin slides off like silk.

Vegetables
Leafy vegetables such as lettuce and spinach deteriorate fast – within an hour of being picked. Root vegetables such as carrot and parsnip can be

stored successfully for months if the conditions are right. Fruit shows just the same wide range of behaviour. While strawberries demand to be eaten as soon as picked, citrus fruit will maintain equilibrium over a long period. All produce, however, needs to be handled very carefully if it is to be stored. Cuts and bruises quickly lead to disease. Where you have harvested a range of different-sized fruit and vegetables, store them in such a way that you can use the small ones first. These will be in greater danger of drying out.

LEAF AND SALAD VEGETABLES

Harvest soft leafy vegetables such as salad crops, oriental brassicas and spinach early or late in the day when they are at their coolest. On sunny days, a lettuce may have heated up by 5–10°C/41–50°F at midday. Store salad crops in a cool place (for most people, the salad box of a refrigerator), in a polythene bag, loosely folded over. Cabbages of the white and red type, which are not frost hardy, can be pulled whole and stored on wooden slats, the stalks and roots dangling below the slats. They can also be trimmed and hung in nets in a cool, frost-free place. Other winter cabbages and chard are harvested as they are needed.

FRUITING AND FLOWERING VEGETABLES

Late crops of frost-tender vegetables such as courgettes, cucumbers, aubergines, peppers and chillies can be stored in a cool place in polythene bags, loosely folded over. Sweetcorn can also be stored but the flavour soon deteriorates. Tomatoes keep successfully in a cool place. Marrows, pumpkins and winter squash should be 'cured' by leaving them to dry and harden in the sun. They will keep for several months in a cool, frost-free store. Chillies dry successfully. Pull up plants and hang them upside down before picking the chillies and putting them in jars or threading them on a string.

PODDED VEGETABLES

Pick French and runner beans before frost can get to them and store in a cool place in polythene bags loosely folded over. They will only keep for a few days. Haricot beans and peas can be dried. Pull up the plants whole when the pods are mature and hang them in a cool, airy place. When they are completely dry, shell and store in jars.

BULB AND STEM VEGETABLES

Leeks can be wrapped in newspaper and kept in a cool place if the ground is likely to freeze hard. Onions, shallots, garlic and celeriac can all be stored successfully. Proper harvesting is the key to keeping onions, shallots and garlic. Make sure that the bulbs have been properly dried off before storing in shallow trays stacked in a well ventilated but frost-free place. Onions with thick juicy necks will not keep for very long. Use these up first. You can also tie onions in strings to hang from the ceiling, or pack them in cotton or plastic nets. Onions need drier storage conditions than other vegetables. Damp starts them into growth again.

ROOT VEGETABLES

Harvest potatoes when the ground is dry so that they are not covered in mud. Store in thick paper sacks, not polythene, which makes them rot. Tie the neck of the sack to exclude light, which stimulates the poisonous alkaloids that make green patches on the tubers. Leave carrots, beetroot, turnips, swedes, parsnips, winter radishes, salsify and scorzonera in the ground as long as possible. Covering them with straw will make lifting easier in frosty weather. They can also be stored in layers in boxes of damp sand, in a cool place. Twist the foliage off first. If you have enough space you can make a clamp, the traditional method of storing root vegetables. Kept like this, they should last through most of the winter. Put down a 20–30cm (8–12in) layer of straw on the floor of a cool store room, cellar or outhouse, and pile the vegetables in a tidy heap on top. Cover them with another layer of straw at least as thick as the first and finish by adding a layer of earth 15cm (6in) deep. Vegetables in a clamp are, of course, much easier to get at than ones stuck firmly in frozen ground, but they may attract vermin.

Fruit

Soft-fleshed fruit such as peaches and plums deteriorate quickly once harvested, so the most important fruit to store are those such as apples and pears.

APPLES

The ideal store is one free of frost and mice with a temperature of 3–5°C/37–40°F. In practice, it is difficult for ordinary gardeners to keep stores as cool as this. Aim for a steady 8°C/45°F. Pick apples when the stalk parts easily from the branch. Early maturing cultivars such as 'George Cave' should be eaten straight from the tree. Other apples can be stored in wooden boxes, laid out on slatted shelves or packed into polythene bags that can hold 2–3kg (4–6lb) of fruit. Tie the bags loosely and punch holes in them so that air can circulate freely. Apples in boxes and on shelves store slightly better if individually wrapped, but the gain must be weighed against the extra work involved. Keep fruit as far as possible from any strong smelling things such as onions or paint, which may taint the flavour.

PEARS

The same general principles apply as for apples, but pears are the more volatile of the two. The lower the temperature, ideally 0–1°C (32–34°F), the longer they keep. Do not wrap the fruit, as they need picking over frequently. Pears are at their best for a very short period. Bring a few at a time from the store into a warm room to finish the ripening process. Do not store pears in polythene bags, as it encourages rot.

QUINCES AND MEDLARS

Store quinces on trays in a cool, dark place where they will keep for up to a month. Keep them as far as possible from other fruit, which may pick up their strong aroma. Medlars must be stored until soft (see page 180).

CITRUS FRUIT
Citrus fruit last a long time provided they are cool and dry. Store fruit in boxes or on slatted shelves.

Freezing
The quality of frozen produce is greatly affected by the rate at which it has been frozen. If food is frozen slowly, large ice crystals will form and these spoil the texture of fruit and vegetables. Fast-freeze produce (the instruction booklet that comes with the freezer will give details of how to do it) and do not try to do too much at the same time. If you know you are going to freeze crops, look out for those cultivars of fruit and vegetables that have been specially selected for the process.

VEGETABLES
- **Broad beans**: freeze while beans are still small and not yet starchy.
- **Broccoli and calabrese**: cut the florets into suitable lengths.
- **Brussels sprouts**: choose small firm sprouts and trim off outer leaves.
- **Cauliflower**: break into florets about 5cm (2in) across.
- **French beans**: pick beans while still small and freeze them whole.
- **Peas**: freeze only young peas. Shell them first.
- **Spinach**: wash thoroughly, drain and trim the stems.
- **Sweetcorn**: remove the husks and tassels before freezing.
- **Tomatoes**: freeze whole. To use, slip off skins under the tap.

HERBS
- **Mint and basil**: freeze leaves in small polythene bags.

FRUIT
- **Apples**: freeze after cooking to a pulp or purée.
- **Apricots, nectarines, peaches and plums**: cut in half and stone the fruit. Freeze halves in light syrup.
- **Blackberries, hybrid berries, mulberries and raspberries**: spread the fruit on trays to fast-freeze before packing it in containers.
- **Cherries**: stone acid (Morello) cherries before freezing.
- **Currants**: strip fruit from the bunches before freezing.
- **Gooseberries**: top and tail fruit before freezing.

A harvesting calendar for vegetables to store
MID-SUMMER
- **Garlic** Ease the bulbs out of the ground and dry them off thoroughly, as for onions, before storing in ropes or bunches.

LATE SUMMER
- **Shallots** When the foliage withers, dry the bulbs off thoroughly before storing them in ropes or bunches.
- **Onions** As the foliage bends over, sprouting inhibitors are transferred from

leaf to bulb. Spread bulbs to dry thoroughly before storing. Onions grown from sets are likely to mature earlier than those grown from seed. To make a rope of onions, first hang a long loop of string from a nail. Push the neck of an onion through the loop. Tighten the string and at the same time bend the neck of the onion so that it is firmly held. Push the neck of the next onion between the two strings, then take the onion itself around both strings and push it back between them to make a loop round the string. Twist the rope in a half turn before securing the next onion in the same way as before.

EARLY AUTUMN
- **Peas/beans** Lift haulms and hang upside down before storing crops.
- **Potatoes** Lift maincrops and store in paper sacks or clamps.

MID-AUTUMN
- **Beetroot** Lift the roots, twist off the leaves and store in boxes of damp sand.
- **Carrots** Lift the roots, twist off the leaves and store in boxes of damp sand or clamps (see above).
- **Pumpkins/squash** Harden off the fruit in the sun before storing.

PESTS & DISEASES

Some people only seem to see their gardens in terms of its pests and diseases, as a battlefield where a long war of attrition has to be waged by the gardener against mangold fly, mustard beetle, blight and rust. These are probably the same people who write 'Disgusted of Tunbridge Wells' letters to their local papers and as a matter of principle challenge their bills in a restaurant. Gardening does not have to be confrontational in this way. In mixed plantings of herbs and flowers, vegetables and fruit, there is little likelihood that your crops will be wiped out by bugs. That is a problem of monocultures, when large areas are covered with single crops such as potatoes or peas. Diseases can best be prevented by attending to the conditions in which plants grow. If they are growing strongly and enjoying life, they are much less likely to succumb to illnesses.

Nature's balance
Bugs exist to feed other creatures. If you annihilate them with insecticide, the predators will go, hungry, elsewhere. Then, when the pests come back, they will not have any enemies. The reason for the existence of diseases such as black spot or botrytis is not so clear to the gardener, but with plants, as with humans, your best strategy is prevention rather than cure. In part two of this book, Growing Vegetables, Fruit & Herbs, you will find, under each specific fruit or vegetable, a heading 'Pests and diseases', under which are

listed the most common complaints to which that plant is prone. There, too, you will find a few suggestions about ways to deal with specific problems. Some gardeners still like to know what potion they can turn to if the aphids get out of hand, or what preventative sprays they can use in a season when blight is most likely to strike the potatoes and the tomatoes.

But serenity in the garden is more easily achieved if you learn to be tolerant of pests and diseases. Up to a point . . . There is no need to fling the netting off the raspberries and invite the local blackbirds in for a feast. Most likely, they will already have discovered the hole you forgot to block off and be nipping in on their way back from the hedges for a taste of some classier food. But it is not the end of the world if your cabbages have a few of their outer leaves nibbled by caterpillars, or if a slug has taken an hors d'oeuvre from your lettuce. Now that we buy rather than grow so much of our food, we have come to expect an almost unreal perfection in the appearance of fruit and vegetables. The trade-off is a marked decline in taste. A supermarket lettuce may have been sprayed as many as eleven times before it leaves its glasshouse to make the journey to a supermarket shelf. No insects lurk in the folds of its leaves. No downy mildew disfigures its appearance. We would complain bitterly to the manager if it did. But there is a price to pay for this: the lurking suspicion that what we are putting in our mouths is not what is doing our bodies most good.

When you grow your own fruit and vegetables, you eat them confident in the knowledge that you have been the arbiter of what they should or should not receive by way of medicine. If the price to pay for that is the odd bit of root fly to carve out of a carrot when you are preparing it, or a few strawberries lost to botrytis, then that is a price worth paying.

It may sometimes seem to the gardener that there are more baddies than goodies on his patch. There aren't, but the goodies are slower on the uptake and the gardener's patience is limited. Aphids (greenfly and blackfly) are the most common horrors and it *is* slightly offputting when you go to gather your broad beans to find the plant seething quietly with blackfly. You could spray them, but you can just as easily snap the top off the plant – blackfly always congregate on the juicy growing tops – and dispose of it in the dustbin. It is in artificial environments such as greenhouses, often without natural predators, that you may feel most need to reach for a bottle. But you could equally well reach for an encarsia wasp, which can despatch prodigious numbers of whiteflies.

In the natural cycle of events, a build-up of pests is followed by a similar build-up of predators. It is the gap in between that is nerve-wracking, but gradually you learn to trust in nature, which has a longer overview than fidgety humans. We do not help the natural cycle by introducing into the food chain unnatural numbers of predators such as cats. In cities, where there are more cats than could star in a million musicals, there are relatively few species of birds. This in turn has an effect on the numbers of insect pests.

Bottled remedies

Insecticides work in several ways. The simplest are those that kill by contact. You spray the bug; it drops down dead. Other insecticides leave a deposit on the leaf, which is then eaten by the creature. Caterpillar killers work this way. Systemic insecticides are more devious. These are absorbed by the tissues of the host plant and get into the sap. The insects are killed by feeding on the plant that you have sprayed. Sap suckers such as greenfly and blackfly are usually tackled this way.

If you must spray, the least dangerous times to do it are early in the morning (say before 10 a.m.) or in the evening (after 6 p.m.) when there are fewer beneficial insects on the wing and bees are less likely to be working flowers. Millions of bees, which do no harm to anyone, have been killed each year by reckless spraying. Spray when foliage is dry and when there is no wind. But remember your allies. Avoid using kill-all insecticides that get rid of friends as well as foes. Choose chemicals that are as specific as possible to the problem in hand.

Fungicides can be used to fight against a wide range of common diseases. They can combat powdery mildew, which is particularly prevalent in hot, dry summers and are also effective against grey mould (botrytis), which attacks strawberries and other plants. Leaf spots, such as black spot in roses, may also be controlled by a systemic fungicide.

Like insecticides, fungicides work in different ways. The systemic types are absorbed through the leaves into the sap of the plant, there killing any resident fungus spores. Contact fungicides work by making a barrier between the leaf surface and any hopeful external spores. They will be effective only if they are applied regularly, usually at 10–14-day intervals. All fungicides are better at prevention than cure. Unfortunately most gardeners are better at reacting than predicting. Your best defence is to grow your plants in well-nurtured soil and in the kinds of situation that nature intended for them. They will then be less prone to any kind of disease.

PESTS, DISEASES & MINERAL DEFICIENCIES

Pests and diseases sort themselves quite clearly into the general, such as aphids and grey mould, which are attracted to a wide range of plants, and the specific, such as asparagus beetle or cane spot, which are very particular about their targets. The latter are generally less of a problem than the former, though where they attack they may inflict more damage. A gardener also needs to be able to distinguish between those things that can be controlled and those that cannot. Generally pests are more easily dealt with than diseases. There is no sure treatment for problems such as honey fungus, sclerotinia rot and violet root rot.

Pests
APHIDS
The most common aphids are the greenfly and the blackfly, two of the 550 different kinds of aphid that thrive in Britain. Aphids share with slugs the dubious honour of being the most commonly complained about pests in the garden. They breed prodigiously, because for the whole of the summer all aphids are female. Their young grow up in a week and then start to give birth themselves. Don't even *think* about it: it is too frightening. Greenfly are sap suckers and therefore spreaders of virus diseases, which can be more of a problem to the gardener than the pests themselves. Their enemies are ladybirds and hoverflies. Blackfly are most likely to be a problem on cherry trees, where they congregate on the growing shoots, and on broad beans, where they also favour the juicy tips. Pinching out the tops of broad beans is the simplest way of getting rid of them on this crop. On a small cherry, you can also pinch out growing tips regularly, both to keep the tree compact and to deter aphids. Most aphids overwinter on different host plants to those they attack in summer. The black bean aphid often overwinters on euonymus. As well as the problem of their introducing virus diseases, mass attacks by aphids reduce the vigour of a plant, and distort its growing tips. Aphids also excrete a sticky liquid known as honey dew, which in its turn attracts sooty mould. You can help to keep aphids in control by encouraging their natural predators. You can also treat them with insecticide.
ONION FLY
If your onions suddenly turn yellow and keel over, then you may well have this fly on your patch. The adults look like small houseflies and in late spring lay their eggs in the soil around onion or leek crops. The creamy maggots eat the roots of onions and leeks, and then burrow into the bulbs themselves and continue to fatten themselves up at the gardener's expense. The most dangerous time is in early and mid-summer when young plants may be killed by the grubs of the onion fly. The flies themselves overwinter in the ground as pupae. There is no effective treatment. Remove and get rid of any plants affected by this pest. Your best strategy for outwitting it is to shift your onion and leek beds each year – in other words to practise an organized rotation of crops.
WHITEFLY
Whiteflies are a particular problem in greenhouses, where they congregate on crops such as aubergine and tomato. The flies lay eggs, usually on the backs of leaves, and these hatch into tiny scale-like sap-sucking creatures. The scale pupates and then hatches into a fly, and the whole grisly cycle starts again. Yellow

sticky traps are very effective, as is the encarsia wasp, but you can also hoover up whiteflies on the wing by using a battery-operated car vacuum cleaner.

CARROT FLY
Adult flies are inconspicuous. It is their progeny that does the damage. Small underground grubs nibble at carrot roots, causing the tops to wilt or discolour. The first generation of flies hatches in late spring, so damage is most obvious in early summer. As the adult flies are incompetent fliers, you can protect crops with barriers of polythene about 75cm (30in) high, or cover rows of seedlings with a fleecy film. You can also time sowings to avoid the fly's peak hatchings. Sow in early summer rather than late spring.

CELERY FLY
Tiny white grubs, similar to carrot fly grubs, tunnel into the leaves of celery, causing pale blotches that later turn dry and brown. Spring attacks, when celery plants are still young, are the most dangerous. Pick off and destroy affected leaves or spray with a systemic fungicide.

CABBAGE ROOT FLY
The small white grubs of the cabbage root fly feed on the roots of brassicas, causing the plants to wilt. Young plants may be killed altogether. Several generations of the fly hatch in a single season, usually appearing in mid-spring, mid-summer and late summer. There is no cure, but collars fixed round the stem of the plants provide an effective deterrent.

ASPARAGUS BEETLE
The yellow and black beetles are easy to identify. Both beetles and their larvae feed on asparagus foliage and may completely defoliate plants. They are active from late spring to late summer and overwinter, as pupae, in the soil. Spray with a contact insecticide and clear away all debris from asparagus beds.

SCALE INSECT
These small brown, flat creatures may colonize apples and pears, cherries, peaches, plums, figs and vines. They are more likely to be found on stems and trunks than leaves or fruit. They are rarely troublesome.

RASPBERRY BEETLE
The maggots of the raspberry beetle may also attack loganberry and blackberry. The adult beetles hatch from pupae in the soil from mid-spring onwards and lay eggs in the flowers of cane fruit. The grubs eat the centre of the fruit as it develops. When it is ripe, they return to the soil to pupate. You can prevent damage by spraying with a contact insecticide before the raspberries begin to change colour. Loganberries should be sprayed as petals fall, blackberries before the flowers open.

RED SPIDER MITE
Red spider mite is a problem in hot, dry summers. The tiny mites can be seen only through a magnifying glass, but sometimes they produce threads like a spider's web. Affected leaves are flecked with yellow and then turn

brown before they die. Greenhouse crops such as aubergines, cucumbers and melons are worst affected, but in a hot summer the mite moves outside to colonize vines and strawberries. Damp down greenhouses to maintain a humid atmosphere and disinfect them thoroughly in winter. Phytoseiulus is an effective biological control.

FLEA BEETLES

Brassicas of all kinds, including turnips, swedes, radishes, rocket, pak choi and mizuna, as well as cabbages and Brussels sprouts, may be attacked by these tiny beetles, which pepper the leaves with holes and leap into the air when disturbed. Seedlings and new transplants are most at risk. They overwinter in plant debris, so clear this away at the end of the growing season.

MEALY BUG

Mealy bug is a tropical pest that attacks greenhouse crops and vines. The bugs are small, white and covered with a waxy-looking wool. At all stages – adult or larval – they are a nuisance. They feed on plant sap and excrete a sticky liquid, which in turn attracts sooty moulds. They usually tuck themselves into leaf axils and other places from which it is difficult to dislodge them. You can pick them off with a paintbrush soaked in methylated spirits or use the ladybird *Cryptolaemus* as a biological control.

BIRDS

In the summer, soft fruit such as strawberries, raspberries and currants will need protection. In the winter, pigeons may attack brassicas. Both can be protected quite easily with nets, wide-meshed for the brassicas, small-meshed for the soft fruit. Bullfinches sometimes strip buds from fruit trees and starlings are partial to cherries, but full-sized trees are difficult to protect.

MICE

Beans and peas are the crops most likely to attract mice. They burrow down to eat the seeds when you plant them in spring. Netting provides a partial deterrent; so does a scattering of holly leaves along the row. But the only sure way to catch mice is to set traps, baited with something they like even better than the legumes.

MOLES

Gourmet moles sometimes set themselves up in asparagus patches, where they crunch the succulent stems underground, but they rarely become a major problem in vegetable gardens. They are difficult to dislodge, as their underground tunnel systems are so extensive, but you can flood the runs with a hosepipe, which discourages them for a while.

CUTWORMS

Lettuce seedlings seem most often to be attacked by cutworms, which are actually moth caterpillars rather than worms, unpleasantly plump, cream coloured and about 3cm (1½in) long. They nibble through the base of young plants which, even if not severed completely, quickly wilt and die.

Cutworms emerge from the soil to feed at night. You can collect and destroy them by the light of a torch if you are not squeamish. Alternatively, you may choose to drench the ground with a soil pesticide. They are more of a problem in new gardens than old.

EELWORM

Potato eelworm is a baddy with no redeeming features. It is a soil-borne pest that hatches out from an egg protected by a tough brown cyst. Young eelworms home in on the roots of potato plants, and in the worst cases the whole plant dies. Crop rotation is the best defence. Do not grow maincrop potatoes on the same patch more than once every five years. Some cultivars have partial resistance. Look for 'Cara', 'Concorde', 'Jewel', 'Maris Piper', 'Morag', 'Penta' and 'Pentland Javelin'.

CABBAGE CATERPILLAR

You could forgive cabbage caterpillars if they were content with feasting on the outside leaves of cabbages, cauliflowers and Brussels sprouts. But they get where we want to be: right in the heart of the plant. Caterpillars may be of three different kinds: those of the large cabbage white butterfly are yellow and black and hairy, those of the small cabbage white are pale green and velvety, while those of the cabbage moth are yellowish green and scarcely hairy at all. Pick off caterpillars by hand (chickens are very partial to them).

SLUGS AND SNAILS

The most irritatingly bothersome pests in a fruit and vegetable garden are slugs and snails. Although they may not look as impressive as the big overground monsters, small black-keeled slugs are the worst offenders, attacking a wide range of crops including potatoes, tomatoes and strawberries. But many other crops are at risk, particularly when they are young and succulent. Thrushes and hedgehogs feed on snails and slugs. If they are not in evidence, try nematodes (a biological control), or use slug pellets.

Diseases and mineral deficiencies

BACTERIAL CANKER

Apples, cherries and plums are the fruits most affected by bacterial canker, which invades stems through leaf scars or wounds. Drops of amber-coloured gum may ooze out from the affected areas. The stem and then its foliage and flowers begin to wither. You can control the canker by cutting out and burning the affected branches and then spraying the trees with a copper-based fungicide when the petals fall. You will have to spray three more times at three-weekly intervals in late summer.

BLOSSOM END ROT

Tomatoes and occasionally green peppers are most commonly affected by blossom end rot, which is caused by a deficiency of calcium. Underwatering is often the cause, so it is perhaps not surprising that plants in grow bags should be most susceptible. Sunken, blackish patches discolour the base of the fruit, which may rot as a consequence. There is no cure. Prevent it by attending to the correct watering and feeding.

CHLOROSIS

Chlorosis is particularly noticeable in acid-loving plants, such as blueberries, which may be growing in soils that are too alkaline for their tastes. Plants are unable to take up enough manganese and iron from the soil and leaves begin to turn yellow. Prevent it by matching plants to the right growing conditions. You can hold it in check by watering with a solution of sequestered iron.

CANE SPOT

Small purplish spots may appear in late spring or early summer on the canes of raspberries, loganberries and other hybrid berries. The spots eventually split open the surface of the canes and new shoots may die back. Control it by cutting out the worst-affected canes. The fungus overwinters on old canes.

BLIGHT

This is most troublesome on potatoes and their cousins, tomatoes, and is particularly prevalent in damp summers, when spores of the fungus *Phytophthora infestans* cause blotches on foliage. In certain conditions, the disease spreads rapidly, completely rotting the foliage. Brown patches on potatoes spread into the hearts of the tubers. The best way of preventing the disease is to grow blight-resistant varieties of potato.

CHOCOLATE LEAF SPOT

Fungus spores cause chocolate-coloured spots on the foliage of broad beans. The stems may also be discoloured by streaks of dark brown. Most prone to damage are crops that have been sown in early winter to harvest the following year. Spring-sown crops are less likely to be infected. Grow beans in fertile, well-drained soil and destroy badly affected plants. Avoid using fertilizers heavy in nitrogen, or sowing in very acid soils. The disease is rarely fatal.

VIOLET ROOT ROT

Violet root rot attacks asparagus, beetroots, carrots and parsnips. Occasionally it will also infect swedes, turnips, potatoes and celery. Leaves wilt and turn yellow. When you dig up plants you find purple fungus covering the roots and crowns. Spores can remain in the soil for long periods and there is no cure. Destroy affected plants and move crops to fresh ground.

CLUBROOT

The fungal spores of clubroot can remain active in the soil for up to twenty years, causing galls on the roots of the cabbage family (which includes swedes and turnips). The root becomes distorted and swollen and may eventually rot. Leaves turn shades of yellow, red or purple. Crop rotation is the best defence, as there is no cure. Do not compost cabbage roots. Lime the soil if necessary to create a pH level of 7.0–7.5.

DOWNY MILDEW

Downy mildew affects a wide range of crops including beetroot and spinach, cabbages, onions, peas and vines. It is particularly prevalent on lettuce. In humid conditions, fluffy white fungal growths develop on the undersides of the leaves. Growth is stunted. Ventilate greenhouse crops to avoid infection. Some lettuces such as 'Avondefiance' have partial resistance to the disease.

WHITE BLISTER

This is a disfiguring but not fatal disease of brassicas. Green blisters turn into shiny white warty clusters on the undersides of the leaves. Foliage is distorted, but does not die. It is most likely to be a problem where plants are growing too closely together. Adjust spacings between plants and practise crop rotation. Destroy the worst-affected leaves.

SILVER LEAF

Cherries, peaches and plums are most likely to be affected by this disease, which causes silvering of the leaves and may eventually kill an entire tree. The spores infect the tree through wounds or pruning cuts. Prune trees in summer, when there is less risk of the infection occurring. Cut away infected branches, making the cut at least 30cm (12in) below any affected foliage. Take care with strimmers and mowers, which may cause wounds to the bark.

GREY MOULD/BOTRYTIS

A wide range of fruit and vegetables, including courgettes and marrows, greenhouse tomatoes, peas and beans, lettuce, figs, vines and especially strawberries may be affected by this disease, which is worst in damp summers. Buds, fruit, leaves and stems may all be affected, becoming covered in a grey, fluffy mould. It often attacks plants that may be suffering from some other disease, such as downy mildew. Some strains of grey mould are resistant to fungicides, but you can try spraying soft fruit at flowering time, repeating the treatment every two weeks.

HONEY FUNGUS

Your neighbour will probably tell you you've got it as soon as you move into your new house. It is a soil-borne parasite that attacks the roots of trees such as apples, causing slow decay and eventual death. Plants that are strong and healthy can usually resist attack. Remove affected plants, including all traces of root. Avoid members of the *Rosaceae* family when you replant.

SOOTY MOULD

Sooty mould follows aphids, forming on the sticky liquid that they excrete. It weakens a plant, because it prevents it from photosynthesizing. You can wash it off with soapy liquid.

PARSNIP CANKER

The shoulders of affected parsnips discolour and rot. The disease may also spread further into the root, especially where there are lesions caused by carrot fly. The disease, which shows as black or orange patches on the flesh, is worse in wet seasons. There is no cure, but you can prevent outbreaks by rotating crops, improving the drainage of the soil and planting canker-resistant varieties such as 'Avonresister', 'Cobham Improved Marrow', 'Gladiator' or 'White Gem'.

LEAF BLOTCH
White or creamy brown spots, oval in shape, appear on the foliage of leeks and onions. As the leaves age, the spots darken, eventually killing off the foliage. The disease is most prevalent in wet weather and there is no cure. Remove and burn any affected leaves and practise a strict rotation of crops. In Britain, the disease is more of a problem in the south-east than the north.

PEACH LEAF CURL
The leaves of peaches, nectarines and almonds may all be attacked by the spores of the fungus *Taphrina deformans*, which distorts and blisters them. The foliage drops and is replaced by a second healthy crop of leaves. Repeated attacks weaken trees. Protect wall-trained trees with a light polythene shelter to keep off rain between mid-winter and mid-spring. Spray with a copper-based fungicide in late winter and again in autumn, after the leaves have fallen.

SCLEROTINIA
This may attack Jerusalem artichokes, carrots, celery and parsnips. White fluffy mould gathers on the bottoms of the stems of artichokes. Affected plants should be dug up and destroyed. The mould is most likely to attack carrots and parsnips while they are in store. Keep stored crops cool and dry. On celery plants, sclerotinia is most likely to form on the crown. There is no cure. Destroy affected plants and practise a strict rotation of crops.

POWDERY MILDEW
Like grey mould, powdery mildew attacks a wide range of crops including cabbages, courgettes and marrows, peas and beans, apples and pears, cherries, peaches, plums, vines and strawberries. The mildew, which coats leaves and stems, is most likely to be a problem in hot, dry seasons. Do not plant too close. The only certain control is to spray with a systemic fungicide before the disease appears and to continue at fortnightly intervals.

RUST
Powdery brownish spots and streaks appear on the foliage of leeks, and more rarely chives. Individual leaves may die, but the disease is rarely fatal. Destroy affected leaves and prevent the disease by practising crop rotation. Water at the base of the plant rather than over the leaves. Plant rust-resistant varieties of leek such as 'Walton Mammoth'.

SCAB
Apples, pears and citrus fruit may all develop scab, which appears as black, scabby patches on foliage and fruit. Fruit may remain small and distorted. It is worst in mild, damp summers. Plant scab-resistant varieties such as the apples 'Sunset' or 'Winston' and the pears 'Beurre Hardy' and 'Conference'. Clear

away fallen leaves from under trees in autumn. Potato scab, which produces corky growths on the tubers, is commonest on light soils. If necessary, avoid susceptible varieties such as 'Maris Piper'.

STEM ROT

Stem rot is most likely to be a problem where cucumbers and tomatoes are grown in greenhouse borders. Brown sunken patches appear on the stems at ground level and the plants wilt. It is most likely to occur in cold, damp conditions. Rotate crops in greenhouse borders or grow crops in grow bags to prevent the build-up of soil-borne diseases. Spores can remain in the soil for long periods to re-infect future crops.

REVERSION DISEASE

This may be spread by big bud mites, feeding on blackcurrant bushes. The plants become markedly less vigorous and crop less well. The leaves may be narrower than usual and the flowers smaller and brighter pink. There is no cure. Dig up affected bushes and burn them. Plant fresh stock in ground as far away as possible from the old site.

CUCUMBER MOSAIC VIRUS

The virus also attacks courgettes, marrows and melons and is spread by sap-sucking aphids. Foliage is mottled with yellow and the fruits might also be affected, stunting their growth. There is no cure. Destroy badly affected plants and keep on top of aphids, which transmit the virus from plant to plant in the garden.

BIOLOGICAL CONTROL

There is rather a ghastly fascination in peering through a magnifying glass at a purposeful little ladybird hoovering up mealy bugs and cramming them into its mouth with all the delight of a five-year-old at a birthday tea. The brown and black ladybird called *Cryptolaemus* is one of several predators which, given the right conditions, can be effective in demolishing pests such as whitefly, spider mite and mealy bugs. The predators work best in controlled environments such as greenhouses, which is where pest attacks are most often severe.

To use biological controls effectively, you have to understand the life cycle of the pest as well as the predator. Whitefly, for instance, have young offspring that suck in sap at one end and excrete a sticky syrup called honeydew at the other. Only a day or two after maturing, the adult whitefly starts to lay a frightening number of eggs. Having hatched, the larva wanders about a bit until it finds a good feeding station. When it has plugged into a leaf vein, it stays at the same trough until it pupates and itself becomes a fly. Then the whole awful cycle starts again.

The first two here are available to buy by mail order. The following are garden friends to remember before you start spraying your foes.

ENCARSIA FORMOSA, a minute wasp, is the most effective control against whitefly. Its method of attack is grisly. The adult wasp lays its eggs inside the larva of the whitefly and, like revivified mummies in a horror film, the young eat their way out from inside, emerging after about three weeks as fully fledged new wasps. To operate productively, the wasp needs night temperatures above 10°C/50°F and is most effective in day temperatures of 18°C/65°F and above. If the temperature is low, the wasp cannot breed as fast as the whitefly. Encarsia works best if it is introduced three times at two-weekly intervals as temperatures warm up in spring. Hatching at regular intervals, the wasps attack the whitefly when it hurts most: right in the middle of its reproductive cycle. The wasps are powerless against clouds of whitefly on the wing, which is the point at which most gardeners start to think about biological control.

PHYTOSEIULUS PERSIMILIS, a mite, will control red spider and feeds on its prey at any stage, juvenile or adult. But, as with encarsia, the conditions have to be right for it to keep up with its prey.

COMMON LADYBIRDS, whether adult or in their larval form, can dispatch prodigious numbers of aphids – biological control can work with indigenous predators as well as with introduced ones. The larvae are the hungrier and eat about fifty aphids a day each. They are slatey blue with a few orange spots. Nettles help ladybirds build up in spring in time to attack summer aphids. The ladybirds fatten up meanwhile on nettle aphids.

HOVERFLIES and their larvae will help to keep down aphids. Plant marigolds to attract them to the vegetable patch.

LACEWINGS are more likely to visit gardens with a wide range of plants. Their larvae will devour huge quantities of aphids.

ICHNEUMONS are a type of leggy, four-winged wasp that preys on caterpillars. You can encourage them to the garden by planting golden rod and fennel.

CENTIPEDES are also excellent predators. Slugs are their preferred diet, but they will make do with other pests.

GROUND BEETLES, especially the big, black kind, are also keen on slug breakfasts.

WEEDS

New gardeners need to know what weeds look like, especially in their seedling or underground forms. Bindweed roots look quite important, if you are a novice gardener. You feel constrained to replant them tenderly in finely sifted earth. If you do, their gratitude will be boundless. On the other hand, if you think a plant is pretty, keep it, even if know-all gardeners tell you it is a weed. Corydalis, the wall weed with ferny leaves and yellow flowers is a case in point. Daisies are enchanting. So, in the proper place, is speedwell. Call it by its proper name, veronica, if it makes you feel better about it.

Perennials

GROUND ELDER *Aegopodium podagraria*

The worst weeds are perennial ones such as ground elder, which thrives in a wide range of soils and often arrives entangled in the roots of the clumps of Michaelmas daisy or goldenrod that gardeners give away in suspiciously large quantities. It spreads both by seed and by means of its shallow network of creeping rhizomes. Digging and pulling weakens it eventually, but it can be difficult to control amongst permanent plantings, for instance in a fruit garden.

CREEPING THISTLE *Cirsium arvense*

Creeping thistle is another horror that often arrives woven unnoticed through the roots of other plants. A systemic weedkiller is the most effective way of attacking it. Systemic weedkillers travel down through leaves and stems into the roots of pernicious weeds. They do not work immediately, but they are very effective. The active ingredient eventually breaks down in the soil. They work best if you apply them when the target weed is growing strongly. Holding fire in this way tests the nerves, but is the most effective strategy.

BINDWEED *Convolvulus arvensis*

Bindweed makes its presence known in the second half of summer when, having hauled itself unnoticed through raspberry canes and blackcurrant bushes, it opens up a succession of very showy trumpet flowers, each about 5cm (2in) wide at the mouth. If it were not such a bully, it would be grown everywhere as a decorative climber. It is perennial, dying down each winter to a tangle of fleshy white underground roots, which may travel for yards in a season. Dig it, pull it or treat it with glyphosate.

COUCH GRASS *Elymus repens*

Couch grass, which can grow up to 75cm (30in), is supported by a deeply entrenched subterranean network of rhizomes, by which it spreads rapidly through the ground. It flowers in late summer and can also spread by means of seed. Its greatest friend is the rotavator, which chops up its underground rhizomes and spreads them about even faster than the couch can manage to do itself. If you choose to dig it out, you must remove every piece of rhizome, which will sprout afresh if left. Use a non-residual weedkiller if necessary.

DOCK *Rumex* spp.

Docks are well anchored with long taproots. Once dug up they are done for, but if you merely snap them off they will resprout. There is immense satisfaction in drawing a large dock from the ground with all its root intact.

Do not allow it to set seed, which it sheds prolifically, and tackle docks when they are young rather than old, for the root will not be so entrenched. There is little need to use herbicide.

STINGING NETTLE *Urtica dioica*

These are a sign of fertile ground and have some use in the garden as fodder for caterpillars and nettle aphids, on which predatory ladybirds feed. If you cannot learn to love them, dig them out, or spray them with glyphosate when they are in flower.

Annuals

Annual weeds are not so sinister as perennials, as they can easily be kept in check by handweeding or hoeing.

SHEPHERD'S PURSE *Capsella bursa-pastoris*

Shepherd's purse, with its distinctive triangular seedpods, may be in flower all year and so is a prolific self-seeder.

HAIRY BITTERCRESS *Cardamine hirsuta*

This is a landcress which, when young, you can mix into salads. It has a peppery taste, not unlike that of watercress. That is one way of keeping on top of it. It has a staggeringly explosive mechanism for dispersing seeds. Catch it before it lets fling.

ANNUAL MEADOW GRASS *Poa annua*

This is most likely to be a problem where there are grass paths through a kitchen garden, but it is easy to pull. It can be suppressed to a large extent by heavy mulching. As with most annual weeds, the trick is to deal with it before rather than after it has seeded.

GROUNDSEL *Senecio vulgaris*

Each plant of groundsel (and meadow grass) can produce up to 500 seeds, so the best time to pull or hoe them is before they shed it. Hoeing is best done in hot dry weather, when weeds die quickly in the sun. You do not have to uproot annual weeds, just cut off their heads.

FAT HEN *Chenopodium album*

Fat hen, with succulent leaves and heads of green bobbly flowers, can carry up to 28,000 seeds on one plant. Weed seeds germinate in the top 5cm (2in) of soil, so mulches need to be deeper than that if they are going to suppress weeds.

CHICKWEED *Stellaria media*

Common chickweed is one of the most persistent weeds in vegetable gardens, flowering for most of the year. Seeds will germinate in autumn and the plants continue to grow all winter in a mild year. Control it by hand weeding or hoeing.

SPEEDWELL *Veronica persica*

The common field speedwell is one of the large family of speedwells which, though very pretty, may spread rapidly to become a weed in the kitchen garden. Control it by pulling or hoeing.

THE KITCHEN GARDEN CALENDAR
SPRING

Throughout spring
* Hoe regularly between crops to keep down weeds.
* Mulch around plants, trees and bushes to suppress weeds and conserve moisture in the soil.
* Water if necessary, especially newly planted crops.

Early spring
VEGETABLES
* Sow broad beans, Brussels sprouts, calabrese, carrots, cauliflowers, lettuce, parsley, parsnips, peas, radishes, rocket, spinach and spring onions outside when conditions are suitable.
* Continue to force Belgian chicory.
* Sow aubergines, celeriac, celery, cucumbers, leeks, lettuce, parsley, peppers and tomatoes in a frost-free greenhouse or indoors.
* Plant out Jerusalem artichokes, asparagus, onion sets and seedlings, early potatoes and shallots.

FRUIT
* Finish planting fruit trees and bushes.
* Finish pruning fruit trees and bushes.
* Where mildew has been a problem, spray gooseberries just before flowers open and continue at fortnightly intervals.
* Hand-pollinate wall-trained fruit such as peaches and apricots if insects are not on the wing.
* Prune out some of the old wood on Morello cherries if you have not done this after picking the fruit.
* Prune blueberries.
* Check blackberries, loganberries and tayberries. Tie in to wires as necessary.
* Mulch young trees, raspberry canes and fruit bushes.
* Set out young plantlets grown from strawberry runners.
* In cold areas protect blossom of early flowering trees with polythene.
* Feed blackcurrants with bonemeal.

Mid-spring
VEGETABLES
* Earth up early potatoes.
* Hoe between rows of seedlings.
* Pull up stumps of Brussels sprouts and burn them.

* Sow beetroot, broad beans, broccoli, Brussels sprouts, winter cabbages, calabrese, carrots, cauliflowers, kohl rabi, leeks, lettuce, spring onions, parsley, parsnips, peas, radishes, red chicory, rocket, salsify, scorzonera, spinach, swedes and turnips.
* Plant out Jerusalem artichokes, onion sets and potatoes.
* Sow aubergines, courgettes, cucumbers, French and runner beans, squash, sweetcorn and tomatoes in a frost-free greenhouse.

FRUIT
* Pick flowers off new young strawberry plants, which should not be allowed to fruit in their first year.
* Finish planting raspberries, if this was not done in late autumn.
* Check fig trees, prune and tie in new growth if necessary.
* Hand-pollinate wall-trained peaches and nectarines if necessary. If the weather is very dry, spray the trees with a fine mist of water, which will help fruits to set.

Late spring
VEGETABLES
* Plant globe artichokes and cardoons.
* Continue to hoe off weeds.
* Stake peas.
* Earth up potatoes.
* Sow beetroot, winter cabbages, calabrese, carrots, cauliflowers, chard, courgettes, endive, French and runner beans, kohl rabi, leeks, lettuce, parsley, parsnips, peas, radishes, red chicory, rocket, spinach, spring onions, swedes and turnips.
* Sow cucumbers, courgettes, squash and sweetcorn in a frost-free greenhouse or indoors.
* Plant out Jerusalem artichokes, aubergines, celeriac, celery, peppers, potatoes, French and runner beans, sweetcorn and outdoor tomatoes.
* Transplant well-developed seedlings of cauliflowers.

FRUIT
* Start to pick gooseberries.
* Pull out any new young raspberry canes that come up a long way from the original rows.
* Continue to water if necessary, especially wall-trained trees.
* Weed strawberries and put straw around the plants, together with a sprinkling of slug pellets if slugs are known to be a problem.
* Put netting over soft fruit.
* Shorten leaders of trees grown as fans, cordons and espaliers.
* Start to thin out new shoots on wall-trained peaches, apricots and plums.

SUMMER

Throughout summer
* Hoe regularly between crops to keep down weeds.
* Mulch around plants to suppress weeds and conserve moisture.
* Water if necessary, especially newly planted crops.

Early summer
VEGETABLES
* Sow beetroot, calabrese, carrots, chard, chicory, courgettes, cucumbers, endive, Florence fennel, French and runner beans, kohl rabi, lettuce, parsley, peas, radishes, rocket, spring onions, squash and Swedes.
* Plant out aubergines, celeriac, celery, courgettes, cucumbers, peppers, sweetcorn and outdoor tomatoes into prepared ground.
* Transplant broccoli, Brussels sprouts, cauliflowers and leeks.
FRUIT
* Pick strawberries, raspberries, currants and gooseberries regularly.
* Train in new shoots of blackberries, loganberries and other hybrid berries.
* Tie in selected shoots of wall-trained peaches and nectarines. Thin the fruit if necessary.
* Remove runners on strawberries unless they are needed for new plants.
* Pinch out shoots on wall-trained plums and Morello cherries that are growing in the wrong direction.
* Pinch out the tips of new shoots on well-grown fig trees.
* Pick off sawfly caterpillars if they attack gooseberry bushes.

Mid-summer
VEGETABLES
* Watch for blight on maincrop potatoes and lift early if necessary.
* Earth up Brussels sprouts and other brassicas on exposed, windy sites.
* Remove side shoots from tomatoes. Nip out the top of outdoor tomatoes when four or five trusses have set.
* Lift garlic and dry off the bulbs.
* Sow beetroot, calabrese, carrots, chard, chicory, endive, Florence fennel, kohl rabi, lettuce, parsley, peas, radishes, rocket and turnips.
FRUIT
* Continue to train in canes of blackberry and loganberry. If you want to increase stock, tip layer shoots now.
* When strawberries have finished fruiting, cut leaves off old plants and take away the straw. Weed and clean between the rows.
* Thin apples if they have not thinned themselves sufficiently in the 'June drop'.
* When raspberries have fruited, cut out old canes and tie in the new ones.

* Continue to train and tie in tree fruit growing against walls.
* Branches of plum trees that are very heavily laden may need support.
* Give citrus fruit a high-nitrogen feed.

Late summer
VEGETABLES
* Lift onions and shallots and dry them off before storing them.
* Cut off and burn top growth of maincrop potatoes if it is blighted.
* Sow kohl rabi, mizuna, oriental salad leaves, radishes, spinach and turnips.
* Sow curly endive under glass.
FRUIT
* Continue to cut out raspberry canes that have fruited and tie in new ones.
* Prune wall-trained apples and pears as necessary.
* Plant out well-rooted runners in new strawberry beds.
* Prune damsons and plums if necessary when they have fruited and cut out any damaged branches.
* When peaches and nectarines have finished fruiting, cut out the shoots on which the fruit was borne and tie in new shoots to replace them.

AUTUMN

Throughout autumn
* Store root vegetables such as beetroot, carrots, swedes and turnips as you lift them. Keep them in a cool, frost-free place.
* Dig and manure ground once it has been cleared of crops.

Early autumn
VEGETABLES
* Cure pumpkins and winter squash before storing them.
* Continue to earth up brassicas that will be standing outside through winter.
* Sow oriental salad leaves, winter radishes and spinach.
FRUIT
* After fruiting cut out at the base old canes of blackberries, loganberries and other hybrid berries. Tie in new canes in their place.
* Weed well around fruit trees growing in grass.
* Cut off and burn any mildewed top growth on gooseberries.
* Order new fruit trees and bushes from specialist nurseries.
* Finish summer pruning of wall-trained apples and pears.
* Cut out dead wood on wall trained Morello cherries and finish tying in new shoots.

Mid-autumn
VEGETABLES
* Plant garlic.
* Sow broad beans and winter radishes.
* Clear away bean sticks, rotting vegetation, tomato stakes, etc.
* Cut down stems of asparagus and Jerusalem artichokes.
FRUIT
* Store sound fruit in a cool, frost-free place.
* Take cuttings, if necessary, from gooseberry and currant bushes.
* Prepare ground for planting new trees and bushes.
* Tidy up plantings of alpine strawberries, removing dead leaves.
* Prune gooseberries and currants after the leaves have fallen.
* Put greasebands round apple trees to trap codling moths.

Late autumn
VEGETABLES
* In cold areas, protect crowns of globe artichokes by packing them with straw or bracken.
* Sow broad beans and peas.
* Plant garlic and rhubarb.
FRUIT
* Finish picking apples and pears.
* Plant new trees, bushes and raspberry canes as soon as possible after leaf fall.
* Spray peaches and nectarines against peach leaf curl just before leaf fall.

WINTER

Throughout winter
* Finish digging and manuring ground whenever conditions are suitable, and prepare it for spring planting.
* Force plants such as Belgian chicory and rhubarb from mid-winter onwards.
* Inspect stored apples and pears regularly and take out any fruit that is starting to go rotten.

Early winter
VEGETABLES
* Store carrots, turnips and swedes in a cool, frost-free place.
FRUIT
* Check stakes and ties on fruit trees and loosen ties where necessary.

Mid-winter
VEGETABLES
* Order vegetable and flower seeds, seed potatoes and onion sets.
* Sow crops such as chicory and onions in a frost-free greenhouse or indoors.
* Start planting shallots.
FRUIT
* Prune apples and pears if frosts are not too hard.
* Continue to plant fruit trees and bushes if weather permits.

Late winter
VEGETABLES
* Prepare seed beds for early sowings.
* Set out potatoes in boxes to 'chit'.
* Sow peas outdoors in mild areas.
* Sow aubergines, celeriac, leeks, lettuce and onions in a frost-free greenhouse or indoors.
FRUIT
* For an early crop, cover strawberry plants with cloches.
* Prune cobnuts and filberts when the catkins are fully open.

INDEX Numbers in *italics* refer to illustrations.

BIBLIOGRAPHY

Baker, Harry, *The Fruit Garden Displayed*, 1986
Bunyard, Edward, *The Anatomy of Dessert*, 1929
—, *The Epicure's Companion*, 1929
Bunyard, George, *The Fruit Garden*, 1904
Consumers' Association, *The Gardening from Which? Guide to Pests and Diseases*, 1991
Creasy, Rosalind, *The Complete Book of Edible Landscaping*, 1982
Davidson, Alan, *Fruit*, 1991
Doweding, Charles, *Organic Gardening*, 2007
Hogg, Robert, *The Fruit Manual*, 1875
Larkcom, Joy, *Vegetables for Small Gardens*, 1995
—, *Salads for Small Gardens*, 1995
—, *The Vegetable Garden Displayed*, 1992
—, *Oriental Vegetables*, 2007
Lord, Tony (ed.), *The Plant Finder*, 2009
McHoy, Peter, *The Gardening Which? Guide to Successful Pruning*, 1993
McVicar, Jekka, *Jekka's Complete Herb Book*, 2007
Morgan, Joan, *A Paradise out of a Common Field*, 1990
—, *A New Book of Apples*, 2002
Phillips, Roger, and Rix, Martyn, *Vegetables*, 1993
Robinson, William, *The Vegetable Garden*, 1905
Sanders, Rosanne, *The English Apple*, 1988
Wilson, Alan, *The Story of the Potato*, 1995

ACKNOWLEDGMENTS

This book originally came out under the title *The New Kitchen Garden*. I am tremendously grateful to John Nicoll of Frances Lincoln for suggesting that he should publish an updated version, thoroughly revised to take account of all the wonderful new varieties of fruit and vegetables that were not available to gardeners when the book first appeared. I'd like to thank Jo Christian for her constant encouragement, Anne Askwith for editing the text with such scrupulous attention to detail and designer Becky Clarke.